Basil *of* Caesarea

Foundations of Theological Exegesis and Christian Spirituality

Hans Boersma and Matthew Levering, series editors

Available in the Series

Athanasius, by Peter J. Leithart

*Vincent of Lérins and the Development
of Christian Doctrine*, by Thomas G. Guarino

Basil *of* Caesarea

Stephen M. Hildebrand

Baker Academic
a division of Baker Publishing Group
www.BakerAcademic.com

© 2014 by Stephen M. Hildebrand

Published by Baker Academic
a division of Baker Publishing Group
P.O. Box 6287, Grand Rapids, MI 49516-6287
www.bakeracademic.com

Printed in the United States of America

Library of Congress Cataloging-in-Publication Data
Hildebrand, Stephen M., 1973-
    Basil of Caesarea / Stephen M. Hildebrand.
      pages cm. — (Foundations of theological exegesis and Christian spirituality)
    Includes bibliographical references and index.
    ISBN 978-0-8010-4907-1 (pbk.)
    1.Basil, Saint, Bishop of Caesarea, approximately 329–379. I. Title.
  BR65.B36H54 2014
  270.2092—dc23   2013042565

14 15 16 17 18 19 20   7 6 5 4 3 2 1

For Samuel Joseph

Rursus ut aeternae bona volvo perennia vitae,
　　Quae Deus in caelo praeparat innocuis,
Laetor obisse brevi functum mortalia
　　Ut cito divinas perfrueretur opes.
Ne terrena diu contagia mixtus iniquis
　　Duceret in fragili corporis hospitio;
Sed nullo istius temeratus crimine mundi,
　　Dignius aeternum tenderet ad Dominum.

Aut illum gremio exceptum fovet Abramio,
　　· *Et blandus digiti rore Eleazar alit;*
Aut cum Bethlaeis infantibus in paradiso;
　　Quos malus Herodes perculit invidia,
Inter odoratum ludit nemus, atque coronas
　　Texit honorandis praemia martyribus.
Talibus inmixtus Regem comitabitur Agnum,
　　Virgineis infans additus agminibus.

When I ponder the everlasting goods of eternal life,
　　That God in heaven prepares for the innocent,
I rejoice that he, engaging but briefly mortal things,
　　Has departed to enjoy quickly the riches of God.
That he, though mingled with the wicked, did not long experience
earthly contagion in the fragile lodging of the body;
but because he was polluted by no offense of this world,
　　He fittingly inclined to the eternal Lord . . .

Taken away from the bosom of Abraham, either
charming Lazarus comforts, nourishes him with his finger's dew,
Or, in paradise with the infants of Bethlehem,
　　Whom evil Herod in envy slew,
He plays in the fragrant woods
　　And weaves crowns, rewards for honored martyrs.
Mingling with such as these he will attend the King, the Lamb,
　　An infant joined to the ranks of Virgins.

St. Paulinus of Nola, *To the Parents of Celsus,*
poem 35, 15–20; 581–88 (PL 61, 677, 688)

Contents

Series Preface

Recent decades have witnessed a growing desire among Orthodox, Catholics, and Protestants to engage and retrieve the exegetical, theological, and doctrinal resources of the early church. If the affirmations of the first four councils constitute a common inheritance for ecumenical Christian witness, then in the Nicene Creed Christians find a particularly rich vein for contemporary exploration of the realities of faith. These fruits of the patristic period were, as the fathers themselves repeatedly attest, the embodiment of a personally and ecclesially engaged exegetical, theological, and metaphysical approach to articulating the Christian faith. In the Foundations of Theological Exegesis and Christian Spirituality series, we will explore this patristic witness to our common Nicene faith.

Each volume of the present series explores how biblical exegesis, dogmatic theology, and participatory metaphysics relate in the thought of a particular church father. In addition to serving as introductions to the theological world of the fathers, the volumes of the series break new ecumenical and theological ground by taking as their starting point three related convictions. First, at the core of the Foundations series lies the conviction that *ressourcement*, or retrieval, of the shared inheritance of the Nicene faith is an important entry point to all ecumenical endeavor. Nicene Christianity, which received its authoritative shape at the councils of Constantinople (381) and Chalcedon (451), was the result of more than three centuries of ecclesial engagement with the implications of the incarnation and of the adoration of Father, Son, and Holy Spirit in the liturgy of the church. Particularly since the 1940s, when Catholic scholars such as Henri de Lubac, Jean Daniélou, and others reached back to the church fathers for inspiration and contemporary cultural and ecclesial renewal, *ressourcement* has made significant contributions to theological development and ecumenical discussion. The last few decades have also witnessed growing evangelical interest in an approach to the church fathers that reads them not only for academic reasons but also with a view to giving them a voice in today's discussions. Accordingly, this series is based on the conviction that a contemporary retrieval of the church fathers is essential also to the flourishing and further development of Christian theology.

Second, since the Nicene consensus was based on a thorough engagement with the Scriptures, renewed attention to the exegetical approaches of the church fathers is an important aspect of *ressourcement*. In particular, the series works on the assumption that Nicene theology was the result of the early church's conviction that historical and spiritual interpretation of the Scriptures were intimately connected and that both the Old and the New Testaments speak of the realities of Christ, of the church, and of eternal life in fellowship with the Triune God. Although today we may share the dogmatic inheritance of the Nicene faith regardless of our exegetical approach, it is much less clear that the Nicene convictions—such as the doctrines of the Trinity and of the person of Christ—can be sustained without the spiritual approaches to interpretation that were common among the fathers. Doctrine, after all, is the outcome of biblical interpretation. Thus, theological renewal requires attention to the way in which the church fathers approached Scripture. Each of the volumes of this series will therefore explore a church father's theological approach(es) to the biblical text.

Finally, it is our conviction that such a *ressourcement* of spiritual interpretation may contribute significantly toward offsetting the fragmentation—ecclesial, moral, economical, and social—of contemporary society. This fragmentation is closely connected to the loss of the Platonic-Christian synthesis of Nicene Christianity. Whereas this earlier synthesis recognized a web of relationships as a result of God's creative act in and through Christ, many today find it much more difficult to recognize, or even to pursue, common life together. A participatory metaphysic, which many of the church fathers took as axiomatic, implies that all of created reality finds its point of mutual connection in the eternal Word of God, in which it lies anchored. It is this christological anchor that allows for the recognition of a common origin and a common end, and thus for shared commitments. While the modern mindset tends to separate nature and the supernatural (often explicitly excluding the latter), Nicene Christianity recognized that the created order exists by virtue of God's graciously allowing it to participate, in a creaturely fashion, in his goodness, truth, and beauty as revealed in Christ through the Spirit. A participatory metaphysic, therefore, is one of the major presuppositions of the creed's articulation of the realities of faith.

In short, rooted in the wisdom of the Christian past, the volumes of the series speak from the conviction that the above-mentioned convictions informed the life and work of the church fathers and that these convictions are in need of *ressourcement* for the sake of today's theological, philosophical, and exegetical debates. In light of a growing appreciation of the early Christians, the series aims to publish erudite introductions that will be of interest in seminary and university courses on doctrine and biblical exegesis and that will be accessible to educated lay readers with interest in how early Christians appropriated and passed on divine revelation.

Hans Boersma and Matthew Levering, series editors

Acknowledgments

I have incurred many debts in the course of writing this book. I am grateful to Matthew Levering, Hans Boersma, and Baker Academic for the opportunity to participate in the series. The press has been very generous and patient. I owe a particular debt of gratitude to James Ernest and Robert Hand for their help and guidance. The library staff at the Franciscan University of Steubenville was most accommodating.

My family has generously indulged my interest in St. Basil. I am forever grateful to my wife, Sara, and my children, Lucy, Peter, Elizabeth, Paul, Anthony, and George, for the sacrifices that they made on behalf of this project. I make W. K. L. Clarke's prayer my own, "that St. Basil may be allowed to know about my devotion to his memory and to pray for me; also that I may be privileged to meet him one day."[1] I hope that my affection for him has deepened rather than diminished my insight into his life and work, but, of course, that judgment must be left to the reader.

Preface

The Foundations of Theological Exegesis and Christian Spirituality series is, in a sense, an attempt to recover a lost world for theology and ecumenical endeavor today, and the lost world is the "Nicene world." "The world of Nicene Christianity," writes Orthodox theologian John Behr, "embraces not only matters pertaining to dogmatic theology . . . , but also spirituality (liturgy, prayer, piety) and also includes both a history (marked by particular events) and a geography (with its own sacred centers)."[1] Nicene Christianity has not been totally lost, of course, but the synthesis of theology, spirituality, prayer, liturgy, and, we might add, a particular way of reading Scripture that mark the Nicene worldview has largely been displaced, if not in the faith lives of ordinary Christians, then certainly in Christian intellectual circles.

What happened? A full account of this is beyond both the scope of this book and my abilities, but it seems certain that the rise of the historical methods—in particular, their application to the Scriptures and to the Christian tradition—has played a role. This is not to say that modern historical studies have been a wholly negative factor in the practice of theology in modern times. On the contrary, and in spite of harmful missteps, they have made an invaluable contribution to our understanding of the biblical text and the history to which that text witnesses as well as to our understanding of theology as a discipline. Ironically, it has been the flourishing of scholarly and historical study of the patristic age that stands behind the current attempt to heal the fractures in Christianity caused in part by historical studies of previous centuries. "It is perhaps," writes Behr, "the relegation of this 'Nicene world' to books that stimulated the intense interest, in recent times, in the debates of the fourth century."[2]

One of the fruits of this renaissance in the study of the fourth century is the realization of the complexity and range of positions on all sides. It was not simply Arius and the Arians against Athanasius and the Nicenes. Rather,

"Arianism" has become a much less useful label, for it named so many and very different theological positions, and the same is true of "Nicene": it can obscure the variation and independence among the many theologians to whom the label is applied and who applied it to themselves.

In the following pages, we will see that St. Basil lived in the Nicene world, or *a* Nicene world. He has much in common with the theologians who likewise confessed that creed but is nonetheless an original thinker. The overarching argument that I try to make here is that Basil's whole theology and spirituality emerge organically out of his simple desire to live a life faithful to the gospel. This is no revolutionary thesis, but it is my hope that this explanation of Basil's theology will not only contribute to our understanding of him but also suggest what he might offer us today in our own theological endeavors. We will first set out the story of his own life, how he came to embrace more intensely the Christian life (chap. 1). Then, we will turn to his anthropology (chap. 2), for Basil's understanding of man provides the clearest vantage point from which to see the place of both the Scriptures and the whole physical world (chap. 3).[3] Basil sees the Scriptures and the created world as books in which man reads about his salvation, a salvation accomplished above all by the work of the incarnate Son and the sanctifying Spirit (hence, chaps. 4 and 5 on the Trinity). From here we can turn to Basil's understanding of the Christian life under the headings of Christian discipleship (chap. 6) and asceticism (chap. 7). Chapter 8 analyzes Basil's use of the theological and ascetic traditions before him in order to create an appreciation of his theological method. In the last place, I will offer a conclusion that brings together the theological, spiritual, moral, and ascetical aspects of Basil's thought into a single unity.

Abbreviations

I should offer a note on the citations. For oft-cited works, I have used parenthetical citation to avoid the burden of too many endnotes. I give the work, abbreviated as indicated below, followed by the book number (if there is more than one book), paragraph number(s), and the page number(s) in the translation after a semicolon. Thus, (*Ag. Eun.* 1.2; 85) cites *Against Eunomius*, book one, paragraph two, on page 85 of the translation by Mark DelCogliano and Andrew Radde-Gallwitz. Some works exist in more than one translation, and so I indicate below which translation I am citing for each work. I occasionally slightly change a translation and indicate as much with the word *altered*, after the citation. I do not give the page number of the critical edition but think that a particular text could be easily looked up given the information that I do provide. When I allude to a text or wish to refer the reader to a text but do not cite it, I still use parenthetical citation, though without a page number in the translation.

For citations from Scripture I generally use the Revised Standard Version. In some cases, I will cite a translation that includes either an allusion to or an actual quotation of Scripture. In the case of a reference, I provide the scriptural source in brackets if it is not provided by the translation itself, say in parentheses. In the case of a citation, I preserve both the actual translation (often not the RSV) as well as the manner of citation: some use quotation marks, while others use italics. If the italics in a quotation are mine rather than the text's, I will indicate as much. Basil's comments on the Psalms are often unintelligible if one uses a translation based on the Hebrew rather than the Greek. Thus, for quotations from the Psalms, I generally use the English translation embedded within Basil's homilies rather than the RSV.

Ancient Authors

Athanasius of Alexandria

To Serap.   *Letters to Serapion*, trans. Mark DelCogliano, Andrew Radde-Gallwitz,
                 and Lewis Ayres, in *Works on the Spirit: Athanasius and Didymus*, Popular
                 Patristics 43 (Crestwood, NY: St. Vladimir's Seminary Press, 2011)

Augustine of Hippo

Conf.   *Confessions*, trans. Henry Chadwick (New York: Oxford University Press,
                 1991)

Basil of Caesarea

Ag. Eun.   *Against Eunomius*, trans. Mark DelCogliano and Andrew Radde-Gallwitz,
                 Fathers of the Church 122 (Washington, DC: Catholic University of Amer-
                 ica Press, 2011)

ep.   *Epistle(s)*, trans. Roy J. Deferrari, in *Saint Basil: The Letters*, 4 vols., Loeb
                 Classical Library (Cambridge, MA: Harvard University Press, 1926–34)

Hex. 1–9   *Hexaëmeron*, trans. Clare Agnes Way, in *St. Basil: Exegetic Homilies*, Fa-
                 thers of the Church 46 (Washington, DC: Catholic University of America
                 Press, 1963)

Hex. 10–11   *Hexaëmeron*, trans. Nonna Verna Harrison, in *St. Basil the Great: On the
                 Human Condition*, Popular Patristics 30 (Crestwood, NY: St. Vladimir's
                 Seminary Press, 2005)

Hom. Anger   *Homily against Anger*, trans. Harrison, in *On the Human Condition*

Hom. Attend   *Homily, Attend to Yourself*, trans. Harrison, in *On the Human Condition*

Hom. Barns   *Homily, I Will Tear Down These Barns*, trans. C. Paul Schroeder, in
                 St. Basil the Great: On Social Justice, Popular Patristics 38 (Crestwood,
                 NY: St. Vladimir's Seminary Press, 2009)

Hom. Evil   *Homily Explaining that God Is Not the Cause of Evil*, trans. Harrison, in
                 On the Human Condition

Hom. Famine   *Homily in a Time of Famine and Drought*, trans. Schroeder, in *On Social
                 Justice*

Hom. gen. Chr.   *Homily on the Holy Generation of Christ* (I am grateful to Mark DelCo-
                 gliano for the use of his forthcoming translation)

Hom. In Begin.   *Homily on "In the Beginning Was the Word,"* trans. Mark DelCogliano, in
                 St. Basil the Great: On Christian Doctrine and Practice, Popular Patristics
                 47 (Crestwood, NY: St. Vladimir's Seminary Press, 2012)

Hom. Mart. Jul. *Homily on the Martyr Iulitta* (untranslated)

Hom. on Ps.   *Homilies on the Psalms*, trans. Way, in *Exegetic Homilies*

Hom. Rich   *Homily, To the Rich*, trans. Schroeder, in *On Social Justice*

Hom. Usury   *Homily Against Those Who Lend at Interest*, trans. Schroeder, in *On Social
                 Justice*

Lg. Rul.   *Longer Rules*, trans. Anna Silvas, in *The Asketikon of St. Basil the Great*,
                 Oxford Early Christian Studies (New York: Oxford University Press, 2005)

Mor.   *Morals*, trans. W. K. L. Clarke, in *The Ascetic Works of St. Basil* (London:
                 SPCK, 1925)[1]

On Bap.	*On Baptism*, trans. M. Monica Wagner, in *Saint Basil: Ascetical Works*, Fathers of the Church 9 (Washington, DC: Catholic University of America Press, 1962)
On Faith	Trans. Clarke, in *Ascetic Works of St. Basil*
On H. Sp.	*On the Holy Spirit*, in *St. Basil the Great: On the Holy Spirit*, trans. Stephen M. Hildebrand, Popular Patristics 42 (Crestwood, NY: St. Vladimir's Seminary Press, 2011)
On Judg.	*On Judgment*, trans. Clarke, in *Ascetic Works of St. Basil*
On Renunc.	*On the Renunciation of the World* (spurious), trans. Clarke, in *Ascetic Works of St. Basil*
Protr. Bap.	*Protreptic on Baptism*, trans. Thomas Halton, in *Baptism: Ancient Liturgies and Patristic Texts*, ed. André Hamman and Thomas Halton, 76–87 (Staten Island, NY: Alba House, 1967)
Reg. Bas.	*The Rule of St. Basil* translated into Latin by Rufinus (*Small Asceticon*), trans. Silvas, in *Asketikon*
Sh. Rul.	*Shorter Rules*, trans. Silvas, in *Asketikon*

Eunomius of Cyzicus

Apol.	*Apology*, trans. Richard Paul Vaggione in *Eunomius: The Extant Works*, Oxford Early Christian Texts (New York: Oxford University Press, 1987)
Exp. of Faith	*Exposition of Faith*, trans. Vaggione in *Eunomius: The Extant Works*

Gangra, Synod of

Gangra	Trans. Silvas, in *Asketikon*

Gregory of Nazianzus

Ep.	*Epistle*, trans. Charles Gordon Browne and James Edward Swallow, in *S. Cyril of Jerusalem, S. Gregory Nazianzen*, NPNF, 2, 7 (1893; repr., Peabody, MA: Hendrickson, 1994)
Or.	*Oration* (except Or. 27–31), trans. Charles Gordon Browne and James Edward Swallow, NPNF 2, 7; Or. 27–31; trans. Frederick Williams and Lionel Wickham, in *On God and Christ: The Five Theological Orations and Two Letters to Cledonius*, Popular Patristics 23 (Crestwood, NY: St. Vladimir's Seminary Press, 2002)

Gregory of Nyssa

Ag. Eun.	*Against Eunomius*, trans. H. A. Wilson, in *Select Writings and Letters of Gregory, Bishop of Nyssa*, NPNF, 2, 5 (1893; repr., Peabody, MA: Hendrickson, 1995)
Macr.	*The Life of St. Macrina*, trans. Kevin Corrigan (Toronto: Peregrina, 1998)

Origen

Ag. Cel.	*Against Celsus*, trans. Henry Chadwick, in *Origen: Contra Celsum*, rev. ed. (New York: Cambridge University Press, 1980)
On F. Prin.	*On First Principles*, trans. G. W. Butterworth (Gloucester, MA: Peter Smith, 1973)

Socrates

Eccl. Hist.   *Ecclesiastical History*, anonymously trans. in *Ecclesiastical History: A History of the Church in Seven Books, from the Accession of Constantine, A.D., 306, to the 36th year of Theodosius, Un., A.D. 445, including a period of 140 years* (London: Bagster, 1844); rev. A. C. Zenos, *The Ecclesiastical History of Socrates Scholasticus*, in *Socrates, Sozomenus: Church Histories*, NPNF, 2, 2 (1890; repr., Peabody, MA: Hendrickson, 1995)

Sozomen

Eccl. Hist.   *Ecclesiastical History*, trans. Edward Walford, *Ecclesiastical History: A History of the Church in Nine Books, from A.D. 324 to A.D. 440* (London: Samuel Bagster & Sons, 1846); rev. Chester D. Hartranft, *The Ecclesiastical History of Sozomen, comprising a History of the Church, from A.D. 323 to A.D. 425*, in *Socrates, Sozomenus: Church Histories*, NPNF, 2, 2 (1890; repr., Peabody, MA: Hendrickson, 1995)

Other Abbreviations

ANF   Ante-Nicene Fathers
can.   Canon
hom.   Homily
NPNF   Nicene and Post-Nicene Fathers
PG   Patrologiae cursus completus, series graeca, ed. J.-P. Migne.
pref.   Preface
prol.   Prologue
Q.   Question
Silvas   Silvas, *The Asketikon of St. Basil the Great*

1

Awakenings

Living the Gospel at Home and in the Church

In the fourth century there was nothing perfunctory about baptism. There is evidence that the practice of infant baptism was around at least a century earlier, but by St. Basil's time it had not yet achieved the status of a widely used custom. Christianity, moreover, even after the conversion of Constantine and his subsequent toleration of his new religion, had not yet succeeded in creating a culture whose first reflex was to baptize its newest members. Baptism, then, was largely the domain of adults, especially those in danger of death. There developed a robust tradition of postponing the cleansing bath.

From one point of view, the postponing of baptism casts the fourth and fifth centuries in a negative light, for the practice came along with a sense of the inevitability of serious sin and a corresponding complacency. The most famous example of this, of course, we find in Augustine's *Confessions*. Augustine explains why his mother had not had him baptized as a child. He had come down with a fever and himself begged for baptism, and St. Monica made the arrangements. Augustine, however, suddenly recovered, and, he relates, "my cleansing was deferred on the assumption that, if I lived, I would be sure to soil myself, and after that solemn washing the guilt would be greater and more dangerous if I then defiled myself with sins" (*Conf.* 1.11.17; 13–14).

Here, of course, Augustine refers to the severe penitential practice of the early church that only strengthened and encouraged the postponement of baptism. One had only two opportunities in life for the forgiveness of serious sin, baptism (first penance) and second penance, a public ritual that began with the physical separation of the sinner from the community (sometimes separation meant standing in a different part of the church, sometimes it meant staying outside the church) and culminated, after a long and more or less difficult penance, with the public reacceptance of the sinner into the community through the laying on of hands. Moreover, when one applied a cost-benefit analysis to these two options, as Monica had done for Augustine, the first was so much more appealing than the second, whose penances could be very long, very painful, and very inconvenient.

We can also, however, view the custom of postponing baptism more positively, for it was put off not merely because second penance was so difficult and unrepeatable. Baptism was put off, too, because it meant a serious change in one's life. It was no empty ritual, for those who received it were to be zealous for the Lord and his commandments. To be baptized, in other words, was to undertake the Christian life with earnestness and seriousness. Baptism was put off because it was meaningful.

We have no indication that Basil's mother, St. Emmelia, was of the same mind as St. Monica when she postponed her eldest son's baptism. Indeed, there is good reason to think that Basil was expected not to sin, as Augustine was expected to sin. While we will consider Basil's familial background later, suffice it to say here that Basil senior was himself a committed Christian, not a pagan as Augustine's father, Patricius, was.

Though Patricius had become a catechumen around the time of Augustine's adolescence, he seemed then not quite ready to embrace the rigors of the Christian life, for when he saw Augustine at the baths, "showing sign of virility and the stirrings of adolescence," he got drunk to celebrate the imminent arrival of grandchildren (*Conf.* 2.2.6; 26). Augustine says that his father "was drunk with the invisible wine of his perverse will directed downwards to inferior things" (*Conf.* 2.2.6; 27). It is impossible to imagine such a scenario unfolding with Basil and his father.

John Henry Newman offers infant baptism as an example of a development of doctrine; the turning point, in the Eastern Church, is the generation between St. Basil and St. John Chrysostom, who supports the practice of infant baptism. "It is difficult for us at this day," Newman writes, "to enter into the assemblage of motives which led to this postponement" of baptism, but he goes on to mention a few reasons, among which two approximate the two reasons we have mentioned: "a keen sense and awe of the special privileges of baptism which could only once be received" and the "reluctance to being committed to a strict rule of life."[1] Newman's description of Basil's family, which we will consider again later, communicates well that they had a "keen sense and awe of the special privileges of baptism."

> St. Basil was the son of Christian confessors on both father's and mother's side. His grandmother Macrina, who brought him up, had for seven years lived with her husband in the woods of Pontus during the Decian persecution. His father

was said to have wrought miracles; his mother, an orphan of great beauty of person, was forced from her unprotected state to abandon the hope of a single life, and was conspicuous in matrimony for her care of strangers and the poor, and for her offerings to the churches. How religiously she brought up her children is shown by the singular blessing, that four out of ten have since been canonized as Saints. St. Basil was one of these; yet the child of such parents was not baptized till he had come to man's estate.[2]

Newman implies here that the piety of Christians such as Emmelia and Monica led to the near universal observance of the rite of infant baptism in later generations. There must be something more, something else, besides piety that accounts for the development of infant baptism, for there were pious Christians before Emmelia and Monica, and yet the practice of infant baptism did not take off. Nevertheless, if we grant Newman's inference to be at least partially true, then Basil had the piety but not its consequence.

Basil senior and Emmelia postponed Basil's baptism, then, not out of resignation to the power of passion but because baptism was a serious commitment at that time in the church, thought to be best made by adults. The circumstances of Basil's adult baptism bear this out, for it was an important aspect of the spiritual awakening that proved so very important in his life.

Indeed, if we are to understand Basil's theological vision of God, man, the world, the church, and the Scriptures, we must begin with this awakening that he experienced as a young man, just after he finished his schooling to become a rhetor. Basil's awakening was a "conversion,"[3] if we may speak loosely, to a life of Christian asceticism, and this Christian ascetic life is at once the context for Basil's reading of the Scriptures and the key to his understanding of God himself and his role in the economy of salvation. A fuller explication of these claims must await an account of Basil's awakening, which itself is but one example of a much broader movement in the fourth century that has been called "domestic asceticism" or "household asceticism."

Domestic Asceticism

The fourth century marks the beginning of a golden age of monasticism in the church, and in the forefront of our minds here are the great founders and fathers of Christian asceticism. We think, rightly, of Antony the Great (d. 356), about whom several lives were written, though Athanasius's became the most famous. We think of Pachomius (d. 346), whom we regard as the founder of coenobitic monasticism and who wrote the first rule to guide the common life for communities of both male and female ascetics. We think of Rufinus (d. 410) and Jerome (d. 420). The pioneering female ascetics should not be forgotten: Marcellina (d. 398), Demetrias (after 440), Melania the Elder (d. 410) and the Younger (d. 439). And, of course there are our Basil and Macrina (d. 379).

We do well to recognize, however, that this golden age is not limited to the institutionalized forms of asceticism but also embraces the less organized and more inchoate movement, from which some of the more organized forms grew.[4] At least two factors spurred the growth of this movement, as they did of organized asceticism: persecution before Constantine's conversion and the secularization of the church that followed it. While persecution must have affected individual families differently, Gregory of Nazianzus indicates how it affected Basil's paternal grandparents.[5] During the reign of Maximinus, he tells us, Basil's ancestors steered the virtuous mean between cowardice and foolhardiness in the face of persecution (*Or.* 43.5–6). They fled to the mountains of Pontus as a small company without servants and stayed there for around seven years. "Their mode of life," Gregory relates, "delicately nurtured as they were, was straitened and unusual, as may be imagined, with the discomfort of its exposure to frost and heat and rain, and the wilderness allowed no fellowship or converse with friends" (*Or.* 43.6; 397). Gregory describes here a sort of forced ascetic life. The wilderness forced on Basil's grandparents not only the bodily discomfort turned asceticism brought on by the elements but also ascetic isolation, a sort of social abstinence. As a very famous and later example of the former, we can call to mind Augustine's dear friend Alypius, who "tamed his body to a tough discipline by asceticism of extraordinary boldness: he went barefoot on the icy soil of Italy" (*Conf.* 9.6.14; 163). Basil's grandparents and their companions, Gregory tells us, did not grumble as did the Israelites in the desert. Rather, in piety and faith they cast themselves upon the mercy and bounty of God, who provided them wild game for food. These animals were not hunted or chased with dogs but with prayers, at which "their quarry lay before them, with food come of its own accord, a complete banquet prepared without effort, stags appearing all at once from some place in the hills" (*Or.* 43.7; 397). Persecution became the occasion for prayer and ascetic struggle, and Basil's grandparents took advantage of it. Indeed, Gregory wonders at these wild animals presenting themselves as food to Basil's relatives, not hunted by them but "caught by [their] mere will to do so" (*Or.* 43.8; 397). He sees this both as a foretaste of heaven and a reward for the "struggle" (*athlēsin*) in which they had been engaged (*Or.* 43.8).

With the conversion of Constantine, mediocrity and sometimes corruption replaced persecution as a spurring influence on both formal and domestic asceticism, for Constantine's beneficence to the church was a mixed blessing. It meant the production of Bibles, the building of churches, the restoration of property, tax breaks and some civil powers for clergy, and so on, but it also meant lukewarm half-converts from paganism and unscrupulous men seeking ecclesial office for worldly reasons.[6] We will see later that one of the moving forces behind Basil's ascetic thought was his conviction that the church of his time experienced so many difficulties and internal divisions because Christians, especially Christian leaders, had abandoned the commandments of Jesus and the order and peace that flow from keeping them (*On Judg.* 1–2).

Anna Silvas describes well the household asceticism that resulted from Christian families devoting themselves to living the gospel:

> The values of the Graeco-Roman civic *politeia* gradually yielded to more ex-
> plicitly Christian virtues. The cultural shift is seen especially in the fostering
> at home of the Scriptures and church traditions, in the practice of hospitality,
> personal frugality, and a Gospel charity in which the ruling idea is no longer
> philanthropy with a view to civic kudos, but self-effacing succour of the poor
> in imitation of Christ. (Silvas, 68)

We see a shift too from the ascetic practices of Basil's grandparents to those of his parents. There was a movement from the forced and prayerful austerity of living in the woods to avoid persecution to the "community of virtue" notable "for generosity to the poor, for hospitality, for purity of soul as the result of self-discipline, [and] for the dedication to God of a portion of their property" (*Or.* 43.9; 398). This is not quite the shift that Silvas describes above, but, of course, the one type of shift is not exclusive of the other, and we will see in Basil himself as in his family a gradual abandonment of the trappings and values of the secular culture in which they lived as they ever more thoroughly embraced the gospel and its social implications.

Eustathius of Sebaste

Eustathius may have been a friend of Basil's family and certainly exercised a spiritual and theological influence upon him. Born around 300, he belonged to the generation before Basil's and, so, was a father figure to him. The son of Bishop Eulalius of Sebaste,[7] Eustathius was a leader in both formal and domestic asceticism and advanced the former in the Roman provinces of Armenia, Paphlagonia, and Pontus, Sozomen tells us (*Eccl. Hist.* 3.14). He established "a society of monks," Sozomen says, but he also seems to have had a deep connection with St. Basil's family, and presumably other similar families (*Eccl. Hist.* 3.14; 293). We will see later Eustathius's doctrinal elasticity as he moves from one theological and doctrinal camp to another (from the "Semi-Arian" to the Nicene to the Pneumatomachian, who denied the divinity of the Holy Spirit); he also shows himself able to adjust his ascetic ideals in the face of ecclesial opposition.

This first sign of trouble was his condemnation by his own father "for dressing in a style unbecoming the sacerdotal office" (*Eccl. Hist.* 2.43; 72). Eustathius was a priest, but he had adopted the garb of a philosopher. His manner of dress turned out to be symbolic of more serious problems. In 340 or 341, the bishops of the area gathered in council at Gangra and condemned certain ascetic practices and Eustathius by name.[8] Gangra's prefatory letter summarizes the charges against Eustathius and his followers and then anathematizes the alleged beliefs and practices. They "find grave fault with marriage and suppose that none of those in the married state has hope with God, so that many married women, being deceived, have withdrawn from their own husbands and husbands from their own wives" (Gangra, pref.; 487; also can. 1, 9–10, 14). They will not even offer prayers in the houses of the married or take part in the Eucharist celebrated there, and they despise married clergy and their liturgies (Gangra, pref.; 488–89; also can. 4, 11, 20). Their rejection of marriage is made all the worse in the event that these ascetics, unable to control themselves, commit adultery. And it was not only the husband and wife who were the victims of these extreme views, for children were abandoned by their ascetic parents and themselves encouraged to withdraw from their parents and the filial obligations owed to them (Gangra, can. 15–16).

The Eustathians, however, did not stop at the destruction of marriage and the family, for they undermined in various ways not only the social order in the church but also that in secular society. They withdrew from the church and held their own assemblies, drawing away not only people but also their tithes (Gangra, can. 15–16, 5–8). The secular social order was undermined by the encouragement of slaves to withdraw from their masters and by the condemnation of the rich who did not forsake all their possessions (Gangra, can. 3). This social disruption, secular and ecclesial, was given concrete form in the Eustathians' ascetic practices: they wore strange clothes (Gangra, can. 12); women assumed men's dress and cut their hair (Gangra, can. 13, 17); they fasted on Sundays (Gangra, can. 18–19) and mocked the fasts of the church; and some rejected the eating of meat (Gangra, can. 2). All of this accords with the account of both Sozomen and Socrates, who focus on Eustathius's ascetic extremism, which was socially and ecclesially disruptive.

After the Synod of Gangra, Eustathius saw the error of his ways, repented, and suffered little ill repute from the whole affair. Sozomen reports that from this point on, "Eustathius exchanged his clothing for the stole, and made his journeys habited like other priests, thus proving that he had not introduced and practiced these novelties out of self-will, but for the sake of a godly asceticism" (*Eccl. Hist.* 3.14; 294).[9] Indeed, says Sozomen, Eustathius was renowned for his persuasive speech as for his purity of life, for he was able to persuade many to live a life of temperance and even virginity, this time, of course, according to the customs of the church and so in a way that was not offensive to either ecclesial or social order. Another indication that Eustathius was able to enter, and even flourish, in that stream of the ascetic movement that was not at odds with the institutional church was his relationship with Basil's family. They too were impressed with his speech and his purity of life, and he most probably played a role in their choice to continue down the ascetic road on which their persecuted grandparents had embarked. It is in the light of this larger movement in which Basil's family and Eustathius participated in various ways that we should see Basil's awakening.

Basil's Awakening

The first point to be made is that Basil was no Augustine, at least in the sense that he did not live a debauched life before his conversion to Christian asceticism and had not fallen in with a heterodox and schismatic sect. Basil came from a distinguished Christian family. In his funeral oration for St. Basil, St. Gregory of Nazianzus tells us that "the distinction of his family on either side was piety" (*Or.* 43.4; 396).[10] On his father's side were confessors who suffered in the persecution of Maximinus and Diocletian (*Or.* 43.5–8). Gregory of Nyssa mentions by name Macrina the Elder, Basil's paternal grandmother (*Macr.*; 20).

While we can only guess how the piety of his ancestors might have affected Basil, there is ample evidence of the influence that his immediate family had on him. We get a better sense of this from his brother Gregory of Nyssa than from Gregory of Nazianzus, who simply mentions the virtuousness of Basil's parents, Basil and Emmelia, noting especially their generosity to the poor and their hospitality (*Or.* 43.9). Nazianzen, in fact, seems to ignore that there was any significant change in Basil's character or course of life. Gregory of Nyssa testifies not only to Basil's need for conversion but also to the person who effected it: Basil's sister Macrina.

Nyssa writes that when Basil came home from school in Athens (355–56), "he was monstrously conceited about his skill in rhetoric, contemptuous of every high reputation and exalted beyond the leading lights of the province by his self-importance" (*Macr.*; 24). Basil admits that he had labored on the path to worldly success: he aspired to be a rhetor, that most prestigious and respected position in ancient society. In retrospect, however, Basil saw his intense study of rhetoric as time lavished on vanity and futility. "I occupied myself," he writes, "with the acquirement of the precepts of that wisdom made foolish by God [and] one day arising as from a deep sleep I looked out upon the marvelous light of the truth of the gospel, and beheld the uselessness of the wisdom 'of the princes of this world that come to nought' [1 Cor. 2:6]" (ep. 223.2; 3:293).

What is the nature and significance of Basil's awakening? In my later treatment of Basil's understanding of the ascetic life, I will attempt a thorough answer to this question, but suffice it to say here that, on the one hand, Basil's awakening was far more than a career change, for it is invested with deep religious significance and, indeed, presupposes a rich theological anthropology. On the other hand, we must balance Basil's above self-assessment with two others that he offers us. In one of his earlier works, written within a decade of the awakening itself, Basil writes that he was "delivered from the deceitful tradition of those outside, having been brought up from the very beginning by Christian parents." "With them," he continues, "I learned from a babe the Holy Scriptures which led me to a knowledge of the truth" (*On Judg.* 1; 77). Although in this same passage Basil mentions that he "engaged in many business affairs," there is no pejorative connotation and no sense that he departed from the scriptural truth that led him from infancy. He says much the same thing in epistle 223, the same letter in which he described the vanity and futility of his worldly pursuits. Defending himself against a charge of heterodoxy, Basil asserts, "I never held erroneous opinions about God, or, being otherwise minded, unlearned them later. Nay, the conception of God which I received in childhood from my blessed mother and my grandmother Macrina, this, developed, have I held within me" (ep. 223.3; 3:299). All of this conveys the impression that Basil's awakening was above all moral rather than doctrinal, and I will have more to say on this later.

So Basil had a moral awakening. Who woke him up? Anna Silvas presents a very compelling account of the story of Basil's awakening and the persons who lay behind it. Most influential were his sister, St. Macrina, and his brother, Naucratius. Macrina had been engaged to be married late in the 330s when her fiancé died. Upon his death Macrina invoked her right not to marry again and determined to be a consecrated widow and, in her case, a consecrated virgin. Gregory of Nyssa presents Macrina as the religious center of the family, in whose midst she continued to live as a leaven.

Nyssa also tells us the story of Basil's next younger brother, Naucratius. Though a talented rhetorician, Naucratius devoted himself to the ascetic life of "solitude and poverty" (*Macr.*; 26). Naucratius lived in the woods with Chrysaphius, a former servant and now friend, and the two of them provided food for a community of poor and sick old people. Naucratius and Chrysaphius tragically died in a hunting accident that shook Basil's whole family.

Silvas conjectures, very reasonably, that it was the death of Naucratius that brought Basil home from Athens (Silvas, 68).[11] Soon thereafter Macrina converted him to the ascetic life. Gregory of Nyssa writes that Macrina won Basil "so swiftly . . . to the ideal of philosophy that he renounced worldly appearance, showed contempt for the admiration of rhetorical ability and went over of his own accord to this active life of manual labor, preparing for himself by means of his complete poverty a way of life which would tend without impediment towards virtue" (*Macr.*; 25).

This turn to philosophy, in the ancient manner of speaking, with all of its sapiential and religious overtones was not "a *new* call," Silvas writes, "but a *re*-call."

> Makrina was not proposing something new to Basil, but recalling him to the piety of their childhood upbringing and to the intention he had formed even in Athens

to seek a life of "philosophy." . . . She persuaded her brother to make a break once and for all with the conventional life of a catechumen highly educated in the secular curriculum. Now that he was at a new juncture, let him not resume by default the life their father had left off, that of the devout Christian aristocrat and professional man, excellent as far as it went, but seize the moment to embrace baptism and with the life of Christian "philosophy"—virginity and asceticism. (Silvas, 70)

In addition to the counsel of Macrina and the example of Naucratius was the mentorship of Eustathius of Sebaste.

Eustathius modeled for Basil the path on which he should himself embark. In the same letter that we have so far examined for Basil's account both of his awakening and of his consistency in right belief from childhood, he tells us of the role that Eustathius of Sebaste played in his life at this point. "Bemoaning much my piteous life," Basil writes, "I prayed that there be given me a guidance to the introduction to the teachings of religion" (ep. 223.2; 3:293). Basil above all wanted to amend his character, and he realized that the evangelical path to perfection lay in poverty (selling one's goods), charity (giving them to the needy), and detachment (having no concern for the goods of this world). He wanted to find someone who had lived this way of life in order "to traverse with him this deep flood of life" (ep. 223.2; 3:293, altered).

So Basil went looking for such a guide. He tells us that he found many excellent and marvelous ascetic exemplars in Alexandria and the rest of Egypt, as well as in Coele-Syria and Mesopotamia (ep. 223.2).[12] But he also saw some in his own country doing the same. "I believed that I had found," Basil writes, "an aid to my own salvation" (223.3; 295). Eustathius was this aid. Having found what he was looking for, Basil was baptized around 357 by his bishop, Dianius, in Caesarea and retired to Pontus, where he was joined by Gregory of Nazianzus in his pursuit of the ascetic life. Gregory, however, could not stay in Pontus and was drawn back to Nazianzus.

Basil's Pontic retreat was rustic. In epistle 14, to Gregory of Nazianzus, he described some of its features. It had a mountain with a plain at its base, forests, and cool streams. It was secluded, with natural barriers on all sides. Basil calls it an island: two deep ravines on two sides, a river on the third, and the mountain on the fourth. There was plentiful game and fish and much natural beauty, for example, in songbirds and flowers (ep. 14.2). Gregory's response (his ep. 4) to Basil's letter cast these very attributes in a different, humorous light. He calls it a place of exile, and Basil's dwelling there, a mousehole. The air is limited and the sun can be seen only as "through a chimney" (ep. 4; 446). The river is loud and has more stones than fish. The birds sing, surely, but about famine, and Gregory complains about the food he ate there in his next letter.

For I remember those loaves and the broth (so it was called), yes, and I shall remember them too, and my poor teeth that slipped on your hunk of bread, and then braced themselves up, and pulled themselves as it were out of mud. (ep. 5; 447)

When he puts all joking aside, however, Gregory speaks of his Pontic experience with Basil in the highest terms. He longs not only for the "psalmodies and vigils," the "sojournings with God in prayer," and the study of Scripture, but also for the experience of gathering wood and cutting stone; he longed to be "a monk worn out by hard life," sustained by communion with God and "onesouledness" with Basil and the other brethren (ep. 6; 447–48).

It was during this Pontic retreat of the late 350s that we see a crucial shift in Basil's understanding of the Christian life—his realization that he cannot properly worship God except through studying and praying the Scriptures. The evidence for this shift consists of a few early letters (ep. 1, 2, 4, 14, and 22). If we accept Silvas's chronological ordering of these letters (thus, 1, 14, 4, 2, and 22), it is manifest "that Basil's ascetic discourse progresses from a philosophical discourse, virtually indistinguishable from that of the pagan ascetic traditions (Letters 1 and 4), through letters which increasingly combine such discourse with more overtly Christian content (Letters 14 and 2) to one which is thoroughly Christian and scriptural in tone (Letter 22)" (Silvas, 86–87).[13] Silvas notes that in epistles 1, 14, and 4, Basil's ascetic life seems rather classical. In all these letters he heavily uses classical allusions to pagan authors and in epistle 4 indicates that he has taken up the philosopher's mantle.[14]

In epistle 2 (358), to Gregory of Nazianzus, Basil has actually been practicing his new lifestyle for some time, a year or more. The first thing to notice is Basil's realization that the ascetic life is not exactly what he imagined.

> But I am ashamed to write what I myself do night and day in this out-of-the-way place. For I have indeed left my life in the city, as giving rise to countless evils, but I have not yet been able to leave myself behind. On the contrary, I am like those who go to sea, and because they have had no experience in sailing are very distressed and sea-sick, and complain of the size of the boat as causing the violent tossing; and then when they leave the ship and take to the dinghy or the cock-boat, they continue to be sea-sick and distressed wherever they are; for their nausea and bile go with them when they change. Our experience is something like this. For we carry our indwelling disorders about with us, and so are nowhere free from the same sort of disturbances. Consequently we have derived no great benefit from our present solitude. (ep. 2.1; 1:7–9)

So solitude (erēmia), what he later calls "separation from the world,"[15] has not borne the ascetic fruit that Basil had expected.

Basil, however, does not give up on it, not yet. He follows his confession of his lack of success with a statement of the ascetic program that, he thinks, will lead to salvation, and the pair of solitude and tranquility (hēsychia) dominate the program. "We must," Basil writes, "keep the mind in tranquility," without which it is drawn here and there and cannot focus on the truth (ep. 2.2; 1:9).[16] While "tranquility" designates above all a state of the soul rather than a physical place, this state of the soul is much easier to acquire in solitude and separation from the world, for solitude calms the passions and lulls them to sleep (ep. 2.2). So solitude and physical separation from the world engender spiritual tranquility, which is the "beginning of the soul's purgation" (ep. 2.2; 1:13), and "when the mind is not dissipated upon extraneous things, nor diffused over the world about us through the senses, it withdraws within itself, and of its own accord ascends to the contemplation of God" (ep. 2.2; 1:13). From this point, the soul's only concern is to acquire eternal goods, virtues (especially temperance, justice, fortitude, and prudence) that direct those who are zealous to live as they ought (ep. 2.2).

It is only here that Basil mentions a significant role for the Scriptures: they are "a most important path to the discovery of duty," since they contain not only the precepts of conduct but also the lives of the saints as examples for us (ep. 2.3; 1:15). It would be inaccurate, however, to think of the Scriptures as an unnatural appendage to an otherwise purely Hellenistic model of salvation. The whole ascetic program that Basil outlines in epistle 2 he expressly understands as an imitation of Christ. The life of solitude and tranquility enables us "to keep close to the footsteps of him who pointed the way to salvation (for he says, 'If any man will come after me, let him deny himself, and take up his cross and follow me' [Matt. 16:24]" (ep. 2.1; 1:9). Basil also speaks of "divine instruction" and "divine teaching" that may—the context does not make it clear—refer to the Scriptures (ep. 2.2). There is, too, a reference to imitating the choirs of angels by hastening to prayer at daybreak and worshiping the Creator with hymns and songs (ep. 2.2). These seem to be Psalms.

One more feature of Basil's ascetic program in epistle 2 needs to be mentioned: prayer. Prayer stirs the soul, refreshes it, and invigorates it (ep. 2.4). Prayer "engenders in the soul a distinct conception of God. And the indwelling of God is this—to hold God ever in memory, his shrine established within us" (ep. 2.4; 1:17). Thus, in withdrawing from the world, the soul can quiet the passions and, in prayer, ascend to the thought of God alone. "The lover of God," Basil writes, "withdraws into God . . . and abides in the practices that lead to virtue" (ep. 2.4; 1:17).

Basil spends the rest of the letter describing these practices that lead to virtue. One must be moderate in speaking and listening (ep. 2.5). One must attend—or rather, not attend—to one's physical appearance: the hair is to be unkempt and clothes dirty, as they are for the philosophers (ep. 2.6). The tunic ought to be worn in a particular way, and sandals should be cheap but adequate. One must apply to food the same rule of utility that applies to clothing, having consideration only for the true needs of the body so that the mind can remain focused on God. Prayers should be said before and after the one regular meal each day (ep. 2.6). Finally, one must sleep in a way that is conducive to virtue. "Sleep should be light and easily broken . . . interrupted deliberately by meditations on high themes" (ep. 2.6; 1:25).

Silvas sees great significance in epistle 2. The use of Scripture appears for the first time; and there emerge distinctively Christian themes. She comments that

> Basil appears to be straddling two types of discourse and has not quite sorted them out yet. Perhaps the most important new note in ep. 2 is that now, several months into his new life, "prayer" has come to assume a great importance for Basil and the "memory of God" and "yearning" it engenders. Prayer was hardly conceded by the philosophers as a means to divine knowledge; indeed, Plotinus seems to have disdained it. (Silvas, 88)

Basil's shift to a more overtly Christian and scripturally based asceticism continues with epistle 22, "On the perfection of the monastic life." "All talk of 'philosophy' and every classical allusion has fallen away" (Silvas, 88). In epistle 22, Basil writes that "since in the divinely inspired Scriptures many directions are set forth which must be strictly observed by all who earnestly wish to please God, I desire to say . . . a few words based upon the knowledge which I have derived from the divinely inspired Scriptures themselves" (ep. 22.1; 1:129). There follows a catalog of moral guidelines for the Christian with copious allusions to and quotations from the New Testament.

Even if Silvas is wrong on the precise dating, and therefore ordering, of epistles 1, 14, 4, 2, and 22 (as she has it)—even if Basil's progress toward a scripturally based asceticism was not so steady but rather herky-jerky—there is nonetheless a marked change in Basil's ascetic practice after 362. In 362, Basil had left his monastic retreat to return to Caesarea and be reconciled to Bishop Dianius, from whom Basil had withdrawn over his signing of the Homoian creed of Constantinople in 360. After Dianius's death, Basil stayed in Caesarea, and under the new bishop, Eusebius, Basil was ordained a priest and continued to live the monastic life, but in a different form. Indeed, he organized a community of ascetics who looked upon him as their leader. Gregory of Nazianzus gives us some information here in the course of explaining Basil's falling out with Eusebius. Gregory says nothing about the source and character of the dispute, indicating only that Basil was treated unjustly by Eusebius. "All the more eminent and wise portion of the Church," Gregory writes, "was roused against him [Eusebius], if those are wiser than the majority who have separated themselves from the world and consecrated their life to God" (Or. 43.28; 405). These ascetics even threatened schism, Gregory says, as they were so "annoyed that their chief should be neglected, insulted, and rejected" (Or. 43.28; 405). Thus Basil held a significant and loyal following in Caesarea. Not wishing to cause a schism, and with the counsel of Gregory, whose inclination in the face of a difficult situation was often to run, Basil left Caesarea for Pontus "and presided over the abodes of contemplation there"

(*Or.* 43.29; 405). Basil wrote epistle 22 to the monks he had left behind, and it provides us a window into the ascetic life that he had established there.

In some respects Basil's ascetic life in Pontus up to 362 (that we see in ep. 2) is similar to that evidenced by epistle 22. In both, there is an emphasis on poverty, moderation in food and dress, and a constant mindfulness of God. Even in these similarities, however, we can see differences. The most obvious difference is that the counsels of epistle 22 are thoroughly drenched in the language of the Scriptures.[17] We might contrast, for example, the philosophical-sounding mindfulness of God in epistle 2 with the same point scripturally made in epistle 22. "The Christian ought to think," Basil admonishes, "thoughts worthy of his heavenly vocation [Heb. 3:1], and conduct himself worthily of the Gospel of Christ [Phil. 1:27]. The Christian should not be frivolous [Luke 12:29] or easily drawn away by anything from the remembrance of God and from his will and judgments" (ep. 22.1; 1:131).

In Pontus, his ascetic life was marked, we have seen, by isolation and tranquility: it was, Basil says, "city-less" (*apolin*; ep. 2.2). In Caesarea, on the other hand, Basil's ascetic life becomes more socially complex: so much in epistle 22 reflects an elaborate and highly structured common life. First, there are persons in various positions of authority: those entrusted with the dispensation of the Word, for example, and those charged with general discipline (ep. 22.1). When it comes to a monk's necessities or his work, he is under the authority of another and should not grumble (ep. 22.1). Eating and drinking should be done with the approval of superiors (ep. 22.1), and "the Christian should not turn from one work to another without the approval of those assigned for the regulation of such matters" (ep. 22.1; 1:135–37). Second, so many of the counsels in epistle 22 address the malicious and destructive forces that arise in larger communities of persons trying to live a common life, as, for example, the prohibition on evil speech, insults, wrangling, revenge, anger, slander, talking behind another's back, seeking places of honor, disobedience, rivalry, trespassing on another's workshop, envy, rejoicing over another's faults, and resentment. There are also guidelines for fraternal correction, counsel for the attendant hostile feelings that it can engender, and a rule for silence in the workplace out of consideration for other workers. Such prohibitions and counsels would be entirely out of place for, say, Naucratius and Chrysaphius living as friends in the woods of Pontus, or for Basil and Gregory pursuing the philosophic life there. Basil addresses in epistle 22 a set of issues that pertain to a different sort of common life.

Not only is there a complex and structured social life, but social interaction becomes part of the very substance of the ascetic life. The "Christian," who, of course, is the monk, "should not consider himself as his own master, but as having been delivered by God into servitude to his brethren of like spirit, so he should always think and act, 'but everyone in his own order' [1 Cor. 15:23]" (ep. 22.1; 1:133). Here we see an intimation of the other-centered love that would become one of the distinctive features of Basil's mature ascetic thought. Love, rather than authority—though the latter is obviously important—is Basil's guiding principle of social intercourse.

Basil's understanding of the ascetic life and his progress therein illuminate the role of the Scriptures in God's economy of salvation, and, therefore, indicate the context in which we are to read them, the context in which they make sense. Thus far, then, the Scriptures, for Basil, are the directions that we must observe in order to please God, as he says in epistle 22. He sees the Scriptures as divine help and instruction given to Christians so that they might learn, and having learned, remind themselves of the way of life that is pleasing to God. This is the purpose of the Scriptures in the economy of salvation.

In another ascetic work, the *Morals*, at least conceived if not also first written between 359 and 361, Basil advances yet again both his articulation of the Christian ascetic life and the attendant role of the Scriptures.[18] On the surface, the text appears simple, and even primitive, when compared with Basil's ascetic works in their final form. As he says in one of the prefaces to the *Morals*, he wishes "to remind by selections from the inspired Scriptures those who are engaged in the contest of piety what things are displeasing to God and what things he is pleased with" (*On Judg.* 8; 89).[19] Thus the *Morals* seems little more than select passages of the New Testament, with very little commentary by Basil himself, that outline the way of life of an earnest Christian.

Beneath this superficial simplicity, however, lay some profound truths about the Christian life as Basil has come to understand it and some profound differences with his earlier description of the Christian ascetic life. We see in the *Morals*, in its final form, both a deepening of the themes of epistle 22 and the introduction of new ones. As an example, we could take Basil's emphasis on penance at the beginning of the *Morals*. The theme is new in the sense that Basil does not mention it in his ascetic letters, but it nevertheless testifies to a trend we have already seen in his thought—namely, the tendency toward greater social and communal complexity. Basil stresses that "they who believe in the Lord must first repent according to the preaching of John and of our Lord Jesus Christ himself" (*Mor.* 1.1; 101). Moreover, the way in which Basil speaks of the penitents may imply that they are a distinct group within the community: "Those who repent should weep bitterly and show forth from the heart the rest of the things proper to repentance" (*Mor.* 1.3; 101), and the "mere giving up of sin is not sufficient for penitents to win salvation, but they need also fruits meet for repentance" (*Mor.* 1.4; 101). In addition to the penitents, there are also a group of hearers (*Mor.* 72.1).

A clearer example than penance of a theme more deeply considered in the *Morals* than in epistle 22 is authority. Basil devotes rules 70–71 to a consideration of the ordained. The thirty-seven chapters of rule 70 concern bishops:[20] what sort of candidates are to be appointed as deacons and priests, and who is to appoint them; when and how those who are entrusted with the ministry of the Word should preach; what disposition they ought to have to those who are suffering; and how they should treat those in their care (*Mor.* 70). Rule 71, only two chapters long, mentions bishops, priests, and deacons.

In addition to this deepening of the social aspect of the ascetic life there appears in the *Morals* a new and striking emphasis on the sacraments of baptism and the Eucharist. Basil speaks of both sacraments at two different points in the *Morals*. Citing the Great Commission of Matthew 28:19, together with John 3:3 and 5, Basil writes that "those who believe in the Lord must be baptized into the Name of the Father and the Son and the Holy Ghost" (*Mor.* 20.1; 107). Basil then asks, "What is the inner meaning or the power of baptism?" And he answers, "the change of the baptized in mind, word, and deed, and his becoming by the power given, that very thing of which he was born" (*Mor.* 20.2; 107). In the next rule, Basil quotes John 6:54–55 and derives from this text the obvious point "that participation in the body and blood of Christ is necessary for eternal life" (*Mor.* 21.1; 107). He mentions here, too, the necessity of communicating worthily and the appropriateness of praising the Lord with hymns after communion (*Mor.* 21.2–4).

Baptism and Eucharist make a second and significant appearance at the very end of the *Morals*. Basil concludes the work with a rousing summation of the Christian life in question-and-answer format, and the key and oft-repeated question is "What is the distinguishing mark of a Christian?" (*Mor.* 80.22; 129). In the earlier parts of rule 80, the last in the *Morals*, Basil summarizes the qualities that Scripture would have Christians possess as disciples of Christ (*Mor.* 80.1–11), as well as the qualities that Scripture would have the clergy possess (*Mor.* 80.11–21). In the final part of rule 80 and the last chapter of the *Morals*, Basil returns to the theme of Christian identity. He offers several answers to his question "What is the distinguishing mark of a Christian?" all derived from the Scriptures and all focusing on love of God and Christ and love of neighbor. Baptism and Eucharist are seamlessly integrated into the distinctively Christian life. It is the mark of a Christian "to be born anew in baptism of water and Spirit" (*Mor.* 80.22; 130). The one who is born of water is dead to sin, and the one born of the Spirit becomes, "according to the measure given him, that very thing of which he was born" (*Mor.* 80.22; 130). To be a Christian is also to participate in the blood of Christ, "to perfect holiness in the fear of God and love of Christ" (*Mor.* 80.22; 130). Those who receive the Eucharist keep Jesus in perpetual remembrance and "live unto themselves no longer, but unto him who died for them and rose again" (*Mor.* 80.22; 130).

We have seen in Basil's earlier thought that mindfulness of God was very important to the ascetic life, as too was the life of virtue. This remains true, of course, in the *Morals*, but here there is a much stronger focus on Jesus: one must focus the mind not simply on God but on the death and resurrection of Jesus. Thus Basil's ascetic life becomes not only more scripturally centered but more Christ-centered. Earlier Basil spoke of the mind, freed from passions, ascending of itself to God (ep. 2.2). In the *Morals*, the Christian must always set his sight on the Lord Jesus; he must "watch each night and day and in the perfection of pleasing God to be ready, knowing that the Lord cometh at an hour he thinketh not" (*Mor.* 80.22; 131).

Conclusion

I hope to have intimated here, and to illustrate more fully in the chapters that follow, that at the root of Basil's Nicene theology—the foundation of his Nicene world—is a religious and spiritual awakening, or a series of awakenings. The seeds of these awakenings were planted in Basil's childhood, both in the piety of his parents and the memory of his grandparents. The seeds lay dormant for a while until they were germinated by the example and death of Basil's brother Naucratius, and watered by the courage and encouragement of his sister Macrina. The initial awakening grew and matured over time and in stages, from philosophical to sacramental and scriptural, from rustic to urban, from socially simple to socially complex. In the following chapters we will explore the theology that stands behind and emerges from Basil's spiritual awakening, beginning with his theological anthropology.

2

Man

Body and Soul, "Made" and "Molded"

In an article on Basil's two homilies on man, Philip Rousseau has made the astute observation that for Basil, man is, at the heart of his identity, a reader and an interpreter. "Human identity," Rousseau writes, "is at root the identity of a hearer or reader (albeit inspired by the Spirit and alert to the presence of Christ)."[1] We might fill out Rousseau's point by saying that man is both reader and book or text, reader in soul and book in body. This insight illuminates not only Basil's view of man, body and soul, but also his view of the Scriptures and the whole of material creation. The present chapter will explore this claim in regard to Basil's anthropology, while the Scriptures and the rest of creation will be considered later.

Man as Reader

What is the significance of defining man as a reader? Basil sees man as a reader, but a reader must have a text. Man's texts, for Basil, are principally two, the Scriptures and the whole of creation, including the human body. The author of man's two books is God himself. One important implication here is that both the Scriptures and creation, being texts, are full of meaning and significance. The posture that the French poet Paul Claudel took before reality expresses well St. Basil's too. Claudel "in front of a piece of reality—a flower, a mountain, a woman—always felt the need to ask, 'Qu'est-ce que ça veut dire?'"[2] We might typically translate this as "What does it mean?" but literally it is rendered "What does it want to say?" For Basil, the Scriptures and the world want to say something, or God wants to say something through them.

So man is the reader, and creation and the Scriptures are the texts, the books. Basil tells his flock, "This whole world is as it were a book that proclaims the glory of God, announcing through itself the hidden and invisible greatness of God to you who have a mind for the apprehension of truth" (*Hex.* 11.4; 51).[3] The text, whether creation, the Scriptures, or the human body, calls for a response from the reader. Rousseau offers as an example the implication that Basil draws from his trinitarian interpretation of the "Let us make" of Genesis 1:26. It is not just that Scripture communicates to us that "the Father created through the Son, and the Son created by the Father's will" (*Hex.* 10.4; 33). This is revealed so that we may glorify the Father in the Son. The proper response of the reader is worship. "Thus you have been made a common work," Basil addresses his people, "that you may be a worshipper of both together, not dividing the worship but uniting the Godhead" (*Hex.* 10.4; 33). This character of the text, that it calls for the response of the reader, implies that we have in it more than *historia*, more than a story or a history. As Basil says about Genesis 1:26, "We have, on the one hand, you see, what looks, in its form, like a story, but is, on the other hand, at the level of power, a theology" (*Hex.* 10.4).[4] God, then, is not concerned merely to communicate so much information, even useful information, about himself or about us. The Scriptures are not just informative, but, if you will, performative, and here the action that God wishes us to perform is the worship of him as Father, Son, and Holy Spirit. As a reader, man is constantly called to relate to God and to his own salvation what he finds in the two great books, Scripture and creation, that have been given to him. This is why Basil is never interested in mere history or mere observation.

Furthermore, to be created a reader is to be created in an intermediate state. If man already possessed his end, if he already understood God and offered God the worship that God is due, he would not have to read the text of creation or his own body or the Scriptures in order to understand God and be led to worship God as he ought. Even more than existing in an intermediate state, man is an intermediate *being*: he both can read and needs to read. The angels have the ability but not the need (at least not in the same way), while the animals have neither. Man is a reader, an intermediate being, for two reasons: first, he is a rational creature, and second, he is a rational creature with a body.

First, then, let us ponder the significance of man being a rational creature, and here man is in the same position as the angel. Basil often compares men and angels, constantly calling the former to be more like the latter. Man will be pleasing to God when he offers to him servitude and honor like the angels (*Hom. on Ps.* 116 [114].5).[5] Angels are the measure of men, and we can ascend quickly toward equality with them through good conduct (*Hom. Attend* 6). They are intermediate beings insofar as they are created but not insofar as they are bodily.[6] What Basil writes of angels in *On the Holy Spirit*, though, would equally apply to men: These "pure, intelligent, and other-worldly powers," Basil writes, "both are and are called holy because they have acquired holiness as a gift given to them by the Holy Spirit" (*On H. Sp.* 16.38; 70). Basil asserts that holiness and abiding in holiness is the perfection of angels, and they do not have this by nature as the Holy Spirit does. Angels have a measure of holiness from the Holy Spirit, but, unlike the Spirit, their "holiness is extrinsic to their substance," and "they protect their own dignity by remaining steadfast in the good, and while they have freedom of choice, they never fail to attend to what is truly good" (*On H. Sp.* 16.38; 72). Men, like angels, have choice and must attend to the good in order to arrive at perfection.

Men, unlike angels, have bodies. In spite of the profound similarity, a similarity rooted in reason and in a common creatureliness, men and angels differ in that the latter "are perfected not by their making progress but at the moment of their very creation" (*On H. Sp.* 16.38; 73), while the former, by contrast, do make progress, a progress that is achieved, above all, through action in the body. Basil's understanding of man as a rational bodily creature who comes to perfection progressively by the exercise of his rational powers and the gift of the Holy Spirit is reflected in his interpretation of Genesis 1:26.

This text is, for Basil, replete with meaning, and he unfolds its meaning word by word. First, there is *poiēsōmen*, "Let us make." We have already seen one of the truths that Basil sees in this word—namely, the Trinity. The "*poiēsōmen*" of Genesis 1:26 finds its correlative in the "*epoiēsen*" of Genesis 1:27, "And God made man." In the first, which is plural, we are taught to "recognize Father and Son and Holy Spirit"; in the second, which is singular, to avoid the inference of polytheism from the multiplicity of persons by uniting not the hypostases (as, we might add, the Sabellians would do) but by uniting the Godhead and the power (*Hex.* 10.4; 33).

In addition to this "theology," "let us make" signifies the dignity of man. Man is the only creature, Basil points out, whose creation followed a deliberation (*boulē*). Light, the heavens, the stars, the sea, wild and domesticated animals—all came to exist by a simple command without deliberation. God, Basil, writes, "did not say, as with the others, 'Let there be a human being'" (*Hex.* 10.3; 33). "Learn well," Basil writes, "your own dignity [*timion*]. He did not cast forth your origin by a commandment, but there was counsel [*bouleuthērion*] in God to consider how to bring the dignified living creature into life. . . . The wise one deliberates [*bouleuetai*], the Craftsman ponders" (*Hex.* 10.3; 33).

If we read Basil's two points about "let us make" together—the theological, trinitarian one and the anthropological, deliberative one—we can see that the Trinity is the foundation of human dignity. "So it is *boulē* that guarantees dignity," Rousseau writes, "and what makes that discussion possible is the relationship between the two *prosōpa*, the Father and the Son—which in turn

makes the communicative vitality of the Trinity itself an essential precondi-
tion of a human being's *timē* [honor]."[7] Man is the issue of a special act of
divine rationality, a fitting sign of man's own rationality, the source of his
distinction from the animals and of his dignity. It is as if God did not have to
put much thought, so to speak, into the creation of the lower creatures. Or
rather, because he did not think or deliberate about their creation, they are
less reflective of his wisdom. He was more thoughtful and wiser, if we may
put it so, with man's creation, and so man more clearly reflects the wisdom
from which he comes.

Proceeding, again, word by word, Basil turns to "in our image." This is not
to be thought of, of course, in a material way, for God has no shape or size.
He cannot be enclosed "in bodily concepts," for he is "incomprehensible in
greatness" (*Hex.* 10.5; 34). If we read the first sentence of Genesis 1:26 with
the second, "And let them have dominion over the fish," the meaning of "in
our image" emerges. The ruling power is in the soul, not the body, and the
ruling power is reason. The Scripture says that "the human being is according to the image of God"; "the rational part is the human being" (*Hex.* 10.7;
36). Basil uses St. Paul to confirm his interpretation, for St. Paul distinguishes
between our outer man (*ho exō hēmōn anthrōpos*) and our inner man (*ho
esō hēmōn anthrōpos*) (2 Cor. 4:16). Though we are somehow double, "it is
truly said that we are that which is within," and man "is principally the soul
in itself" (*Hex.* 10.7; 36).

In a turn of phrase that accords well with the image of man as reader, Basil
says that the divine voice that says, "let them rule," is *written* (*anagrapton*)
in our nature: "Where the power to rule is, there is the image of God" (*Hex.*
10.8; 36–37). Thus, when we serve the passions and become a slave to sin, we
throw away our dignity and renounce "the nobility of our nature" (*Hex.* 10.8;
37). Basil makes his point with irony, using the master-slave relationship: he
who is a slave according to the body and yet rules his passions has no reason
to lament, for he is a slave in name only, while his master, a slave to pleasure
and passion, is the true slave.

Genesis 1:26 lists the creatures over which man exercises his ruling authority,
and Basil tends to each in turn. He then returns to the question of likeness, for
he had not yet explained what it means to say that man is created "according
to the likeness." He dismisses out of hand the suggestion that "according to
likeness" and "according to image" mean the same thing: "It is perverse to say
the same thing twice, [and] to say that there is an idle word in Scripture is a
terrible blasphemy" (*Hex.* 10.15; 43). To be made, then, according to likeness
is to have the ability, through the exercise of free choice, "to become like God"
(*Hex.* 10.16; 44). God has given us room, as it were, to participate in our own
coming to be like him. He has given us "that which is according to the image"
and "left incomplete" that which is according to the likeness, precisely so that
we might complete what he has left undone (*Hex.* 10.17; 45). As Basil puts

it, God "let us be artisans of the likeness to God, so that the reward for the work would be ours" (*Hex.* 10.16; 44). "He has left it to me," Basil says, "to become according to the likeness," so that the praise for the likeness and the marvel "may become mine and not another's" (*Hex.* 10.16; 44).

If I have, by creation, what is according to the image, how do I "become according to the likeness"? The answer is by becoming a Christian (*Hex.* 10.16; 44). In short, one becomes like God by putting on Christ.

> If you become a hater of evil, free of rancor, not remembering yesterday's enmity; if you become brother-loving and compassionate, you are like God. If you forgive your enemy from your heart, you are like God. If as God is toward you, the sinner, you become the same toward the brother who has wronged you, by your good will from your heart toward your neighbor, you are like God. (*Hex.* 10.17; 44)

To act out of sympathy is to put on Christ, and "drawing near to him is drawing near to God" (*Hex.* 10.17; 44). Basil puts it another way: "How," he asks, "do we come to be according to the likeness? Through the Gospels. What is Christianity? Likeness to God as far as is possible for human nature" (*Hex.* 10.17; 45). Or again, he says that to put on Christ is to be sealed in baptism and to receive the garment of incorruption (*Hex.* 10.17).

Basil finishes his treatment of image and likeness with a fascinating exchange. He takes on the voice of the women in his congregation to offer an objection to all that he has said so far about man's creation according to the image.[8] Basil's objector says that the text has "God made man." He continues:

> "Man [*ho anthrōpos*]," says the woman, "what does that have to do with me? The male [*ho anēr*] came to be, for it does not say *woman* [*hē anthrōpos*]" she says, "but by setting forth *man* [*anthrōpos*], it implies masculine [*to arrenikon*]." (*Hex.* 10.18)

Basil points out that Scripture here uses "man" (*ho anthrōpos*), even in its grammatically masculine form, inclusively. This is made obvious by the text that follows, "male and female he created them." Thus, "nobody may ignorantly ascribe the name 'man' only to the male" (*Hex.* 10.18). Basil affirms that woman "also possesses creation according to the image of God" (*Hex.* 10.18; 45). There is equality of nature in honor, virtue, struggle, and judgment. In a sermon preached in commemoration of the martyr Julitta, Basil has her say, "We are made of the same dough as men. Just like them we were created in the image of God. Woman, just like a man, was made by the creator capable of virtue. Are we not their equals in everything?" (*Hom. mart. Jul.* 2).[9]

If woman is weaker than man, it is in the body only, and not in the soul. Even here, however, the matter is not so simple. The female body "is vigorous in patient endurance and earnest in vigils" (*Hex.* 10.18; 46). "When," Basil asks, "has the nature of man been able to match the nature of woman in patiently passing through her own life? When has man been able to imitate the vigor of women in fastings, the love of toil in prayers, the abundance of tears, the readiness for good works?" (*Hex.* 10.18; 46).

While we will treat Basil's understanding of the body below, we do well here to note that many of the examples that Basil gives of achieving likeness to God involve the body. Fraternal love and compassion, good works, fasting, tears in prayer, dominating the passions of sin—all are summed up in what Basil will later call "bodily service" (*sōmatikēn hypēresian*) (*Hex.* 11.5). We can now describe more clearly how man's intermediate state involves the body. Man is a reader, we said, because he is in an intermediate state and because he is an intermediate being: he has what is according to the image but not yet what is according to the likeness. The latter he possesses, the former he must achieve. Man is made incomplete and must complete himself by becoming a Christian. But being a Christian involves, in the various ways just mentioned, the body and work in the body. Thus we attain what is according to the likeness of God not in the sense that our bodies become like God but in the sense that the soul must use the body in pursuing its likeness to God.

"According to likeness" is closely bound up with "according to image," for we achieve likeness to God by exercising our "own authority." We become like God when we exercise the power to rule, the power given us by God and by which we are made according to his image. Basil nicely brings together image and likeness when he says, "You have become like God through kindness, through endurance of evil, through communion, through love for one another and love for the brethren, being a hater of evil, dominating the passions of sin, that to you may belong the rule" (*Hex.* 10.18; 46).

So far we have emphasized the intermediate character of human existence, as created in the image of God and progressing in his likeness. There is another respect in which man occupies the in-between, what Morwenna Ludlow calls the liminal space. Like angels, men are on the threshold not only of being and becoming but also of good and evil. "Demons," as Ludlow puts it, "occupy a liminal space: their wills are utterly opposed to God and thus evil, and yet these wills exist in a nature which is part of God's good creation."[10] Man, too, occupies this liminal space, and human existence is "a tension between good and evil."[11] The predicament of the demons, the "drama" of their creation and fall "was an exaggerated version of humans' own" and a warning that "humans too could lock themselves into their own lives of sin."[12]

In the first rule of his *Longer Rules*, St. Basil takes up the question of whether there is an order or sequence in the commandments of God and offers in response a beautiful discourse on the twofold commandment of love wherein he presents man as created imperfect or unfinished and in an intermediate state. Of this passage, Silvas writes that "it presents a sophisticated religious anthropology, perhaps with some Stoic and Origenistic colouring, but above all scripturally sourced" (Silvas, 22).

Basil treats not only love but also the anthropological foundation of it. That is to say, he grounds love and the commandment to love in the very creation of the human person. In a few words, we were made to love. God made us in such a way that we have within ourselves "the impulses which tend of their own accord towards love" (*Lg. Rul.* 2.1; 162). Basil speaks of this natural capacity as a "seed-like word" "implanted" in us. The seed grows to maturation in the school—Basil mixes his metaphors—of God's commandments. "It is germinated in the school of God's commandments, where it is carefully cultivated, skillfully nurtured, and so, with God's grace, brought to maturity" (*Lg. Rul.* 2.1; 162). Even though "love for God is not something taught" (*Lg. Rul.* 2.1; 162), for it is given in nature, nature alone does not bring the seed of love to blossom.

Introducing a third metaphor for the innate tendency to love and the process whereby it is brought into activity, into bloom, Basil speaks of himself as stirring up "the spark of divine yearning hidden" within his monks. He tells them that he welcomes their "zeal as necessary for attaining the goal" and that "by God's gift" and their prayers he will be able to enkindle in them the love of God, "according to the power given us by the Spirit" (*Lg. Rul.* 2.1; 162–63). Thus three conditions must obtain for these monks to be aflame with the love of God: first, they themselves must strive after it; second, Basil must do his part as their father in the ascetic life; and third, God must help, the Holy Spirit must give Basil power. These, in fact, are the three essential features, not only of formal religious life but also of any genuine life of holiness or of likeness to God, and all three appear in the preface of the *Longer Rules*, though two dominate.[13]

The first thing to say is that the monks have sought out Basil's direction. Basil responds with a strong exhortation. "I appeal to you," he pleas, "by the love of our Lord Jesus Christ, who gave himself for our sins, let us take thought for our souls" (*Lg. Rul.* prol. 1; 153). Basil numbers himself with the monks when he says "let us." We should lament the vanity of our past life, stop being slothful, consider the final judgment, and no longer defer obedience. We have to not only desire the kingdom but also do those things by which we can gain it. "Whoever," Basil asks, "at the time of sowing stayed at home idle or asleep, yet as soon as the harvest has come, filled his arms with sheaves?" (*Lg. Rul.* prol. 2; 155). We must labor if we are to receive the fruit and conquer if we are to receive the crown. Thus Basil stresses the importance for salvation of human striving. In the language of the *Hexaëmeron*, striving brings image to likeness; in the language of the *Longer Rules*, it brings seed to fruit, the impulse to love to the act of love.

I will later treat more extensively Basil's role as the leader of monastic communities, but suffice it to say for now that human striving finds its complement in human direction. "Let us pray therefore," he writes, "that I may dispense the word blamelessly (Acts 6:4) and that the teaching may bear fruit in you" (*Lg. Rul.* prol. 4; 160). Twice Basil cites the words of the apostle Paul and applies them to himself. Like St. Paul, he must not "cease night or day to admonish every one with tears" (Acts 20:31) and "woe to me if I do not preach the gospel" (1 Cor. 9:16). While in this preface to the *Longer Rules* Basil seems to attend only to two of the three features, indeed leaving aside the most important—namely, the help of God—I believe his point is that God brings about salvation in us, he brings about likeness to him, and makes the latent power to love blossom precisely through Basil's preaching of the gospel and the monks' searching. The last point of the exhortation in the preface of the *Longer Rules* is that the monk confesses his weaknesses to the brethren (and to Basil), so that it be subject to "common examination" (*Lg. Rul.* prol. 4; 159). This confession will be the occasion for the manifestation of the Holy Spirit. "The hidden," writes Basil, "is more easily uncovered by the labour of several looking into the matter together, since . . . God bestows on us the finding of what we seek through the teaching and reminding of the Holy Spirit" (*Lg. Rul.* prol. 4; 159).

The Body

So far, then, we have seen that man is in the position of a reader, and that a reader is necessarily a rational creature, made in the image of God with the power to reason, though not like God by nature. The rational creature, angelic or human, comes to be like God through choice. With angels, the choice is singular and so one cannot speak of any significant sense of progress and certainly not progress over time. With men, there is progress (or regress) over time, and, for Basil, this progress is necessarily bound up with life in the body.

Basil was the heir to a tradition, both philosophical and theological, pagan and Christian, that struggled to appreciate the body, and at the head of the tradition is Plato. It will suffice for our purposes to take note of Plato's account of the making of man in his *Timaeus*.[14] The Father of the universe commissioned, according to Plato, the gods whom he had made to "weave mortal and immortal together and create living creatures."[15] The Father of the universe thus sowed the seed of man's immortal and divine element but himself did not create the mortal body, leaving this inferior work to his inferior gods. The gods, in turn, "fastened the two divine orbits of the soul into a spherical body," the head, and to the head attached the body as a "vehicle" to provide it with locomotion.[16]

At a later point in the *Timaeus*, Plato sums up the creation of man as an immortal principle encased in a mortal physical globe.[17] Lest the soul be polluted by association with the lower passions, the neck serves to insulate the divine element from mortal flesh: it is a "kind of isthmus and boundary between head and breast to keep them apart."[18] Plato makes it clear that the body is a place of temporary sojourn, from which the soul is freed upon good behavior.[19]

Plotinus was often a more immediate source than Plato for Christian theologians, and his view of the body is likewise very negative. Although Plotinus is notoriously difficult to understand, and so has generated a vast body of disputed interpretations, it seems clear enough that for him the body and life in the body are no cause for celebration.[20]

At first sight, Plotinus seems more closely to approximate the Christian view of the material world, for in his thought, matter comes ultimately and, of course, by mediation from the One. This view is complicated, however, by Plotinus's statements that matter is evil, and not just evil, but "primary evil," "evil *per se*," and even "non-being."[21] Matter, of course, is not the same thing as "body." For Plotinus, matter, "the offspring of soul 'becomes body' by its reception of 'form' and, as body, 'provides a receptacle for the principle that has brought it to birth.'"[22] Body, by its association with matter, can never be said to be good except in the most qualified sense, for matter in the sense-world, "while it does accept determination, is not living or intellective, but a dead thing decorated."[23]

This ambivalent account of matter is rounded out by the work that it does in Plotinus's philosophy: on the one hand it accounts for evil in such a way as to protect higher realities from any responsibility for it, and, on the other hand, matter's production by soul avoids the unhappy consequence of a metaphysical dualism in which there are two ultimate first principles.[24]

Stephen R. L. Clark, while acknowledging Plotinus's dualism, wishes to distinguish his dualism from that of other philosophers, especially Descartes.[25] Clark stresses that Plotinus's dualism is more subtle than the Cartesian sort that posits a stricter separation between extension (body) and thought (soul). For Plotinus, "without soul there could be no bodies—and therefore no body separate from soul," and "there can be no body at all, not even the smallest visible unit, without soul."[26]

Even still, while the body needs the soul, the soul is better off without the body. "Our living bodies," writes Clark, "are like maggots in a plant, or like the rotten part of a plant which, qua gardener, we should care for."[27] Clark cites a few passages from the *Enneads* that speak of the fall into matter, the care of the body but the neglect of bodily advantage, and the insulation of the inner self from the experiences of the body.[28] This relationship of dependent animosity is well expressed in the Christian apologetic *Letter to Diognetus*, wherein the author uses the relationship between body and soul as an analogy for that between Christians and the world.

What the soul is in the body, that Christians are in the world. The soul is dispersed through all the members of the body, and Christians are scattered through all

the cities of the world. The soul dwells in the body, but does not belong to the
body, and Christians dwell in the world, but do not belong to the world. . . .
The flesh hates the soul . . . ; so the world hates Christians. The soul loves the
flesh that hates it . . . ; in the same way, Christians love those who hate them.[29]

While the *Letter to Diognetus* preexists the work of Plotinus, they seem to
breathe the same spirit.

In spite of the animosity that the soul has for the body (for the body is a
hindrance to the life of the soul), Plotinus does not draw the inference that
one ought to commit suicide so as to free the soul from the body. "As long
as we have bodies," Plotinus writes, "we must inhabit the dwellings prepared
for us by our good sister soul (the All-Soul) in her vast power of labourless
creation."[30] Plotinus makes the same point in *Ennead* 1.9 but adds that "when
a man contrives the dissolution of the body," some passion is present—revolt
or grief or anger.[31] Clarke sums up this last passage: "Suicide, in most cases,
actually shows that we think too much about our bodies, not too little."[32] He
also makes the point that Plotinus's dualism did not make him inhumane or
uncompassionate. While it is true that Plotinus counseled not to be "inwardly
affected by the suffering of others," this must be balanced by the fact that he
offered the same advice in the face of one's own suffering, but especially by
the fact that he "was compassionate in a better sense."[33] Clark cites Plotinus's
care of orphans as a concrete instance of this general point.[34]

Origen's estimation of the body was more optimistic than Plotinus's,
for Origen leaves behind the paradox at the heart of Plotinus's position
on matter and evil:[35] matter is "evil itself"[36] and the "source of evil in the
soul,"[37] and yet it ultimately comes from the One "through the mediation of
soul."[38] For Origen, the body is without question made by God and therefore good, but it is good in the way that crutches are good—if I may use my
own images—or medicine, or penance, and not in the way of maggots or
rotten parts. "All rational creatures," writes Origen, "who are incorporeal
and invisible, if they become negligent, gradually sink to a lower level and
take to themselves bodies suitable to the regions into which they descend"
(*On F. Prin.* 1.4.1; 40–41). Thus is Origen's crucial argument against Gnostic
determinism. There are no classes of men given in nature, no one determined
from his first existence to be spiritual (*pneumatikos*) or to be a flesh-clod
(*sarkikos*). Rather, all differences between rational spirits—whether one is a
throne or a principality or some other rank in the choir, whether one has a
body or not, whether one is an invalid or not, whether one is born Greek or
barbarian, and so on—all differences whatsoever result from choice and so
are just (*On F. Prin.* 2.9.2–8). If one finds oneself in a particular "region,"
one is there because of one's negligence or cooling off in the pre-existent
bodiless vision of God, and the more severe the negligence or the cooling,
the lower the region.

One can gain insight into a particular theologian's view of the body and its value and significance through that person's teaching on the resurrection. Origen defends the church's belief in the resurrection of the body against the attacks of both the Gnostic heretics and the pagan intellectual Celsus—the first in *On First Principles* and the second in *Against Celsus*. Origen's first point against the Gnostics is that the very word *resurrection* implies a body, for we believe in the resurrection *of the dead*, and it is the body that has died (*On F. Prin.* 2.10.1).[39] What rises, then, is a body, but it is *our* body. "If bodies rise again," Origen writes, "undoubtedly they rise again as a clothing for us, and if it is necessary, as it certainly is, for us to live in bodies, we ought to live in no other bodies but our own" (*On F. Prin.* 2.10.1; 139). Origen goes on to say, drawing on St. Paul (1 Cor. 15:44), that the body is spiritual, which means that "corruption [is] banished and mortality laid aside" (*On F. Prin.* 2.10.1; 139). A spiritual body, however, has no shape (*On F. Prin.* 2.10.2) and is not "entangled in the passions of flesh and blood" (*On F. Prin.* 2.10.3; 140).

On several occasions Celsus had ridiculed—and Origen would add misrepresented—the Christian doctrine of the resurrection of the dead. One of Celsus's overarching themes is that Christians are "lovers of the body" (*philosōmatoi*), which, following Plato, Celsus sees as the opposite of "lovers of wisdom" (*philosophoi*).[40] Thus Christians are uneducated, blind, and hopelessly obtuse, and the absurdity of the Christian position, for Celsus, is especially evident in their belief in the resurrection of the dead. Celsus attributes to Christians the belief that Christians long since dead will rise in the same bodies that they had while alive (*Ag. Cel.* 5.17–18), that resurrection is a sort of reincarnation (*Ag. Cel.* 7.32), and that the body is longed for as if there were nothing more precious as well as despised (*Ag. Cel.* 8.49). In response, Origen both corrects Celsus's caricatures and offers a deeper explanation of the resurrection. The basic principle here is that "when the soul, which in its own nature is incorporeal and invisible, is in any material place, it requires a body suited to the nature of that environment" (*Ag. Cel.* 7.32; 420). Thus the body required for life on earth is superfluous in heaven: "It puts a body on top of that which it possessed formerly, because it needs a better garment for the purer, ethereal, and heavenly regions" (*Ag. Cel.* 7.32; 420).

Just as Origen correlates various states of bodily life with each soul's original sin, so the resurrected body correlates with the level of holiness achieved by the soul in its life in the body. All souls, that is, are created the same in the beginning, and each falls into a particular form of bodily life according to the degree of its pre-existent negligence. So also, "in the case of those who shall be counted worthy of obtaining an inheritance in the kingdom of the heavens," a spiritual body is fashioned that "can dwell in the heavens; while to those who have proved of inferior merit, or of something still meaner than this, or even of the lowest and most insignificant grade, will be given a body

of glory and dignity corresponding to the dignity of each one's life and soul"
(*On F. Prin.* 2.10.3; 141).

Origen treats the resurrection of Christ in his *Commentary on Matthew*,
but briefly, obscurely, and indirectly, for he considers it in the course of explaining the transfiguration. The glorification of Christ in the resurrection, Origen
says, "was akin to his transfiguration,"[41] and of the transfiguration, he writes
that Jesus "appeared to them [Peter, James, and John] in the form of God, in
which he formerly was, so that he had to those below the form of a servant,
but to those who had followed him after the six days to the lofty mountain, he
had not that form, but the form of God."[42] It is not clear what Origen means
by this text, but one can sympathize with those who take this to effectively
deny the bodily character of the resurrection. What he seems here to say about
Christ, he was later understood to say about all souls. According to Justinian, he is supposed to have said that "those rational beings who sinned and
on that account fell from the state in which they were, in proportion to their
particular sins were enveloped in bodies as a punishment; and when they are
purified, they rise again to that state in which they formerly were, completely
putting away their evil and their bodies" (*On F. Prin.* 2.8.3; 126).[43]

Origen's response to Celsus's attack on the Christian view of the body,
according to Enrica Ruaro, is far less satisfying than Tertullian's. Origen's
"defense of the body," she writes, "is very tepid and often elusive (as testified
even by his problematical theory of the resurrection) and he remains unmistak-
ably stuck to the soul['s] primacy: he basically accepts the negative association
of the expression 'lovers of the body' and simply rejects the definition."[44]
Ruaro points out that Origen's theory "seems to deny material continuity
between the actual body and the resurrected one" and thus contradicts the
very core of the doctrine of the resurrection.[45] Origen, she thinks, so focuses
on the transformation involved in the glorification of the resurrected body that
he undermines "the value of the actual body," so that "in the end the 'new'
body has lost every 'bodily' characteristic and is becoming almost 'fleshless,'
ethereal, a kind of body that Celsus himself would very likely have been well
disposed to accept."[46]

Moreover, by Origen's principles, the pre-existent soul would have some
sort of body, a heavenly body, and would exchange it for—or it would be
transformed into—a grosser body upon cooling off in its zeal for God and the
consequent fall. It is difficult to see in what significant sense such a heavenly
body would be physical, since it, like the soul, would pre-exist the creation
of the physical world. In addition, in Origen's thought, the whole purpose of
the economy is to restore fallen rational souls to the state that they enjoyed
before their fall. All of this implies that the spiritual and glorified body of the
resurrection lacks any meaningful physicality.

Tertullian's defense of the Christian view of the body is, by contrast, vigorous and thorough: he is a true lover of the flesh. Ruaro summarizes Tertullian's

view under three headings: body and soul are both created by God, body and soul are profoundly and closely bound together in this life, and body and soul are reunited in the next.[47] The first point would be common to most Christian theologians, but Tertullian goes so far as to say that the flesh is made in God's image. Indeed the excess characteristic of so much of his thought and argument is wonderfully displayed here:

> God forbid, God forbid, (I repeat), that he should abandon to everlasting destruction the labour of his own hands, the care of his own thoughts, the receptacle of his own Spirit, the queen of his creation, the inheritor of his own liberality, the priestess of his religion, the champion of his testimony, the sister of his Christ![48]

On the second point (on the bond between body and soul), Ruaro mentions the simultaneous creation of body and soul, their common working in human knowledge, and the fact that together they form the whole man—"the soul alone is not the man."[49] Finally, on the third point, Tertullian offers no ethereal resurrection, for "the flesh will rise, indeed all of it, its very self, and whole."[50] It must be admitted, as Ruaro does, that Tertullian's high view of the body is tempered by negative statements in other works and contexts, and this makes it difficult to determine what belongs to Tertullian's stable belief about the body and what to his shifting and temperamental polemic.

The great fourth-century disciple of Origen, Eusebius of Caesarea, spiritualized the resurrection of Christ. Constantine's sister, Constantia, had written to Eusebius asking for an image of Christ, and Eusebius's response is more an admonishment for asking rather than an answer.

> You wrote to me regarding a certain icon of Christ and your wish for me to send you such an icon: what did you have in mind, and of what kind should this icon of Christ be, as you call it? . . . Which icon of Christ are you looking for? The true, unchangeable image that by nature shows the likeness of Christ, or rather the other image that he has taken on for our sake when he clothed himself with the form of a servant (cf. Phil. 2:7)? . . . I cannot imagine you are requesting an icon of his divine likeness. Christ himself has instructed you that nobody knows the Father except the Son, and that nobody is worthy to know the Son except the Father alone who has begotten him (cf. Matt. 11:27).
>
> Thus, I presume, you desire the icon of his form as a servant, the form of the humble flesh with which he clothed himself for our sake. Yet about this we have learned that it is intermingled with the glory of God, that what is mortal has been swallowed up. . . . The servant's form has been transformed, entirely and thoroughly, into ineffable and intangible light, the same light that equals God the Word. . . . How could anybody presume to paint an icon of this marvelous and unfathomable form, provided such divine and spiritual essence can at all be called a "form."[51]

Thus the body of Christ was spiritualized out of existence, dissolved, as it were, into his divinity. This communicates clearly that there is no value in the flesh of Christ apart from that which it possessed as an instrument of the Logos in his earthly sojourn.

Eusebius's view of the body of man fits well with his understanding of the body of Christ. As it was for Origen, for Eusebius the body is a function of the fall. Man, according to Eusebius, "is the beloved offspring of the Logos, of the common redeemer of all, who perfects him as to his nature according to the image and likeness of his own Father."[52] Moreover, if man had lived according to his nature, "he might perchance have been free from all earthly and corruptible life," but out of mercy God clothed him with a body, so that he might return to the state from which he had fallen.[53] The body is, thus, the instrument of the salvation of the soul.

Toward the end of the fourth century, just before the death of Basil, Origenist views—real and attributed—became the focus of controversy. Epiphanius of Salamis attacked Origenist views of the Trinity and the resurrection of the body and influenced other anti-Origenists like Jerome, Theophilus of Alexandria, and Shenute. Elizabeth Clark describes the polemic of these four against Origenism and concludes that Christian belief concerning the body dominates their concern.[54] While Basil's death spared him involvement in the Origenist controversy, he nonetheless seems to have quietly left behind certain of Origen's teachings and to have qualified others. As an example of the former is the soul's pre-existence of the body: I see no evidence that Basil held this position.[55] Moreover, Basil's understanding of angels tends against a view that humans were once bodiless souls; for angels, "while they have freedom of choice, they never fail to attend to what is truly good" and do not progress in holiness but are such "at the moment of their very creation" (*On H. Sp.* 16.38; 72–73). For the former we turn to an explanation of Basil's view of the body.

What, then, does Basil say about the body? First, Basil applies St. Paul's distinction between the inner and the outer man (2 Cor. 4:16) to Genesis 1:26, "Let us make man in our image." Basil takes this text to refer to the "inner man," for it is our rational part that is made according to the image of God. "I recognize two human beings," Basil writes, "one the sense-perceptible, and one hidden under the sense-perceptible, invisible, the inner human" (*Hex.* 10.7; 36). The outer man, then, is the body. "I am," Basil writes, "what concerns the inner human being, the outer things are not me but mine" (*Hex.* 10.7; 36).[56] I am the rational soul, and the body is not me, but mine. Or as Basil puts it, "The human being is principally the soul in itself," and "the body is an instrument of the human being" (*Hex.* 10.7; 36). So far, Basil sounds very much like Origen and Eusebius.

Basil, however, departs from them in his interpretation of Genesis 2:7, "Then the LORD God formed man of dust from the ground." As the fathers are wont to do, Basil asks why Scripture tells us twice that God made man.

We had already learned as much in Genesis 1:27, "So God created man." God would not needlessly repeat himself and so must be telling us something more here. First he adopts an earlier interpretation, whereby Genesis 1:27 refers to the creation of the soul and Genesis 2:7, to that of the body.

> Already some have said [Basil writes] that "molded" is said of the body while "made" is said of the soul. Probably the idea is not outside the truth. . . . The Psalmist teaches the difference between making and molding when he says, "Your hands made me and molded me" [Ps. 119 [118]:73]. (*Hex.* 11.3; 50)

Thus, the inner man, the soul, is made; the outer man, the body, is molded.

Basil offers a second interpretation, however: the first text tells us that God created us; the second, how. And God tells us how we were made to distinguish us from the wild creatures. "If," Basil writes, "it simply said that he created, you would have thought that he created us in the same way as the domestic animals, as the wild beasts, as the plants, as the grass" (*Hex.* 11.4; 51). Thus Scripture communicates to us our dignity: unlike the animals, we were made by the very hands of God, with "loving skill," and so we must "flee fellowship with the wild creatures" from whom we were made differently (*Hex.* 11.4; 51). Here, it is very important to note, Basil includes our bodies in this account of our dignity. Earlier Basil had given the impression that the making of the soul and body were to be kept separate, and that our dignity clearly lay in the former. But in this second sermon on man, "Basil had," to use the words of Philip Rousseau, "dismantled, or at least smoothed over, the distinction between *poiēsis* [making] and *plasis* [molding]."[57] While Basil allows an interpretation of *making* and *molding* that refers the first to the creation of the soul and the second to that of the body, he prefers the interpretation that applies both to the whole man and accounts for the difference not in the object made, but in the manner of its making. In his first sermon, as we saw above, he grounded human dignity in God's *boulē*, his deliberation, before he made man (or man's soul). In the second sermon, to borrow again the eloquent words of Rousseau, "he had allowed the dignity bestowed by God's *boulē* to affect every level or stage of the creative process."[58] "Let us *make*" (the soul, the inner man) here becomes, as it were, "Let us *mold*" (the body, the outer man), and thus the body participates in the dignity of deliberation that was earlier reserved to the soul.

Basil exhorts his congregation, "Ponder how you were molded. . . . May what is molded by God not be defiled by evil, not be altered by sin; may you not fall from the hand of God" (*Hex.* 11.4; 51). This text clearly separates Basil from Eusebius and Origen. The body does not come as a consequence of sin but precedes sin. Basil, in a stroke of rhetorical genius, "makes his audience present at the creation," and so identifies them with man straight from the hand of God.[59] As Philip Rousseau observes, Basil "is not interested in *mere historia*," mere history, but in bringing "the reality of creation into their own lives."[60]

As we saw with Origen and Eusebius, so with Basil: what is said about the resurrection (ours or Christ's) can help us to understand the place of the body. For Basil, the end is like the beginning. Before the fall, man was vegetarian, as were all the animals too (*Hex.* 11.6). "Behold," the Lord says, "I have given you . . . every tree with seed in its fruit; you shall have them for food" (Gen. 1:29). As a clever proof of the point in regard to animals, Basil offers the example of the vulture. They must have eaten something when there were no dead bodies upon which to feast. "All," writes Basil, "followed the diet of swans and all grazed the meadows" (*Hex.* 11.6; 53). So neither man nor animal was carnivorous before the fall, but there is more. Pleasure in eating comes from sin. Man needs very little, in fact, to sustain himself, but with the introduction of sin and the fall from paradise, we invented other delights to console ourselves for the loss of the delight that attached to the tree of life. Now we have "variety in diet," "adulterated delicacies," "cooks and bakers," and "pastries and aromas" (*Hex.* 11.7; 54). The Christian is to live without such things, to live now as Adam did then.

> As we wish [Basil writes] to conduct ourselves in imitation of the life of paradise, we avoid this excessively material enjoyment of foods, conducting ourselves as far as is possible according to that life, using fruits and grains and the produce of fruit trees for passing through life, but what surpasses these things we reject as unnecessary. (*Hex.* 11.7; 54)

The Sabbath is a forecast of the eschaton, indeed, of the final judgment. "There will be no more works of this world in that day, no more marriages, nor more business dealings, no more agriculture. But the whole earth will be terrified, all the creation in turmoil, the sweat inconsolable, even the just in turmoil regarding what lot then will be disclosed for them" (*Hex.* 11.11; 57). "That seven," writes Basil, "is prefigured by this seven," the eschaton by the seventh-day rest of God (Gen. 2:2) (*Hex.* 11.11; 58).

Thus, Basil's argument that man was vegetarian before the fall is still another indication of his view of the body. It was not the body itself that was created because of the fall, for before the fall God had given to man fruits and vegetables for food (*Hex.* 11.6–7). As we have seen, Basil posits that even lions and vultures, indeed the whole animal kingdom, were not carnivorous before the fall. Sin brings not bodily existence itself, but variety in diet, delicacies, pastries, and other enjoyments centered on the flesh. Moreover, the eschaton brings not the dissolution of the body or its absorption into divinity, but rather a return to paradise.

Though Basil sees the end as a return to the beginning, it is not wholly so, for the resurrected body differs in important respects from the prelapsarian body. Now, "it is impossible for us . . . to be capable of the sight of the glorious appearance [of the countenance of God] because of the weakness of the flesh which envelopes us" (*Hom. on Ps.* 34 [33].11; 268); then, however, at the resurrection, we will acquire face-to-face knowledge as the angels have (*Hom. on Ps.* 34 [33].11), and nothing will distract us from our vision of God. For in the "country of the living," nothing interrupts the "constancy and tranquility of reason" (*Hom. on Ps.* 116 [114].5; 358). In that country the body and the things of this world cannot distract for there, there is no night, no sleep (the "image of death"), no eating or drinking ("the supports of our weakness"), "no disease, no pains, no remedies, no courts of justice, no business, no arts, no money," which is "the beginning of evil, the excuse for wars, [and] the root of hatred" (*Hom. on Ps.* 116 [114].5; 358–59). Even before the fall, man needed to eat, if not meat, then plants and vegetables. "Life in the world to come," however, "is angelic and in need of nothing" (*Mor.* 68.1; 19).

We, obviously, were able to fall from paradise, but the resurrected life is "immutable," for "there is neither rebellion of the flesh, nor cooperation of a woman in sin" (*Hom. on Ps.* 116 [114].5; 357). Basil goes so far as to say that in heaven the body has no gender. "Therefore, there is no male and female in the resurrection, but there is one certain life and it is of one kind, since those dwelling in the country of the living are pleasing to their Lord" (*Hom. on Ps.* 116 [114].5; 357).

Basil is not here saying that there will be no body at all but that the body will no longer be a source of corruption and distraction. In the country of the living, he writes, "there is no alteration either of body or soul" (*Hom. on Ps.* 116 [114].5; 358). Verna Harrison points out that Basil is not speaking here of a kind of androgyny, "a diminished humanity stripped of the good qualities commonly associated with men and women"; rather, she writes, Basil indicates "a genuine wholeness, a fullness of participation in divine life, in which all the virtues come to fruition."[61]

If the body is not the medicine of sin, the temporary remedy of evil, what is its purpose? Basil answers this question in his interpretation of God's threefold command to man: "grow, and multiply, and fill the earth" (see Gen. 1:28). Here, says Basil, God has not commanded bodily growth, but growth in soul, growth in the inner man. This, he writes, is "growth into God" (*Hex.* 11.5; 51). It is growth in visions, piety, works of virtue, from self-control to justice to courage. "Multiply," again Basil takes spiritually, but here speaks of the church rather than the individual soul. God commands the church to proselytize, proclaiming the gospel to the whole earth. Finally, and more to the point, "fill the earth" means "fill the flesh which has been given you for serving through good works" (*Hex.* 11.5; 52). The body's purpose is service (*sōmatikēn hypēresian*). "Let the eye be filled with seeing duties. Let the hand be filled with good works. May the feet stand ready to visit the sick, journeying to fitting things. Let every usage of our limbs be filled with actions according to the commandments" (*Hex.* 11.5; 52).

In *Hexaëmeron* 11.4, Basil exhorts his congregation to ponder their molding, the manner of their creation, so that they might glimpse their dignity and live according to it. At the end of sermon eleven, Basil ponders the molding with them: he elucidates some of the significance of the way in which God created the body. First, there is the matter of human posture. God made man upright. Man's head does not incline downward as the sheep who finds its happiness in grazing to fill its stomach. Man is made not to look down, but up. His natural inclination is to focus not on earthly things "but on heavenly things, where Christ is" (*Hex.* 11.15; 61). Thus the body, Basil tells his people, "is a lesson about the purpose for which you were created. You were created that you might see God, not that your life might be dragged down on the earth, not that you might have the pleasure of beasts, but that you might achieve heavenly citizenship" (*Hex.* 11.15; 61, altered).

Basil makes the same point in an earlier sermon on Deuteronomy 15:9, "Be attentive to yourself, lest an unlawful word come to be hidden in your heart."[62] Here he exhorts his hearers to "be attentive also to the structure of the body and marvel at how appropriate a dwelling for the rational soul the sovereign Fashioner has created" (*Hom. Attend* 8; 104). We can see, with Rousseau, that Basil's use of the Pauline image of the inner and outer man is "not just a contrast, but the setting up, by the creator, of a pathway that humans themselves can follow in their progress from an earthly to a heavenly way of life."[63]

Indeed, Basil expands in *Hexaëmeron* 11 upon many of the themes that he briefly treated in *Hexaëmeron* 3. In addition to posture, there is the placement of the head at the top of the body, the nature of the tongue and teeth, and the wisdom of the respiratory and circulatory systems. He makes a lot of the particular position and attributes of the eyes. We have two in case one fails, and, in any case, two yield stronger vision than one. Moreover, the eyes have three protective membranes in addition to eyelids and eyelashes. And the eyebrow projects "as a kind of protuberance" to keep the vision of the eyes straight, while the nose directs sweat away from them (*Hex.* 11.16; 63).

We can see that in the smallest details our bodies direct us to what is above, where Christ is. "The very baseness of material experience is made the means to a true understanding of human dignity."[64] To use the image with which I began this chapter, man must "read" his body. As the whole of creation, man's body is a book in which is written the plan of God for man. When one attends to the body, one can see traces in it of God's wise deliberation, that trinitarian *boulē* of which man is the image and from which he derives his dignity.

So is Basil a true lover of the body? Or, if we borrow Ruaro's analysis, is Basil more like Origen or Tertullian? Does he offer a tepid or a robust view of the body and its value? On the one hand, we can see that Basil very much comes out of an Origenistic and Eusebian framework. Most important, there is the tendency to treat the body merely as the instrument of the soul and thus to identify the soul alone with the true self. Basil can also speak of the fall in terms reminiscent of Origen. The soul was attentive to God and united to him through love but "has fallen away from this . . . [and has been] made evil by various and manifold weaknesses" (*Hom. Evil* 6; 74). Because the soul "came into being according to the image of God, it understands the Good and knows his joy . . . , abiding in the contemplation of the beautiful" (*Hom. Evil* 6; 74). But, as Origen had earlier said, the soul became satiated and fell. Basil says that it "received a satiety of blessed delights and was as it were weighed down by a kind of sleepiness and sank down from things above, being united with the flesh through the disgraceful enjoyment of pleasures" (*Hom. Evil* 6; 74).

On the other hand, against these similarities with the tradition that under-values the body stand some very significant features of Basil's thought. First, there is his interpretation of "made and molded." Here, the body shares in the dignity of the soul and is set apart, along with the soul, from the rest of creation. It points toward and shares in the life to which the soul is called. Second, unlike the apologist who wrote to Diognetus, Basil does not unam-biguously set the body against the soul. While he sometimes speaks of body and soul each flourishing at the expense of the other,[65] he also says that the flesh gives sympathy, not hatred, to the soul and that "the body receives life from the soul, [while] the soul receives pain from the body" (*Hom. Attend* 7; 103). That is to say, body and soul are so united that what the body suffers, the soul suffers.

It is clear, moreover, that in his understanding of man before the fall and at the resurrection, Basil is as different from Origen as he is like him. The soul does not pre-exist the body, and the body is not created as a remedial punishment for the sin of the soul. The resurrected body does not seem, for Basil, overly spiritualized, or at least not spiritualized to the point of losing all physical qualities whatsoever.[66]

Basil distinguishes more clearly than Origen between angels and men, and this has important implications for his view of the body. The most obvious difference in their respective views is that for Basil the angel comes to perfec-tion in an instant and by a singular choice whereas the soul of man progresses toward its perfection. Moreover, the angel's choice is permanent and irrevers-ible, whereas the choices of men (save the last) are not. The body, we have seen in some of Basil's texts, is naturally and divinely ordered, down to the place-ment of the nose and eyebrows, to aid the soul in its pursuit of the likeness of God. These stand in tension with the texts wherein the body obstructs the soul's coming to God. In addition, while the body, at its best, complements the soul, the soul does not seem to complement the body. Surely, "the power of . . . the soul has been bound together with the body" and "penetrat[es] to its extremities" and "leads the many separate limbs and organs to one convergence and sharing of life" (*Hom. Attend* 7; 103). But even still, one never gets the impression from Basil that the soul would be worse off without the body or that the soul would suffer from the absence of the body. If Ruaro is right about Tertullian, then we might say that Basil loves the body more than Origen, but that Tertullian loves it more than Basil.

Conclusion

In sum, when we look at Basil from the vantage point of the later Christian tradition, in some important respects he anticipates the mature doctrines of later periods while advancing on the views of his predecessors, and in other respects the later tradition will advance on his thought. Like the earlier Origenist tradition, Basil identifies man with his rational soul. The soul, the inner man, is the ruling power and, we might say, the reading power. Man for Basil, and not for Origen, is a reader from the hand of God, for he must study his way to God. This would be so even if man had not fallen, for it is natural to him to have to progress toward God. The body, from the beginning, reminds the soul of the end toward which it must progress and provides the soul with the occasion for this progress. It retains this purpose after the fall. For Origen, man is created in a state of perfection; he is complete from the hand of God, rather than unfinished as in Basil's thought. He needs a body, not because he is an intermediate being, a creature, of the sort who progresses toward God through bodily service, but because he has fallen. Put another way, the "space" between God and man is different for Basil and Origen. For Origen, the space results from sin; for Basil, from mere creatureliness. Just as Origen and Basil view the body—one of man's texts—differently, so, in spite of profound similarities, they will view the other texts—creation and Scripture—differently. Above all, the physical world is not a remedy for sin but the theater in which man progresses toward God, a theater created before sin rather than for sinners. To this world and to the Scriptures we now turn.

3

The Two Books

Creation and Scripture

Having considered the very fruitful image of man as a reader, we turn to the books that God has given him to read.[1] There is obviously the Scriptures, but, as Basil says, "this whole world is as it were a book that proclaims the glory of God" (*Hex.* 11.4; 51). So there are two books, two texts, that must be studied in order to read (if not decipher) the message that God wishes to communicate to us.

The Book of Creation

Basil calls the created world a book, but he also calls it a "training place for rational souls and a school for attaining the knowledge of God" (*Hex.* 1.6; 11). Indeed, the created world is designed by God with this specific purpose. Moreover, it is not simply to the knowledge of God that the world will bring us but to the worship of him. We not only form "an idea of him who is more than beautiful" from beautiful things but also are led on to revere him (*Hex.* 1.11; 19). Basil urges his flock to "contemplate the wonders" of creation (*Hex.* 3.1; 37) and to "glorify the Master Craftsman" for his wisdom and skill (*Hex.* 1.11; 19).

Especially in the *Hexaëmeron*, but also in his other sermons, Basil displays a vast knowledge of ancient natural science and of the behavior and character of all sorts of plants and animals. He is quite familiar with the positions of different natural philosophers and current with the disputed questions of natural science. He shows that he has at least very good secondhand knowledge of Aristotle's *On the Heavens, On the Soul, Metaphysics, Meteorology, History of Animals,* and *On the Parts of Animals;* of Plato's *Timaeus* and *Republic;* of Theophrastus's *Enquiry into Plants;* of Hippocrates's *Aphorisms;* of Aratus's *Phenomena;* of Strabo's *Geography;* of Aelian's *On the Nature of Animals;* of Empedocles's theory of reincarnation; and of Herodotus's *History.* Basil uses what he has learned from pagans to show his audience both the folly of human wisdom and the sagacity of the Scriptures. He uses his knowledge of natural science both to praise God and to put reason in its proper place. After offering a number of different explanations of how the four elements make up the earth, Basil tells his flock: "Should any of these things which have been said seem to you to be plausible, transfer your admiration to the wisdom of God which has ordered them so. . . . If . . . not, still let the simplicity of faith be stronger than the deductions of reason" (*Hex.* 1.10; 17).

One acute difficulty arises in the study of Basil's use of Greek philosophy: it is impossible to tell just how familiar he was with the actual works of the great Greek thinkers. Though oftentimes it is clear enough that he had recourse to primary sources, we cannot deduce from his familiarity with certain Greek ideas that he closely read and studied the primary sources in which these ideas were articulated. For, just as we do, the ancients had handbooks by which students could study the thought of the philosophers.[2] This means more than that Basil would have had some of his knowledge secondhand. Much of *Hexaëmeron* 7 and 8, for example, draws on an epitome of Aristotle, but John Rist points out that "this epitome does not reproduce Aristotle particularly faithfully; in it traces of Aelian, Oppian, Theophrastus and others may be detected."[3] We need not be disappointed in Basil for using manuals, but his use of them makes more difficult an analysis of his appropriation of Greek thought. It confirms the fact—otherwise demonstrable—that Basil was not a Stoic, an Aristotelian, or a Middle- or Neoplatonist pure and simple; rather, as the manuals were, his education was a mixed bag of them all.

Many scholars have done the onerous work of tracing out the precise philosophical sources of Basil's sermons, especially the *Hexaëmeron.* The *Hexaëmeron* and Plato's *Timaeus* share a number of common themes—for example, that time was made with the universe (*Timaeus* 37C–39E; *Hex.* 1.5), that the elements are proportioned and held together in a bond of friendship (*Timaeus* 31C and 32C; *Hex.* 2.2), and that there are two kinds of fire (*Timaeus* 45B and 58C; *Hex.* 6.3). Basil shows himself familiar with Aristotle's theory of the interaction of elements,[4] as well as with his theory of a fifth element (*Hex.* 1.11). The *Hexaëmeron* also reflects some Stoic thought—for example, "the notion that the commands of God create the nature of things and that these divine commands remain in nature and, for example, cause the earth to continue to bear fruits."[5] Basil, like the Stoics, thought the world perishable because its parts are destructible.[6] These and other instances are known to us by the work of Giet improving upon the work of Y. Courtonne[7] and J. Levie,[8] who themselves advanced the studies of nineteenth- and early twentieth-century scholars like M. Berger,[9] E. Fialon,[10] Theodore Leslie Shear,[11] and Frank Robbins.[12] There is no need to repeat further their work here, where we are interested in the use that Basil made of philosophical knowledge as an exegete and preacher to give the world its place in the economy of salvation.

In his first homily on the *Hexaëmeron*, Basil shows that he is familiar with the various theories about the constitution of the earth and the heavens (also *Hex*. 3.3). After rejecting the godless atomic cosmogony of Leucippus and Democritus and Plotinus's eternal world, he urges his congregation not to puzzle over contradictory theories, for it will make their minds "dizzy, with the reasoning going on to no definite end" (*Hex*. 1.8; 14). There is no point in entertaining questions that cannot possibly be answered and that do not serve the edification of the church. Rather than idly chattering about these theories, we should turn our attention to the truly important point: God created the heavens and the earth. Basil exhorts his people:

> Let us glorify the Master Craftsman for all that has been done wisely and skillfully; and from the beauty of the visible things let us form an idea of Him who is more than beautiful; and from the greatness of these perceptible and circumscribed bodies let us conceive of Him who is infinite and immense and who surpasses all understanding in the plenitude of his power. (*Hex*. 1.11; 19)

Basil makes this same point in other ways. He tries, for example, to enumerate the many genera and species of fish to show that such a thing is in fact impossible. He goes on about mussels, scallops, sea snails, lampreys, eels, sharks, dogfish, and the like, only to ask, "Who of those who have grown old around the shores and beaches is able to acquaint us accurately with the history of all fishes?" (*Hex*. 7.2; 108). The answer, of course, is no one.

Natural science becomes more directly relevant to the Christian life when Basil speaks of the behavior of animals who serve in some measure as models to be imitated or examples to be avoided. We should not, for example, follow the crab who inventively feasts on the flesh of the oyster by inserting a pebble in its valves to prevent it from closing and defending itself (*Hex*. 7.3). We should shun the fickle and inconstant octopus, who assumes the color of the rock to which it is fastened (*Hex*. 7.3), but imitate the bees' sense of communal order and the common good. Basil describes the virtues of different kinds of birds and calls for emulation: the social responsibility of cranes, the military service and maternal love of crows, the solicitude for the aged of storks, the inventiveness and spousal fidelity of the swallow, and the faithful trust in providence of the halcyon (*Hex*. 8.5–6). The behavior of animals—and many more examples could be cited—is designed by God to instruct men in the way of virtue and awe them with divine wisdom. "Does not the gratitude of the dog put to shame any man who is ungrateful to his benefactors?" Basil asks. "In fact, many dogs are said to have died beside their masters, murdered in a lonely place. In the case of [a] recent murder some dogs have actually become guides for those seeking the murderer and have caused the evildoer to be brought to justice." The virtue of the dog convicts the vicious man. "What can they say," Basil asks, "who not only fail to love the Lord who created and nourishes them, but even treat as friends men who use offensive language against God, share the same table with them, and even at the meal itself permit blasphemies against Him who provides for them" (*Hex.* 9.4; 143). Creation, indeed, has much to say to us about the life of virtue and the God to whom our lives through virtue are to be directed. With the help of the guidebook of Scripture, Basil reads the book of creation just as he read the book of the human body. We turn now from the books to the guidebook, from the book of creation to the inspired Book.

The Book of Scripture

Scripture, as we saw in the previous chapter, is the primary means whereby man is brought from image to likeness. Given this purpose, a few qualities of Scripture stand out. First, the sacred writings are about, above all, the Christian life for which God has created man and to which he now leads him. This overriding concern of the Scriptures well explains Basil's tendency to attend to moralizing Christian meanings rather than historical ones, for example, or literal ones. Second, the purpose and meaning of Scripture are given them by God himself: God is the true author of the biblical text. Let us, then, take the last issue first.

Inspiration and the Biblical Text

Second Timothy 3:16 says that the Scriptures are inspired (*theopneustos*), and, naturally, the fathers agreed.[13] Their teaching on inspiration, however, is not monolithic or narrowly or technically understood. Conciliar decisions and even other nonscriptural writings can be "inspired." Moreover, it need not name specifically the divine influence upon the sacred author; it may designate as well the doctrine of the Scriptures. Origen admitted even degrees of inspiration in the biblical text.[14]

Basil, of course, shares the view of the ancient church that the Scriptures are inspired by God, and he thinks of inspiration as primarily prophetic and oracular. David and Moses are then, above all, prophets,[15] moved not so much by the Logos, as one can find in Origen, but by the Spirit. Citing Scripture against Eunomius, Basil wrote, "We are going to give you the very words of the Holy Spirit" (*Ag. Eun.* 2.17; 153).[16] The prophets, he says in his homilies on the Psalms, are flutes. "The flute is a musical instrument which needs wind for the melody. Wherefore, I think that every holy prophet was called figuratively a flute because of the inspiration of the Holy Spirit" (*Hom. on Ps.* 30 [29].7; 224). The sacred authors do not bring forth words of human invention but from God. Basil speaks for the prophet, saying, "The things that I teach from the Spirit, these I proclaim to you, saying nothing of my own, nothing human; but . . . I have been hearkening to the propositions of the Spirit, who hands down in mystery to us the wisdom of God" (*Hom. on Ps.* 49 [48].2; 314–15).

If the sacred author is a flute, then there is not a single note out of tune. The Holy Spirit is not careless or sloppy. Every word has its rightful place, and Basil draws attention to this fact in a few sermons. "Notice the exactness of the wording" (*Hom. on Ps.* 1.3; 156), he says in expounding Psalm 1, and "marvel at the accuracy of each term," in a sermon on John 1:1 (*Hom. In Begin.* 4; 256). In the sixth sermon of the *Hexaëmeron*, Basil goes on for some time about the great size of the sun and moon. He explains that he has "mentioned these things as a demonstration of the great size of the luminaries and as a proof that none of the divinely inspired words, even as much as a syllable, is an idle word" (*Hex.* 6.11; 101). Indeed, "to say there is an idle word in Scripture is a terrible blasphemy" (*Hex.* 10.15; 43). As William Tieck points out, for Basil even the silence of the Scriptures is instructive, for Moses "left unsaid, as useless for us, things in no way pertaining to us" (*Hex.* 9.1; 136).[17]

Basil often applies this principle even when he does not call attention to it, and his belief in the exactness of inspiration corresponds to his tendency to explain the Scriptures word by word. He explains why Genesis 1:5 reads, "And there was evening and there was morning, one day" instead of "the first day," as one might expect (*Hex.* 2.8; 34–35). He often reads very much into the customary parallelism of the Psalms. He explains the difference between "saved" and "delivered" (*Hom. on Ps.* 7.2; 167), "made" and "created" (*Hom. on Ps.* 33 [32].6; 238–39), "ripeness" and "beauty" (*Hom. on Ps.* 45 [44].5; 285–86), and "sought" and "ask" (*Hom. on Ps.* 34 [33].3; 253–54). In the title of Psalm 45 [44], the Holy Spirit inspired the psalmist to use the future tense rather than the present, and this makes Basil think of the resurrection (*Hom. on Ps.* 45 [44].2; 277). Indeed, one could not read very far at all into Basil's exegetical sermons without coming upon an explanation of the meaning of the Spirit's use of a single word.

In Basil's view, if the prophet requires the presence of the Spirit in order to speak the Word of God, then the reader does so in order to understand it. Sometimes Basil sounds much like the allegorists when he insists upon the conditions for the right interpretation of Scripture. The Scriptures are not written for all but only for those "who have ears according to the inner man" (*Hom. on Ps.* 45 [44].2; 277). Meditation yields the hidden meaning of the Scriptures, for "it is not the privilege of any chance person to gaze at the divine mysteries, but of him alone who is able to be a harmonious instrument of the promise, so that his soul is moved by the action of the Holy Spirit in it instead of by the psaltery" (*Hom. on Ps.* 46 [45].1; 297–98; ep. 204.5). Even when Basil takes a more literal than allegorical reading of the text, he requires much of the reader; he must be free of passion, unburdened by life's cares, industrious, and inquisitive (*Hex.* 1.1; 3).

While the Scriptures presuppose curiosity, they also produce it. God has made them purposefully obscure, not because he "begrudges us the knowledge," but to kindle our desire for the mysteries there hidden; moreover, we cherish what we have gotten by much labor while despising what comes easy (*Hex.* 3.2; 39).[18] The understanding of these obscure passages comes not only by our labor but by the Holy Spirit, for "the Spirit writes thoughts in us" but "in proportion to the size of the heart." He writes upon the heart "either things evident to all or things more obscure, according to its previous preparation of purity" (*Hom. on Ps.* 45 [44].3; 281–82).

Given his prophetic view of inspiration and his concern for the exact wording of the Scriptures, one might guess that Basil would have an interest in textual criticism, in the establishing of just which reading of a text is the right one, the divine one. Somewhat surprisingly, when Basil is given two (sometimes wildly) different translations of the Hebrew text, he will take both of them rather than one or the other. He notes, for example, that there are various translations for Psalm 60 [59]:8: "Moab is the pot of my hope" or "a pot for washing" or "a pot of security" (*Hom. on Ps.* 60 [59].4; 339). The Moabite, an excommunicant, hopes to enter the church, and he does so through baptism, the "pot for washing," which grants remission of sin and produces security (*Hom. on Ps.* 60 [59].4; 339). Or again, Basil has access to two different copies of Psalm 33 [32]:7—"gathering together the waters of the sea, *as a vessel*" and "gathering together *as in a vessel* the waters of the sea." The former reading he takes to describe the sea as it naturally swells and shrinks, while the latter reading "refers us to ancient history, when the Red Sea, although no one was dividing it nor enclosing it, of itself stood firm, as if held in some vessel" (*Hom. on Ps.* 33 [32].5; 235–36).[19]

When Basil finds a shorter and a longer version of the same text, he most often is not curious as to which is authentic. He simply offers an interpretation of the additional words in the longer version and does not seem to think of the possibility that they may be an interpolation. Basil's rejection of a variant reading in Genesis 1:10 is the exception that proves the rule.[20] Explaining Psalm 29 [28], Basil notes that he has found in many copies the added words "Bring to the Lord, O ye children of God" (*Hom. on Ps.* 29 [28].1; 194). He judges the addition to be most appropriate, not on textual grounds but because of its meaning: only the children of God, those who are holy and worthy to call God Father, should bring an offering to him (*Hom. on Ps.* 29 [28].1).

Basil does not always place two different texts or translations on equal footing. Genesis 1:2, for example, tells us that the spirit of God was "stirring above the waters" in the Septuagint or "warmed with fostering care," as in the Syrian translation of the Hebrew, which, Basil notes, is a closer translation (*Hex.* 2.6; 30–31). On the LXX reading, "spirit" can be "the diffusion of air, understanding that the author is enumerating to you the parts of the world" (*Hex.* 2.6; 30). On the Syrian reading, "Spirit" is the Creator. Basil offers the interpretation of an unnamed Syrian, that the Holy Spirit "endued the nature of the waters with life through his [the Syrian's] comparison with a bird brooding upon eggs and imparting some vital power to them as they are being warmed" (*Hex.* 2.6; 31). Basil does not reject the creaturely reading of "spirit" altogether but says that the divine reading, as it were, is "truer and approved by those before us" (*Hex.* 2.6; 30).

Stressing as he does the Scriptures' divine authorship, it is an obvious consequence for Basil that they can speak only the truth. There can be, then, no real contradictions in what the Scriptures communicate. Basil writes that when the Gospels seem to contradict one another, "it is better for each one to reproach himself as not yet having arrived at an understanding of the riches of the wisdom, and to remind himself of the fact that it is difficult to penetrate the inscrutable judgments of God" (*On Bap.* 2.4; 398).

Basil considers different sorts of tensions. First, there is the problem of a precept (*prostagma*) of the gospel that is contradicted by a word or action of one of its protagonists. Basil does not offer an example here, perhaps because he sees the problem as an easy one to solve. We might think of St. Paul, who reprimanded St. Peter for keeping the law but himself had Timothy circumcised (Acts 16:3). When such things occur, the safe approach and the one that is pleasing to God is to "obey the precept and not search the depths of the riches and the wisdom nor make excuses in sins" (*On Bap.* 2.4; 398).

For other sorts of apparent contradictions, however, we must "search the Scriptures" (John 5:39; *On Bap.* 2.4). That is, when a precept contradicts a precept, we must study their respective contexts and discern the ultimate compatibility that we trust is there so that we can obey both precepts (*On Bap.* 2.4). Here Basil does offer an example. On the one hand, the Lord commanded us to let our light shine by letting others see our good works and glorifying the Father, while, on the other hand, he tells us that in almsgiving not to let the left hand know what the right is doing. Strangely, Basil illustrates the tension but not the resolution, though we might easily guess how the tension is resolved. When we look to the context of the precept concerning private almsgiving, we see that the Lord is concerned with our motives. If we give alms or pray or fast, we should not do so that we "may be praised by men" (Matt. 6:2), for then we already have our reward. We should not then draw attention to ourselves for our own glory, but this is not what is happening when we let our light shine to glorify the Father. In a way, both precepts reduce to humility: we must proclaim what God has done for us; and yet we must recognize and confess that he has done it and not we.

The final category of apparent contradiction—if we can really call it that—is the giving of a command without any indication of how we might carry it out. As an example, Basil offers the Lord's command to lay up treasure in heaven (Matt. 6:20). When we are given such a command but not the manner of carrying it out, we must "learn the true and salutary course from his words in another place" (*On Bap.* 2.4; 399). We have treasure in heaven, Basil quotes one of his favorite texts, when we sell what we have and give to the poor (Matt. 19:21). No matter the nature of the problem we may encounter, whether between a precept and the example of an apostle, or between two precepts, or between a precept and the manner of its execution, our disposition must be one of humility and trust. Basil quotes St. Paul, "'who hath known the mind of the Lord' [Rom. 11:34], who," he continues, "came down from heaven and announced the words of his Father to us. In him it is necessary and salutary to place our trust, as children in their parents, as boys in their teachers, according to the words of our Lord Jesus Christ himself: 'whosoever shall not receive the Kingdom of God as a little child, shall not enter into it' [Mark 10:15]" (*On Bap.* 2.4; 400).

In sum, Basil's approach to the Scriptures is that of a pastor who believes it to be the Word of God rather than that of a scholar interested in sorting through textual problems. It was not, of course, the case in the ancient church that a father had to be one or the other, believing pastor or textual scholar: Origen and Jerome prove as much, though the label "textual scholar" hardly does them justice. Basil's great learning, evident throughout his sermons, did not give him quite the interests of Origen. While Basil was interested in variant readings, he was not interested in textual criticism; he would never have made the *Hexapla*, though he would have (and perhaps did) use it. Variant readings often provoked for him spiritual insights into the meaning of the text, but not all readings were equally acceptable. He even once rejected a reading as spurious.

Antiochene or Alexandrian? Literalist or Allegorist?

In the Scriptures, then, God has provided a text to his reader and creature, man, and the purpose of this text is to bring man to his end by guiding him to the worship of Father, Son, and Holy Spirit, to his own deification. All in the ancient church, save the Gnostics who had reservations about the Old Testament and the "Jews" who had reservations about the New, were agreed that God had inspired such a text, but in the fourth century an important disagreement emerged over how God used the text that he inspired, in particular the text of the Old Testament, to communicate himself to man. The disagreement was institutionalized into the two great schools of patristic exegesis: the Alexandrian and the Antiochene.[21]

The story has been told many times, and it goes something like this. Pantaenus founded the Alexandrian school of exegesis, but Origen is its outstanding representative, and it is characterized above all by the spiritual or allegorical interpretation of the Scriptures, a spiritual interpretation that need not be beholden to the literal meaning of the text. Indeed, Origen is quite well known for his claim that some texts do not have a literal meaning. Alexandrian exegesis, if we suffer the oxymoron, is usually judged by moderns to be arbitrary, reckless, and irresponsible.

The Antiochene school, though, has secured moderns' goodwill and sympathy. Diodore of Tarsus founded it in the fourth century in conscious opposition to the Origenist excesses. As John O'Keefe writes, "Since, according to the standard reading, Antiochene exegetes rejected the allegorical methods of Alexandria in favor of a more literal interpretive style, the Antiochene approach was superior."[22] They, like us, respected the literal, the historical, and the human. Their project failed in the ancient world for two reasons. First, they "simply did not have the tools to fulfill the promise of their experiments; that day had to wait until the philological innovations of the nineteenth century." Second, their ancient colleagues were not large-minded enough to appreciate them; they never got a fair hearing for their ideas.[23]

It is not difficult to marshal texts that reinforce the typical description of the Antiochenes as opposed to allegory and for the literal sense, and the Alexandrians as for allegory and indifferent to the literal sense. Let us consider a couple of examples from Origen and Theodore. The spiritual interpretations of Origen and the Alexandrian school are often benign and sometimes fanciful. Consider, for instance, Origen's interpretation of the angel Gabriel striking Zechariah mute for doubting the truth of his message that Elizabeth will bear a son. Origen writes that "Zechariah's silence is the silence of prophets in the people of Israel."[24] The Word no longer speaks to the Jews and has passed over to the Christians. Zechariah, while mute, nodded and made signs to others, and this too has an allegorical significance. Zechariah's noddings are empty signs—gestures or deeds that lack the rational character of words. These represent the Jewish practices that "lack words and reason. . . . To this very day the people of Israel are mute and dumb. The people who rejected the Word from their midst could not be anything but mute and dumb."[25]

Most of Origen's spiritual interpretation is not so outlandish even if nonetheless free from the constraints of the literal sense. The angel, Luke reports, announced the news of the savior's birth to shepherds. Origen asks, "Do you think that the words of the Scriptures signify nothing else, nothing more divine, but only say this, that an angel came to shepherds and spoke to them?"[26] God's Word cannot be trite. These shepherds to whom the angel speaks, then, are the church's pastors, and the shepherds of the church are unable to guard and lead their flock unless the Good Shepherd accompanies and helps them. But a given text need not have only one spiritual meaning. The shepherds of whom Luke speaks are also the angels who govern human affairs. "It was a great joy," Origen writes, "to these shepherds [the angels], to whom the care of men and provinces had been entrusted, that Christ had come into the world."[27]

Select passages from Diodore and Theodore also confirm the impression that the real difference between the two schools is their use or nonuse of allegory. "We demand them to know," Diodore wrote, "that we prefer much more the historical comprehension of the text than the allegorical."[28] Nothing but fragments of Diodore's voluminous work survives, but the church historian Socrates reports that he "wrote many treatises in which he limited his attention to the literal sense of Scripture, avoiding that which was mystical" (*Eccl. Hist.* 6.3; 139). Sozomen reports the same, simply saying that Diodore "avoided allegory" (*Eccl. Hist.* 8.2; 399). Diodore's school taught much more than biblical exegesis; the students there were "ardent aspirants after perfection" in the monastic life under the guidance of Diodore and Carterius (*Eccl. Hist.* 6.3; 139). Sozomen sees this school as a sort of Christian higher education. Many of Diodore's students had studied Greek philosophy before attending his school wherein they exercised themselves in the sacred books and practiced "philosophy according to the law of the Church" (*Eccl. Hist.* 8.2; 399). This impressive institution produced a series of notable bishops and theologians: John Chrysostom and Theodore of Mopsuestia, who himself taught John of Antioch, Theodoret of Cyrus, Ibas of Edessa, and Nestorius.

Theodore of Mopsuestia, whom the Syrian church calls simply "the Interpreter," railed against the Alexandrian method of interpretation. Theodore sought to undermine what the Alexandrians took to be the scriptural authorization of their method: Paul, they claimed, used allegory in Galatians 4 just as they do, and he even used the word *allegorical* to describe his interpretation of the children of Hagar and those of Rachel. Theodore thought the Alexandrians misread Paul and, in fact, interpreted the Scriptures in a way opposite of Paul's. Of them, Theodore writes:

> Their wish is to deny any difference between the whole of the history recorded in the divine Scripture and dreams that occur at night. Adam, they say, is not Adam—this being a place where they are especially prone to interpret divine Scripture in a spiritual way (spiritual interpretation is what they like to have their nonsense called)—paradise is not paradise and the serpent is not a serpent.[29]

These texts from Origen, Diodore, and Theodore, then, appear to give some credence to the standard account of Antiochene and Alexandrian categories, but the story is far more complicated.

The standard account has come under increasing scrutiny recently. Frances Young and John O'Keefe, for example, have shown that the typical employment of the categories is misleading.[30] We cannot responsibly anoint the Antiochenes as the fourth-century forerunners of the historical-critical method. "No Antiochene," says Frances Young, "could have imagined the kind of critical stance of the Biblical Theology movement, explicitly locating revelation not in the text of scripture but in the historicity of events behind the text, events to which we only have access by reconstructing them from the texts, treating the texts as documents providing historical data."[31] In fact, she continues, "they are anxious about precisely those stories which modern historians are most disposed to treat as mythological."[32]

O'Keefe agrees with Young's criticism but adds one of his own; the difference between the two schools turns not on their stand toward allegory as a literary method but on their stand toward spiritual interpretation and the unity of the Old and New Testament. O'Keefe shows that Diodore and Theodore use allegory in order to make Psalm 29 [28] "fit into the chronological framework of the book of Kings,"[33] but, in general, they are opposed to using it for christological or ecclesial interpretations. It is not, properly speaking, allegory that gives them trouble, but spiritual interpretation. O'Keefe, borrowing the terminology of Erich Auerbach, suggests that the Antiochenes drank deeply of the ancient grammatical-exegetical tradition and adopted the opposition to the *vertical figuration* that attended it;[34] "History is about human things, and these should not be confused with things divine."[35]

This point is crucial. What has God really done in inspiring the Scriptures? What kind of text has he given his reader, man? In inspiring the texts of the Old and New Testament, is God connecting events and persons that history has not connected (e.g., the psalmist and the baptized Christian)?[36] Or do the distinct narratives of the Old and New Testament remain theologically distinct because they are historically distinct? O'Keefe makes a persuasive argument that Leontius of Byzantium—a sixth-century opponent of the Antiochene school, and especially of Theodore of Mopsuestia—was basically right when he charged that the exegesis of Diodore and Theodore was not truly Christian. Leontius described Theodore's exegesis as "Jewish" because he refused to treat the Psalms as a Christian text. Diodore, Theodore, and Theodoret, to a lesser extent, "press and squeeze the Psalms into the historical frame of the books of Kings, all but eliminating any theological connection to Christ."[37] O'Keefe locates the source of this failure of Antiochene exegesis in a slavish use of ancient grammatical methods. The ancient grammatical and exegetical tradition simply could not suffer a text to have "multiple meanings and multiple layers of meaning."[38] O'Keefe concludes his treatment of the question by drawing an interesting parallel between Antiochene exegesis and Antiochene Christology. Just as in their exegesis, "when the theological reading of a text collides with the accepted standards of interpretation, one should choose the latter," so also, when philosophical commitments concerning God and the world clashed with the scriptural revelation that God became man, "philosophical commitments won."[39] O'Keefe's final judgment is no less devastating than Leontius's: Antiochene exegesis is, in the final analysis, rationalistic, reductionistic, and closed to the breadth and scope of God's economic activity.

Where does Basil stand in all this? He is commonly placed in the Antiochene school, conventionally understood. William Tieck calls Basil a proto-Antiochene, a literalist, a proto-Protestant, and so on. All who hold this position inevitably found their arguments upon the *Hexaëmeron*. But one gets quite a different sense of Basil's scriptural interpretation in the homilies on the Psalms, wherein he seems rather close to the Alexandrian way. Indeed, Richard Lim has argued that Basil never abandoned his Alexandrian and Origenistic heritage.[40] Given the recent progress in understanding the Antiochene and Alexandrian categories, we cannot simply ask whether Basil was one or the other; we must be clear about what we are asking. It is better to ask about his attitude toward and use of spiritual interpretation and his position on the unity of the two Testaments rather than whether he was for or against allegory as a literary method. It is unlikely that the categories of Antiochene and Alexandrian will fall out of use, and they can certainly be salvaged, so long as we are precise in our use of them. Perhaps, then, we can frame our question in this way. Is the Basil of the homilies on the Psalms, wherein he used almost exclusively spiritual interpretation, the same as the Basil of the *Hexaëmeron*, wherein he disparages allegory? And if Basil changed his approach to the Scriptures, was this due to his correspondence with Diodore?

Theodore, the quintessential Antiochene (no matter how the word is understood), showed great interest in the history behind the Psalms, and we can certainly say that Basil less diligently and less consistently sought to illuminate the Psalms by placing them in historical context. Most of the time he turns to questions of history only when there is some problem, such as a contradiction between a historical account and a psalmic inscription. The inscription of Psalm 7, for example, has Chusi, David's companion, as the son of Jemini, while 2 Samuel has him as the son of Arachi (2 Sam. 17:5). Basil solves the problem explaining that "son of Jemini" means "son of the right hand" (*Hom. on Ps.* 7.1; 165–66). The psalm thus designates Chusi by his goodness: he informed against Absalom in order to protect David from him. But Basil quickly leaves behind the intrigue among David, Absalom, and Chusi and interprets the psalm as though the prophet were speaking in the name of a Christian.

Even when Basil holds a historical interest beyond the inscription, it is not long before he spiritualizes the text. Considering Psalm 34 [33], Basil asks, "Now, how is it that the inscription names Abimelech, but history mentions Achis, as king of the Gethites?" Tradition, he maintains, has handed down the explanation that "Abimelech" is a title designating a kingly office, like "Caesar" or "Pharaoh" (*Hom. on Ps.* 34 [33].1; 247–48). So the king of the Gethites is named Achis by birth but Abimelech by office. In the case of Psalm 34 [33], Basil maintains a historical interpretation beyond the inscription. He places words in the mouth of David to draw out the historical context of Psalm 34 [33]:3 ("In the Lord shall my soul be praised; let the meek hear and rejoice"):

"since with the help of God, by deceiving my enemies . . . I have successfully obtained safety without war, by only the changing of my countenance" (*Hom. on Ps.* 34 [33].2; 251). He does not, however, apply the whole psalm to these events in the life of David, even where it would be the natural interpretation. By the time Basil gets to Psalm 34 [33]:5 ("And he delivered me from all my troubles") he has begun a moralizing interpretation that pertains more to the life of the Christian than that of David.[41]

Although Basil shows little concern for the historical context of the Psalms except when so provoked by the inscription, he does apply Psalm 7:7 to David and Absalom. "And arise, O Lord my God, in the precept which thou hast commanded" refers to the resurrection of Christ from the dead as well as to Absalom's transgression of the fourth commandment. David "urges God," writes Basil, "for the correction of that son himself and for the restraint of the many, not to be long-suffering, but to rise in anger and, having risen up, to avenge his own command" (*Hom. on Ps.* 7.4; 170). Psalm 7:12 also applies to Absalom. Lest one think that God's providence has failed with Absalom's temporarily unavenged wickedness, David proclaims that "God is a just judge, strong and patient" (Ps. 7:12). "Do not be so poorly disposed toward God," Basil explains, "as to think that He is too weak to avenge, for He is also strong. What reason is there, then, that swift vengeance is not inflicted on the sinner? Because he is patient" (*Hom. on Ps.* 7.7; 177).[42]

While Basil rarely provides a historical and literal interpretation of the Psalms, he often offers spiritual interpretations of varying sorts. Most refer to Christ or to an event in the life of Christ, while the remaining refer to the Holy Spirit, the Christian life, the soul, or the church. One spiritual interpretation does not preclude another, as Basil will offer many for a single text. His spiritual interpretations vary not only in their referent (be it Christ, the soul, or the church) but also in their character. That is to say, Basil will employ allegory properly speaking as well as the more common spiritual reading, which simply applies the text in a Christian setting rather than makes the text an allegorical code having to be deciphered. For example, Psalm 46 [45]:4 reads "the mountains were troubled with his strength." "Mountain" here has no deeper sense built upon the literal sense. Rather, it stands for something to which it bears no intrinsic connection. "Mountains" betokens the arrogant, the rulers of the world, and the fathers of perishable wisdom.[43]

When Basil reads the Psalms, he thinks above all of Christ. It is Christ of whom David speaks in Psalm 45 [44]:8 when he says, "God, thy God, hath anointed thee with the oil of gladness above thy fellows." The oil of gladness, moreover, is the Holy Spirit, and the fellows are Christians (*Hom. on Ps.* 45 [44].8). Christ is the sword of Psalm 45 [44]:4—"Gird thy sword upon thy thigh, O thou most mighty." Basil explains that the thigh is the symbol of "efficiency in generation," and just as Christ is called life, way, bread, grapevine, and light, "so, too, he is a sword that cuts through the sensual part of the soul and mortifies the motions of concupiscence" (*Hom. on Ps.* 45 [44].5; 285).

Indeed, many psalmic verses make Basil think of the incarnation itself. On one occasion he finds a pregnant demonstrative. The psalmist said, "This poor man cried, and the Lord heard him" (Ps. 34 [33]:7). This verse first calls to Basil's mind the Christian believer. "By the demonstrative word for the man who was poor because of God, and hungry and thirsty and naked," explains Basil, "he calls forth your understanding . . . all but pointing with his finger: this disciple of Christ" (*Hom. on Ps.* 34 [33].5; 256). But the text equally applies to Christ himself, "who being rich by nature, became poor for our sakes in order that by His poverty we might become rich" (*Hom. on Ps.* 34 [33].5; 256). There is also the title of Psalm 30 [29], which indicates that the canticle was written for the dedication of the house of David. In its "material form" the psalm was delivered in the time of Solomon, but spiritually it signifies the incarnation of the Word (*Hom. on Ps.* 30 [29].1; 213). Finally—though we could find many more examples besides—Psalm 34 [33]:19 refers to the incarnation. "The Lord is nigh unto them that are of a contrite heart." Basil writes that "these words hold openly the prophecy of the coming of the Lord" in the flesh (*Hom. on Ps.* 34 [33].12; 269).

Basil refers many psalms to events in the life of Christ. Psalm 45 [44]:3— "Grace is poured abroad in thy lips"—refers to the advancement of Christ's human nature in wisdom and grace (*Hom. on Ps.* 45 [44].5), while when David says, "But God will redeem my soul from the hand of hell" (Ps. 49 [48]:16), he "predicts the descent of the Lord into hell, who will redeem the soul of the prophet along with the others" (*Hom. on Ps.* 49 [48].9; 328). Psalms 33 [32]:10 and 45 [44]:8 make Basil think of the passion of the Lord, but the latter reference is more patent (*Hom. on Ps.* 33 [32].6; and 45 [44].9). "Myrrh and aloes and cassia perfume thy garments" (Ps. 45 [44]:8) more readily calls the passion to mind than "the Lord bringeth to nought the counsels of nations" (Ps. 33 [32]:10).

The prophet, as Basil is wont to call him, spoke not only of Christ but also of Christians. As we have seen, the Christian is the poor man of Psalm 34 [33]:7. When the psalmist writes, "Let the meek hear" (Ps. 34 [33]:3), it "means the same as 'Let the disciples of Christ hear'" (*Hom. on Ps.* 34 [33].2; 252). Christians are also the blessed nation whose God is the Lord and "the people whom he hath chosen for his inheritance" (Ps. 33 [32]:12; *Hom. on Ps.* 33 [32].7). In Psalm 15 [14]:5 the prophet praises "the perfect man who is about to arrive at the unchangeable life" for not loaning money at interest (*Hom. on Ps.* 15 [14] bis. 1; 181). And in Psalm 34 [33]:12 the children whom the Father will teach the fear of the Lord are the baptized. Basil paraphrases the psalmist: "'Come,' that is, 'because of your good deeds approach me, children, since you are considered worthy because of your regeneration to become sons of light'" (*Hom. on Ps.* 34 [33].8; 263). Our spiritual son of Origen does more than apply the words of the psalm to Christians, a kind of *sensus plenior*; he also allegorizes certain texts, decoding the references to Christians. Basil discerns the allegorical meaning of Psalm 29 [28]:3—"The voice of the Lord is upon the waters." The verse can refer to the baptism of the Lord wherein the voice of the Father thundered "a mighty voice of testimony." "Waters" here also stands for the saints, "because rivers flow from within them (John 7:38), that is, spiritual teaching which refreshes the souls of the hearers" (*Hom. on Ps.* 29 [28].4; 200).[44]

Very similar to the texts about Christians are those applied to the church and to the soul. Psalm 49 [48]:2–3, for example, addresses all the nations, all the inhabitants of the earth,[45] and Basil refers this to the Holy Spirit summoning a universal church "from all classes of life" (*Hom. on Ps.* 49 [48].1; 312). The psalmist writes of Jerusalem in Psalm 46 [45], and Basil thinks of the church and the soul. The river whose streams make the city of God, the church, joyful is the Holy Spirit (Ps. 46 [45]:5; *Hom. on Ps.* 46 [45].4). God is in the midst of the city and "will help it in the morning early" (Ps. 46 [45]:6). Basil takes Jerusalem to be the soul or the church, and morning is the beginning of spiritual illumination (*Hom. on Ps.* 46 [45].5). Sometimes the prophet speaks in the name of the church, as in Psalm 45 [44]:7 when he says, "I shall remember thy name throughout all generations." The church remembers by praising (*Hom. on Ps.* 45 [44].12). One more striking example will suffice. In Psalm 45 [44]:10, David speaks of the queen, standing on the right, "arrayed in gilded clothing embroidered with varied colors." Basil furnishes the spiritual meaning: the queen is the church and the soul, clad in various pious doctrines and virtues (*Hom. on Ps.* 45 [44].9–11).

Basil recognizes as least two basic levels of meaning in the Psalms: a material, historical, literal meaning and a spiritual one. Most of Basil's spiritual readings are christological, but a good many are ecclesial or sacramental. Although he does not explicitly say that some Scriptures have only a spiritual meaning, he gives only a spiritual interpretation for many of the psalms that he considers. Sometimes the literal meaning does not make sense. Psalm 34 [33]:21 proclaims the protection of the Lord for the bones of the just: "not one of them shall be broken." "Is it necessary," Basil asks, "to hold fast to the word and to be satisfied with the thought which readily falls upon our ears?" (*Hom. on Ps.* 34 [33].13; 271). He is clearly thinking of the literal sense here. In point of fact, to hold fast to it here is absurd for many of the just, many Christians, have suffered broken bones for the sake of the Lord and in witness to him. Again Basil asks, "Do you know the nature of intellectual bones?" (*Hom. on Ps.* 34 [33].5; 273). His exegesis of the Psalms clearly calls to mind the methods of Origen, and for that many would deny it the name "exegesis." At least in his homilies on the Psalms, Basil finds the spiritual meaning more interesting and more relevant: it is the "meaning which is noble and fitted to the divine Scriptures" (*Hom. on Ps.* 29 [28].1; 193). In the case of the

Psalms, the prophet belches forth words with noble meanings because he has consumed a spiritual feast. Prophecy is a spiritual belch, air from the bursting bubbles of effervescent spiritual food. The prophetic soul has fed on the bread of heaven (John 6:51–52) and is filled by every word that comes from the mouth of God (Matt. 4:4). "This soul," says Basil, "nourished with the divine learning, sends forth an utterance proper to its food" (*Hom. on Ps.* 45 [44].3; 280), and this food generates not merely literal utterances but spiritual ones of profound meaning.

Certainly Basil's exegesis of the Psalms have not gained for him the reputation that he now enjoys among scholars. It is not for the homilies on the Psalms that his scriptural interpretation is called responsible, literal, practical, and based in common sense.[46] It is not the homilies on the Psalms that display what William Tieck calls a "wholesome and positive respect for the natural meaning of words without their being tortured or twisted."[47] Tieck is not alone in this judgment, though he lavishly praises Basil. Nearly all modern commentators place Basil on the side of Antioch, on the side against allegory and for the literal sense. Clearly, moderns esteem him not for his homilies on the Psalms but for his *Hexaëmeron*.

Basil wrote the *Hexaëmeron* late in life and it has been taken as his crowning achievement. His invective against allegory here makes readily understandable why so many place him with the Antiochenes, at least if one understands the Antiochene hallmark as opposition to allegory. First, there is the passage in his second homily on creation, by far the mildest of his rebukes of allegorical interpretation. "Passing over in silence all figurative and allegorical explanation at the present time, let us accept," Basil exhorts, "the concept of darkness simply without curiosity, following the meaning of Scripture" (*Hex.* 2.5; 29). Indirectly calling the allegorists "curious" becomes a serious charge when one thinks of Basil's attacks against the curiosity of the pagans.

His condemnation of allegory grew progressively stronger, for in his next sermon he called allegorical exegesis "dream interpretations" and "old women's tales." In the context Basil is disputing some ecclesiastical writers' reading of the waters above and below the firmament (Gen. 1:6–7), according to which the waters above are good spirits and the waters below, evil spirits. "Let us," Basil writes, "consider water as water." Interestingly, as we have seen, he himself had offered an allegorical reading of the water in Psalm 29 [28]:3—"The voice of the Lord is upon the waters." Indeed, he interprets them in nearly the same way as the allegorists do in Genesis 1:6–7. The waters upon which the voice of the Lord rests are nothing other than good spirits, "saints" (*Hom. on Ps.* 29 [28].3; 200).

We find the most important anti-allegorical text in Basil's last sermon on creation. He writes:

> I know the laws of allegory although I did not invent them of myself, but have met them in the works of others. Those who do not admit the common meaning

of the Scriptures say that water is not water, but some other nature, and they explain a plant and a fish according to their opinion. They describe also the production of reptiles and wild animals, changing it according to their own notions, just like the dream interpreters, who interpret for their own ends the appearances seen in their dreams. When I hear "grass," I think of grass, and in the same manner I understand everything as it is said, a plant, a fish, a wild animal, and an ox. (*Hex.* 9.1; 135)

Basil goes on to say that the allegorists "bestow on the Scriptures a dignity of their own imagining," and they consider themselves "wiser than the revelation of the Spirit," introducing their own ideas "in pretense of an explanation" (*Hex.* 9.1; 136).

There is nothing ambiguous about this rejection of allegory; it is interesting, however, to compare it with Basil's own practice in the *Hexaëmeron*. He says in *Hex.* 9.1 that when he hears "grass" he thinks of grass, but earlier he admonished his congregation to think of human nature whenever they see grass (*Hex.* 5.2; 69). For today man "is vigorous in body, grown fleshy from delicacies, with a flowerlike complexion, in the prime of life, fresh and eager, and irresistible in attack; tomorrow that same one is piteous or wasted with age, or weakened by disease" (*Hex.* 5.2; 69). Again in *Hex.* 9.1 Basil says that he understands a plant "as it is said"—that is, as a plant. Previously, though, when he read "plants" he thought of insidious and divisive heretics "who, not being truly instructed in the Scripture but corrupted by the teaching of the evil one, join themselves to the sound body of the Church in order that they may secretly inflict their harm on the more guileless" (*Hex.* 5.5; 73). Finally, reproving the allegorists, Basil says that he takes a fish to be a fish, but he also offers much moral instruction in meditation upon the animal kingdom. The Lord has made animals to behave in certain ways so that we can be instructed in piety when contemplating creation. He encourages husbands and wives to use the "marriage" of the viper and the sea lamprey as an example (*Hex.* 7.5–6; 114). He calls the fickle and the "wind veins" among us octopuses (*Hex.* 7.3; 110). And the greedy are big fish who eat smaller ones (*Hex.* 7.3). So it seems too simple to say that, for Basil, a fish is a fish.

While Basil's use of allegory in the *Hexaëmeron* tempers his invective against it, it is nonetheless true that in this work on creation he uses far less spiritual interpretation than in the homilies on the Psalms. There is also the striking fact that the *Hexaëmeron* contains the anti-allegorical polemic at all; one is quite surprised to find it after a reading of the homilies on the Psalms. Nearly certainly the homilies on the Psalms were written before the *Hexaëmeron*, and this leads us to ask what happened to Basil in the meantime.[48] Did his correspondence with Diodore convince him of the dangers of allegory? Can the difference between the two works be explained by a difference in audience? Or by the difference between the Psalms and Genesis?

Basil knew Diodore before he wrote the *Hexaëmeron* and corresponded with him. Diodore was present in Armenia when Basil had gone there, and he witnessed the trouble that Basil was having with Theodotus of Nicopolis (ep. 99.3). We have two letters of Basil to Diodore. In one, Basil admonishes Diodore for wanting to marry the sister of his dead wife. Basil supposes that someone has put on the person of Diodore in order to ask such an unseemly question (for it was not consistent with the Antiochene's character), but he goes on to refute the practice just in case (ep. 160). The other letter (ep. 135) interests us more, for here we learn that Basil read two of Diodore's works. He praised one for its brevity and simplicity and criticized the other as esoteric and laborious to read. If only we knew which of Diodore's works Basil read, and if only the works of Diodore had survived. In their absence, it is impossible to say whether and to what extent Basil adopted from Diodore the methods of the Antiochene school. Richard Lim, indeed, thinks that Basil did not employ Diodore's method. Basil, for example, does not employ etymology in the Antiochene way; his use rather is "derivative and unsystematic."[49] But as Lim himself admits, it is speculative to draw firm conclusions from so little evidence. Lim argues that Basil's anti-allegorical invective is better explained by a consideration of his audience than by positing a late-in-life conversion to the Antiochene method and a renunciation of his own heritage.

Allegorical interpretation is not for the unlearned and the simple but for the advanced and mature; one cannot give meat to babes. Moreover, allegory in the hands of the unlearned leads to heresy. This, Lim argues, is Basil's concern in the *Hexaëmeron*. He is not rejecting allegory simply, but allegory for his particular congregation. Lim makes a good argument. First, he shows that the anti-allegorical invective is not necessarily anti-Origenist. Origen was not the only father to practice allegory, for it had become a very successful weapon in the hands of heretics like the Gnostics.[50] Second, Lim describes the audience of the *Hexaëmeron*, clearly showing that they are not the sort ready for advanced scriptural study. Basil's flock included tradesmen, we know (*Hex.* 3.1), and he addressed primarily "the proverbial man in the street."[51] "Basil's audience," Lim writes, "was not a select group of Christian intellectuals or those whom he considered spiritually advanced. Some he accuses of being libertines and inhumane husbands and he openly" fears that some of his flock would rush to the dice after church.[52] Clearly, Basil is not preaching to the choir.

Lim's explanation of Basil's attitude toward allegory, however, does not explain the difference in character between the *Hexaëmeron* and the homilies on the Psalms. As his argument goes, because Basil employs allegory in the homilies on the Psalms, it would stand to reason that he had a different audience there, an advanced audience, that could benefit from allegory without falling into its heretical pitfalls. Jean Bernardi has shown, though, that this is not the case. He shows that the homilies are addressed "*au grand public.*"[53] The words of Psalm 30 [29] inspire Basil to admonish his congregants. "Sing to the Lord,

O ye his saints" (Ps. 30 [29]:5). "How many stand there, coming from fornication?" Basil sharply demands. "How many from theft? How many concealing
in their hearts deceit? How many lying? They think they are singing, although
in truth they are not singing" (*Hom. on Ps.* 30 [29].3; 217–18). Apparently he
had reason to think that he was not among the holy without spot or wrinkle.
Indeed, Basil thought these to be few. Not many say "God is our refuge" (Ps.
46 [45]:2) and mean it; few "depend wholly upon God and breathe him and
have all hope and trust in him" (*Hom. on Ps.* 46 [45].2; 299). Basil then turns
to chide his flock directly. "Is a child sick? You look around for an enchanter
or one who puts superstitious marks on the necks of the innocent children;
or finally, you go to a doctor and to medicines, having neglected him who is
able to save" (*Hom. on Ps.* 46 [45].2; 299). For a troubled dream they run to
the interpreters, and in fear of an enemy, secure a patron. "In short," Basil
rebukes them, "in every need you contradict yourself—in word, naming God
as your refuge; in act, drawing on aid from useless and vain things" (*Hom.
on Ps.* 46 [45].2; 299). One final example will show that Basil addresses in
the homilies on the Psalms not the spiritual elite but the unbaptized and the
baptized who have much room to grow in holiness. Again, he asks his people
a series of pointed questions: "Have you reviled? Bless. Have you defrauded?
Make restitution. Have you been intoxicated? Fast. Have you made false pretensions? Be humble. Have you been envious? Console. Have you murdered?
Bear witness, or afflict your body with the equivalent of martyrdom through
confession" (*Hom. on Ps.* 33 [32].2; 299). So, then, Basil did not deliver the
homilies on the Psalms and the *Hexaëmeron* to different audiences, but in
the one he liberally uses spiritual and allegorical exegesis while in the other
he severely criticizes it. This is where Lim's otherwise persuasive argument
falters. If his answer is not the right one, what is?

Basil's exegetical method remained basically the same, although later in
life it became more sober, mature, and critical. In comparing the homilies on
the Psalms and those on Genesis, we must remember the very great difference
between these biblical books, as well as their different handling among the
fathers. Genesis, of course, was unusually subject to perverse allegorical interpretations, especially in the hands of the Gnostics. The Psalms, of course,
were (and continue to be) especially open to christological readings. Basil's
exegetical method did not radically change in the years during which he wrote
homilies on the Psalms and creation: he never let go of a theological reading
of the Old Testament and never restricted God's communication to historical
narrative, though it is true that he became far more sensitive to the abuses of
the allegorical method. Perhaps he acquired this sensitivity from Diodore, but
one certainly cannot say that Basil took over Diodore's theological position of
the priority of history over providence, of the literal over the spiritual, of the
human over the divine. The best evidence for Basil's fundamental consistency
is not the character of the audiences that he addressed but the use of spiritual

interpretations in the *Hexaëmeron*. These spiritual interpretations, akin to those of the homilies on the Psalms, soften the force of the anti-allegorical invective. God created the moon with its changing shapes, for example, to remind us of the inconstancy of our nature (*Hex.* 6.10; 100). Or again, Genesis 1:11—"and fruit trees bearing fruit in which is their seed, each according to its own kind, upon the earth"—leads Basil to expound upon those trees more essential to human life. He mentions vines and calls to his flock's mind Jesus's words in John 15 and Matthew 21:33 about the householder who "planted a vineyard, and set a hedge around it, and dug a wine press in it, and built a tower." The Lord "calls the human souls the vineyard," and the hedge is the commandments and the protection of angels, while the stakes that the vinedresser would use to prop the vines are the apostles, prophets, and teachers of the church (*Hex.* 5.6; 76). "Our soul is 'dug about,'" Basil explains, "when we put aside the cares of the world, which are a burden to our hearts" (*Hex.* 5.6; 76).

> He who has laid aside carnal love and the desire of possessions, or who has considered the violent desire for this wretched little glory detestable and contemptible, has, so to say, been "dug about" and, freed of the vain burden of the earthy spirit, has breathed again. (*Hex.* 5.6; 76)

Such texts indicate that Basil had become more mindful of the perils of allegory without substantially changing his method. He remains throughout committed to the unity of the two Testaments and to the freedom of God to communicate truths about Christ and the life of Christians through the texts of the Old Testament: these things are the immediate and obvious consequences of the text's divine authorship. Basil's practice in the fourth century bears out Leontius's theory in the sixth.

Conclusion

In sum, Basil sees the Bible and the world as two principal instruments whereby God teaches and forms man. Mindfulness of God is a most important concept for him, and it well expresses the role of the physical creation as well as the Scriptures in our salvation. "I want the marvel of creation," Basils preaches to his people, "to gain such complete acceptance from you that, wherever you may be found and whatever kind of plant you may chance upon, you may receive a clear reminder of the Creator" (*Hex.* 5.2; 69). Or, again, Basil writes that "when the day is ended, a mere glance at the starlit heavens is sufficient to call forth from the heart a fervent prayer of thanksgiving and adoration to the Mighty Architect of the universe" (*Hom. Mart. Jul.* 3).[54] Of course, it is not just plants or stars that will remind us of God but any creature whatsoever.

However, the Scriptures for Basil clearly have a greater power than creation to remind us of God. First, there is the fact that the book that is the Bible is itself a guide to the book of creation: God instructs us in the former how to read the latter. Even more, Basil does not speak of creation itself bringing us to a knowledge of the Father, the Son, and the Holy Spirit; only the Bible does so, and not just in the New Testament. We have seen how Basil takes the "Let us make" of Genesis 1:26 (*Hex.* 10.4). We see another example in the third homily on creation, wherein Basil points out that God could have simply reported the creation of the world. Instead of a simple report, however, we get the hint of a co-worker. God speaks and commands, and this speaking and commanding implies that there is someone commanded, someone spoken to. "This way of speaking has been wisely and skillfully employed so as to rouse our mind to an inquiry of the Person to whom these words are directed" (*Hex.* 3.2; 39). That is to say, God is inviting us to wonder about his Son and raising our minds to a consideration of the divine life; God introduces *theology* (*Hex.* 10.4).

What Basil says about the Bible and the world, both in relation to God and in relation to man, highlights the position of man as a reader. On the one hand, a reader is in a position of receptivity and passivity in relation to a text. Thus, man receives the Bible and the created world. On the other hand, man must read. The texts of the Bible and the world, like any text, yield what the author wishes to communicate only with active engagement of the text. So we must receive the guidance that God offers us, but we must act. One might think most basically here of the moral and intellectual effort that is required to read God's two books.

4

The Trinity, Simply

As We Are Baptized, So We Believe

Basil wrote two prefaces to the *Morals*. In the first, *On the Judgment of God*, he briefly describes his own formation in the faith and laments the disorder and disharmony that he has witnessed in the church. "There arises dissension of the many with one another, because we render ourselves unworthy of the attention of the Lord," and because of our insubordination to the Lord's commands (*On Judg.* 3; 79). This sorry state of affairs moved Basil to remind others what the Scripture says about the kind of conduct that is pleasing to God.[1] To follow these directions is to have the charity by which faith works. The faith that works, however, comes first. And so, Basil writes that he deems it "appropriate and necessary . . . [to] expound the sound faith and godly tenets concerning the Father and Son and Holy Ghost, and then add the Morals" (*On Judg.* 8; 89). This setting forth of the sound faith he does in the second preface, *On Faith*.

In *On Faith*, Basil introduces an important distinction in his trinitarian expositions—namely, a distinction between his polemical and non-polemical works. He urges his readers to take into account the audience that he is addressing in order to arrive at an accurate understanding of what he is saying. Indeed, some have read his polemical works, most probably *Against Eunomius*, and gotten the wrong impression.[2] The person for whom he wrote *On Faith* seems to be such a one, and this person had apparently written Basil, asking for reassurances. Basil obliged. "We thought it necessary," he writes, "and incumbent upon us so to do, that no one's mind should be disturbed by the variance of our words, should they differ from those which were spoken on different occasions but were always dictated by our need of replying to objections brought by men antagonistic to the truth" (*On Faith* 5; 97). In a polemic work, Basil explains, the weakness in faith of those whom he addresses required that he glean arguments from various sources, even from nonscriptural and pagan sources (*On Faith* 1).[3] But it is different with believers. Just as one does not use the same implements for waging war as for farming, so one cannot use the same approach with heretics as with believers (*On Faith* 2).

The question of the audience of the *Morals* and its prefaces requires some more attention. While *On Faith* is clearly a preface to the *Morals* (Basil says as much both in *On the Judgment of God* and in *On Faith* itself), it opens in a perplexing way: Basil seems to be addressing a bishop, while the *Morals* itself is addressed to "the brethren in Christ" who "eagerly demanded" that Basil fulfill his long-standing promise (*On Faith* 6; 98). At the beginning of *On Faith*, Basil indicates that he is writing the work in response to someone—no name is given—who had asked him for a written profession of faith. Basil confesses that he hesitated to answer, but out of love for the other and concern for his own salvation, he placed his confidence in Christ, "who also made the apostles then, and now also us—and this through you—sufficient as ministers of a new covenant" (*On Faith* 1; 90, altered). Thus at the time of his writing, Basil was a presbyter or a bishop, a minister of the New Testament, and the man to whom he is writing had something to do with his election or ordination.[4] Moreover, Basil implies that his addressee is also a minister of the New Testament when he writes, "You yourselves also know full well that it is a function of a faithful minister, whatever things his good master has entrusted to his charge, for the benefit of his fellow-servants, to preserve these for their use without adulteration or tricks of the trade" (*On Faith* 1; 90).[5]

We have seen already the evidence that Basil himself was a bishop when the *Morals* achieved its final form, however early the work was conceived and drafted. Thus, Basil was writing as bishop to a bishop, as one who had the charge of a group of ascetics to another likewise positioned. He wrote the *Morals* for a group of ascetics who were nonetheless under the supervision of a bishop who wished to have from Basil an explanation of the faith that would clear up some perceived deficiencies that the bishop had seen in Basil's polemic writings.

Who this bishop is, I cannot surmise, but his significance is not lost. He and the community of Christians to whom Basil is addressing this work are fellow believers. Thus Basil can leave behind the weapons that must be used against an enemy and offer a "simple confession and manifestation of the sound faith," an exhortation on "sound teaching" (*On Faith* 2; 92, altered). Basil is confident that this genre will yield a more accurate understanding of his confession of faith in the minds of his readers than did his polemic work, and so clear himself of any suspicions in the eyes of his brother bishop and his brethren in the ascetic life.

Trinitarian Confession in *On Faith*

Basil summarizes his trinitarian faith in a Scripture-packed creed but begins with a disclaimer on the incomprehensibility of God: "The nature of the majesty and glory of God, being inexpressible in word and incomprehensible by mind, cannot be explained or understood by one phrase or thought" (*On Faith* 2; 92). Not only is it the case that any one "name" cannot express the fullness of God's majesty; even more, every word, used according to its ordinary meaning, is positively misleading (*On Faith* 3; 94). "Godly thoughts about God," writes Basil, "must be pure so far as is possible for the human mind" (*On Faith* 3; 94). It is the incomprehensibility of God that explains why Scripture employs "several names and words for a partial setting forth, and that darkly, of the divine glory" (*On Faith* 3; 94).

Basil then delivers on his promise to offer his faith purely in the words of the Scriptures. It is, essentially, a declaratory creed.

We believe therefore and confess one only true and good God,
Father almighty, of whom are all things,
the God and Father of our Lord and God Jesus Christ:

And his one, only-begotten Son, our Lord and God, Jesus Christ, only true, through whom all things were made both visible and invisible [John 1:3]

and in whom all things consist [Col. 1:17].

Who was in the beginning with God and was God [John 1:1]; and afterwards according to the Scriptures "was seen on earth and lived with men" [Bar. 3:38];

Who being in the form of God thought it not robbery to be equal with God, but emptied himself, and through birth from a virgin, took the form of a servant and was found in fashion as a man [Phil. 2:6, 7], and he fulfilled all things written with reference to him and concerning him, according to the commandment of the Father and became obedient unto death, even the death of the cross [Phil. 2:8], and on the third day he rose from the dead, according to the Scriptures, and was seen by his holy disciples and the rest, as it is written [1 Cor. 15:4–8];

And he ascended into heaven and sitteth at the right hand of the Father; whence he cometh at the end of this world to raise all men, and to render to each according to his conduct [Matt. 16:27].

When the just shall be taken up to life eternal and the kingdom of heaven, and the sinners shall be condemned to eternal punishment [Matt. 25:46] where their worm dieth not and the fire is not quenched [Mark 9:43].

And one only Holy Spirit, the Paraclete, in whom we were sealed unto the day of redemption [Eph. 4:30], the Spirit of truth [John 15:26], the Spirit of adoption, in whom we cry Abba, Father [Rom. 8:15]. Who divideth and worketh the gifts that come of God, to each for his good as he wills [1 Cor. 12:7, 11]. Who teacheth all things and bringeth all things to remembrance, as many as he heareth from the Son [John 14:26]. Who is good and who leadeth into all truth and establisheth all that believe both in sure knowledge and accurate confession, and godly service, and spiritual and true worship [John 4:23] of God the Father and of his Only-begotten Son our Lord and God Jesus Christ, and of himself. (*On Faith* 4; 95–96)

This creed, of course, is devoid of any technical expression, preferring, as Basil indicated, to use only the language of the Scriptures. One notable difference between Basil's creed and typical Eastern creeds is that Basil's lacks a developed section on the pre-existent Son. In the Nicene Creed, for example, we confess that the Son is "God from God, light from light, true God from true God." The declaratory creed of Caesarea, Eusebius tells us, has "we believe . . . in one Lord Jesus Christ the Word of God, God from God, Light from Light, Life from Life, only-begotten Son, firstborn of all creation."[6] Basil simply cites John 1:1 and Colossians 1:15: the Word was God and with God, and all things are made through him and hold together in him. His confession of the pre-existent life of the Son, however, is fuller than a typical Western creed wherein the first mention of the Son is immediately followed by a confession of the incarnation.[7]

Basil does, however, offer a moderately technical and very brief commentary on his confession. "Each name," he writes, "explaining to us clearly the characteristic quality [*idiotēta*] of the One named, and in the case of each of those name certain special characteristics [*idiōmatōn*] being with all reverence observed, the Father in the characteristics of Fatherhood, the Son in the characteristics of Sonship, and the Holy Spirit in his own characteristics" (*On Faith* 4; 96). Basil then tersely illustrates the order among the persons, an order manifest in the relations that obtain among them, for the Holy Spirit does not speak of himself, nor does the Son do anything of himself, but the Father sends the Son and the Son sends the Holy Spirit (*On Faith* 4). Basil concludes his profession of faith with a characteristic reference to baptism and to the great commission of Matthew 28:19–20. As Basil puts it, "so we believe and so we baptize, into a Trinity of one substance [*eis Triada homoousion*], according to the command of our Lord Jesus Christ" (*On Faith* 4; 96). This slightly technical gloss on his creed and his preparatory remarks on the incomprehensibility of God are an implicit admission on Basil's part of the limitations of the simple profession of faith. He ultimately recognized that the language of the Scriptures was too vague and open to perverse interpretations. The deficiency here, as Basil sees it, is not in the Scriptures but in the heretics who distort them. Nonetheless, in order to make clear one's own view and to distinguish it from unsound views that are able to be dressed up in scriptural language but devoid of scriptural truth, one must use such technical expressions concerning the characteristic properties of Father, Son, and Holy Spirit and the "consubstantial Trinity." This latter expression is of particular note in *On Faith*, for it is unique. Basil nowhere else confesses the one divine substance in just this way, and it is the closest that Basil comes to saying that the Holy Spirit is consubstantial with the Father and the Son.[8]

These two features of *On Faith*—the stress on the incomprehensibility of God and the distinct properties of the Father, Son, and Holy Spirit, who share the divine substance—figure very prominently in *Against Eunomius*. The question arises as to why Basil was held in suspicion and how the technical features of *On Faith* would have been received by Basil's wary brethren. I find it impossible to say. For Basil, the safe way out of such doctrinal mistrust is to retreat to the safety of scriptural language with just enough technical language to guard against the two great mistakes of "Arianism" and Sabellianism, against which Basil wrote in his polemic works. Thus Basil employs *idiōma* against the latter and *homoousios* against the former.

The moderate use of technical terms in this context makes Basil's retreat to the Scriptures very different from that of the Homoians, those who confess that the Son is "like" the Father. Homoianism found both a theological and a political justification. Theologically and at their best, the Homoians—or at least some of them—exercised theological restraint out of deference to the Scriptures. They had the very laudable position of not wanting to say too much, not wanting to assert something about the Father and the Son that came ultimately from their own minds rather than from Scripture. This conservatism is the heart and soul not only of Christianity but of any revealed religion. Once one's teaching is ultimately grounded in oneself and not in the revelation of God, it is thereby discredited. The Homoians wished to avoid this unhappy result. There were also, however, Homoians who were motivated not by truth as much as politics. Here, above all, we think of Emperor Constantius and his desire for the appearance, if not the reality, of a common confession of faith by the bishops and believers in the church. In fact, it was Constantius's use of *homoios* at the 360 synod of Constantinople that woke Basil up to the dangers of the word (ep. 9.3). To confess that the Son was "like" the Father meant nothing because everybody, from Nicenes to Eunomians, confessed it, or was forced by Constantius to confess it.

Trinitarian Confession in Creedal Letters

On Faith was written both in response to a query that Basil received concerning his faith and as a preface to the *Morals*, but it was not the only time Basil had to deal with suspicions about his orthodoxy. His statement of faith in *On Faith* was occasioned by the fact that his own thought on the Trinity was obscured by the polemical genre in which he had written, and he was asked to clear things up. The slightly defensive posture of *On Faith* turned out to be a portent of something far more serious than polemical obscurity: Basil faced the direct charge of hypocrisy and heresy.

These new charges arose around 372, as Basil's relationship with Eustathius of Sebaste began to fall apart because of a dispute that arose on the occasion of Basil's trip to Armenia. Basil, together with Theodotus of Nicopolis, had been commissioned by the emperor Valens, who had Arian sympathies, and the count Terentius, who had Nicene sympathies, to ordain bishops for lesser Armenia (ep. 214.1). Theodotus refused to work with Basil on the grounds that Basil held communion with Eustathius of Sebaste, whom Theodotus suspected of heresy. At this point Basil did not share Theodotus's suspicions, for Basil had cleared the air with Eustathius and, convinced of his orthodoxy but getting nothing in writing, tried unsuccessfully to persuade Theodotus of the same. Basil then sought from Eustathius a written confession of faith (ep. 125), which Eustathius did, in fact, sign.[9] Andrew Radde-Gallwitz highlights the importance of these events involving Theodotus, Basil, and Eustathius: they all share the assumption that they can offer a creedal statement as a proof of one's orthodoxy or the test of another's.[10] In this case, however, the written confession did not have the desired effect, for Eustathius reneged on the agreement, broke communion with Basil, and began to undermine him and his reputation.

Eustathius attacked both Basil's character and his orthodoxy. In one letter, Basil asks Eustathius to call to heel two of his henchmen, as Deferrari calls them, for they, writes Basil, "assert that our pretended practice of chastity is but a trick to get ourselves trusted and a pose intended to deceive . . . and the result is that no mode of life is so suspected as vicious by the people here as is the profession of asceticism" (ep. 119; 2:243).[11] As for Basil's faith, Eustathius was spreading the calumny that Basil was tainted by association with Apollinaris and his alleged Sabellianism (ep. 223.4–6; ep. 224). For his part, Basil began to see Eustathius as an Arian, for Eustathius renounced his Nicene confession and instead set forth "a creed to which only an Arius could subscribe or a real disciple of Arius" (ep. 130.1; 2:293).

As Basil had earlier fallen under suspicion, for example, in the eyes of Theodotus of Nicopolis, because of his association with Eustathius, he now found himself suspect in the eyes of many because of his break with Eustathius. It was not, however, only in cases of self-defense that Basil offered his *pistis*, a statement of his faith. On two occasions he offers a summary expression of faith, one in an unsolicited and tender letter of praise, and the other in response to a friendly request that seemed not to be motivated by suspicion of Basil. This first is in a letter of gentle admonition to the daughters of Count

Terentius, who was Basil's friend and confidant,[12] and the second to Eupaterius and his daughter, about whom we know nothing.

Having visited Samosata in 372, Basil was disappointed that he missed seeing the daughters of Terentius. He assures them of his good will toward them and praises them as "goodly scions of a goodly stock, fruitful in good works, and in very truth like lilies among thorns" (ep. 105; 2:199). He commends them and offers thanks to God that they have not given way to the deceptions (perhaps of the Eustathians slandering Basil) that surround them.[13] They have not "abandoned the apostolic proclamation of faith and gone over to the popular novelty of the day" (ep. 105; 2:199). Rather, they have believed in Father, Son, and Holy Ghost.

> Do not prove false [Basil admonishes them] to this sacred trust: Father, the source of all things; only begotten Son, born from him, true God, perfect from perfect, living image, wholly showing the Father in himself; Holy Spirit, existing [*hyparchon*] from God, fount of holiness, power that gives life, grace that gives perfection, whereby man is adopted, and the mortal made immortal, wholly joined to the Father and the Son in glory, in eternity, in power and rule, in sovereignty and divinity, as even the tradition of the saving baptism doth testify. (ep. 105; 2:201, altered)

Basil concludes his letter exhorting Terentius's daughters to avoid communion with anybody who speaks of the Son or Spirit as a creature or the Spirit as a slave.

In response to Eupaterius's request for a statement of faith, Basil confesses that he honors the creed of Nicaea above all. He explains that for Nicaea, "the Son is confessed to be consubstantial [*homoousios*] with the Father, and to be of the same nature as the One who begot him" (ep. 159.1; 2:395). Thus, for the council fathers, the Son is Light from Light, God from God, and Good from Good, but they passed the Spirit over in silence since there was no dispute concerning him. Now, however, Basil deems it necessary to add a word of explanation regarding the Spirit.

> As we are baptized, he explains, so also do we believe; as we believe, so also do we recite the doxology. Since, then, baptism has been given to us by our Saviour in the name of the Father and of the Son and of the Holy Spirit, we offer the confession of our faith in accordance with our baptism, and in accordance with our faith we also recite the doxology, glorifying the Holy Spirit along with the Father and the Son, because we are convinced that he is not foreign to the divine nature. (ep. 159.2; 2:397)

Basil's explanation continues with a contrast between the characteristics of a creature and those of the Spirit, as indicated in the Scriptures. So, for example, the creature is enslaved, the Spirit, free; the creature, sanctified, the

Spirit, sanctifying. Just as in *On Faith*, Basil felt compelled to qualify his creed, so also here in these two letters, but the qualifications are different. In the first context, the qualifications concern the incomprehensibility of God; the unique characteristics of Father, Son, and Holy Spirit; and their consubstantiality. In these creedal letters, the qualifications arise not from the debate with the Eunomians but from the controversy around Eustathius. Here the issue is the divinity of the Spirit.

So Eupaterius asked Basil for his creed, and Basil responded, perhaps because Eupaterius asked in good will. Basil, however, did not always respond to such requests. A certain Count Magnenianus had written Basil commanding that Basil write about his faith in response. Basil resolves not to honor the request, for "I do not wish," he writes, "to leave behind me any work on the faith or to compose sundry creeds" (ep. 175; 2:457). Radde-Gallwitz reasonably infers from this statement that Basil is sensitive to the charge of creed making because of accusations made against him around this time.[14] Basil also mentions that fact that Magnenianus is surrounded by men who "slander" Basil and "utter the most shameful lies" about him, surely a reference to the Eustathians. Basil seems to think that it is pointless to respond to Magnenianus in such a context. Indeed, in a letter to ascetics under his charge, Basil defended himself against the accusations of Eustathius and commented that it would be impossible "that the mouths of those who accuse us shall be checked through our letters" (ep. 226.4; 3:341).

Basil's response, however, is not a complete refusal. While he does not give Magnenianus a creed, he does encourage him to cling to the old faith. He exhorts all believers to be baptized just as they believe and to repeat the doxology just as they are baptized (ep. 175). "It is sufficient," Basil writes, "for us to confess those names which we have received from the Holy Scripture and to shun innovation in addition to them," for our salvation lies in "the sound confession of the divinity in which we have declared our faith" and not in innovations (ep. 175; 2:457–59).

Trinitarian Confession in *On the Holy Spirit*

The statements of faith that we find in *On Faith* and in the creedal letters are important because, in the words of Basil, they are a "simple confession and manifestation of the sound faith" (*On Faith* 2; 92, altered). That it is to say, we see in these texts Basil's confession of faith on its own terms, even if sometimes a bit defensive, rather than as a response to someone else's claim.[15] We find something very similar embedded within the polemic work *On the Holy Spirit*. While in many respects his opponents, the Spirit-fighters, are setting the terms of the debate, on three occasions Basil turns aside to offer a more positive and less combative description of his beliefs concerning the Spirit.[16]

In each of these three positive expositions in *On the Holy Spirit*, Basil offers both a series of scriptural texts and an explanation of their basic sense and thrust.[17] As he says, he offers a few thoughts on the greatness, dignity, and energies of the Spirit that he has learned from the very words of the Spirit; that is to say, in the Scriptures the Spirit teaches us about himself (*On H. Sp.* 9.23). What does he say?

The Spirit is called "Spirit of God" (Matt. 12:28), "Spirit of truth, who proceeds from the Father" (John 15:26), "Spirit of righteousness" (Ps. 51 [50]:12), "directing Spirit" (Ps. 51 [50]:14), and "Holy Spirit"; and John says that "God is Spirit" (John 4:24). Basil sums up the power and force of such descriptions. They do not refer to a circumscribed or created nature but to a "necessary, intellectual substance that is infinite in power, unlimited in greatness, immeasurable by time or ages, and generous with the goods that it has" (*On H. Sp.* 9.22; 53). Basil thinks that the Spirit is just as incomprehensible as the Father and the Son, for just as the world would not know the Father,[18] or the Son,[19] so it does not know the Spirit, for it cannot receive him (John 14:17; *On H. Sp.* 22.53). Moreover, unlike the angels, the all-powerful Spirit has no place: he is omnipresent as no creature, even the bodiless angels, is (*On H. Sp.* 23.54). Chief among the goods that the Spirit gives are life and holiness. He perfects but is not perfected, is participated in but does not himself participate (*On H. Sp.* 9.22).[20]

To the soul that is cleansed, the Spirit is the point of access to the Son and the Father. "He will use," Basil writes, "the eye that has been cleansed to show you in himself the image of the invisible, and in the blessed vision of the image you will see the unspeakable beauty of the archetype" (*On H. Sp.* 9.23; 54). This point is crucial to St. Basil's understanding of the trinitarian faith, for we see here the order, the relations, among the persons of the Trinity. Basil makes the point again in his explanation of a passage from St. Paul: "There are differences of gifts, but one and the same Spirit, differences of ministries, but one and the same Lord [the Son], and differences of operations, but one and the same God [the Father], working all in all" (1 Cor. 12:4–6). St. Paul, Basil explains, is not reversing the rank of the persons, "for he begins from our point of view, since when we receive gifts, we first encounter the one who distributes them, then we consider the one who sent them, and then we turn our minds to the source and cause of them" (*On H. Sp.* 16.37; 70).

Trinitarian Confession in *On Baptism*

We can add to the texts treated so far the exposition of the Trinity that Basil offers in *On Baptism*, written between 372 and 375.[21] The title of this work conceals the fact that it originates in a monastic context, the evidence for which is the question-and-answer format that is familiar from the *Longer* and

Shorter Rules. At the beginning of the work, Basil writes that he had been asked to comment on the second part of the Lord's command in Matthew 28:19 ("baptizing them") but not the first ("going therefore, teach all nations"): "you ask me," he says, "for a discourse on the second part of the injunction and you say nothing regarding the first part" (*On Bap.* 1.1; 339). Basil again refers to the request at the beginning of the second chapter, which bears the title "How baptism according to the Gospel of our Lord Jesus Christ is conferred." In book two we have a more straightforwardly monastic style, as the book comprises thirteen discrete questions and responses.

In the course of his treatment of baptism, Basil expounds the meaning of the triple immersion, immersion in the name of the Father, and of the Son, and of the Holy Spirit. While we find here no startling surprises in Basil's teaching, his exposition of the triple immersion is an outstanding example of the order that he sees both in the Trinity and in the way in which we relate to it.

The first point of note is that Basil begins with the Holy Spirit, for he is our first point of contact, our entrance to communion with the Son and the Father. Just as parent and child are of the same nature, so "we who are born of the Spirit are, necessarily, spirit" (*On Bap.* 1.2; 377). Basil immediately qualifies this statement, for we cannot be divine as the Spirit is divine: we are spirit not according to the incomprehensible glory of the Holy Spirit, but according to the glory "which is in the distribution to every man for his profit of the gifts of God, through his Christ" (*On Bap.* 1.2; 377). Drawing heavily on St. Paul, Basil goes on to describe what it means for us to become spirit by our birth from the Spirit. We will enjoy the fruits of the Spirit: charity, joy, peace, and patience (Gal. 5:22). Our inner person will be renewed, we will walk in the Spirit, and we will confess that Jesus is Lord (Eph. 3:14–16; Gal. 5:25; 1 Cor. 12:3). Our conversation will be in heaven, and we will keep the company of only the holy (see Phil. 3:20; Ps. 101 [100]:5–7; 1 Cor. 5:11).

Once we are baptized in the name of the Spirit, we can be baptized in the name of the Son.

> And so, planted together with Christ in the likeness of his death, baptized in the Name of the Holy Spirit, born anew as to the inner man in newness of mind, and built upon the foundation of the Apostles and Prophets, we may be made worthy to be baptized in the Name of the Only-begotten Son of God. (*On Bap.* 1.2; 379)

Baptism in the Spirit renews us in such a way that we merit the grace to put on Christ. Basil uses the image of a drawing tablet to explain Colossians 3:11. No matter what the tablet is made of—gold, or wood, or silver—the likeness of the king can be drawn upon it. So whether one is Jew or Gentile, male or female, slave or free, Scythian or barbarian—no matter the "material"—the image, the drawing, is the same. Having "put off the old man with his deeds in the blood of Christ," the one baptized in the name of the Son lives "by Christ's teaching in the Holy Spirit" and "has put on the new, created according to God in justice and holiness of truth, and is renewed unto knowledge according to the very image of the Creator" (*On Bap.* 1.2; 380).

Putting on Christ brings one into relationship and communion with the Father, and Basil describes this communion as one of sonship and love. "When the soul has been clothed with the Son of God," he writes, "it becomes worthy of the final and perfect stage and is baptized in the Name of the Father himself of our Lord Jesus Christ, who . . . gave the power to be made sons of God" (*On Bap.* 1.2; 380). Christ, Basil claims, gives us the grace to keep his commands—that is, the grace to love him. And, as the Lord himself has told us, if we love him, then the Father will love us (John 14:23). Sonship, then, whether ours or Jesus's, is a matter of love, according to Basil, and love is a matter of keeping Jesus's commandments.

We see here why Basil stresses so often, so emphatically, and even so harshly the importance of keeping all the commandments. As he puts it, "the observance of the commandments is the essential sign of love," and "without love, even the most effective action of the glorious gifts of grace and . . . faith itself . . . will be of no avail" (*On Bap.* 1.2; 381).

What is the significance of Basil's explanation here of baptism in the triple name? First, it is obvious but nonetheless worth mentioning that the sequence of baptisms is not a temporal order but an economic one. In the temporal order, of course, baptism in the name of the Father comes first, but in the order of salvation, for Basil, we first relate to the Spirit, and through the Spirit, to the Son, and through the Son, to the Father. Basil himself does not comment here on the fact that he has inverted the baptismal formula, and one gets the impression that he offers here his reflexive and customary understanding of salvation. We got a glimpse of this above in our treatment of a few texts from *On the Holy Spirit* and will see it again in the next chapter. In polemic with the Spirit-fighters, he comes to stress the economic order of the Spirit, Son, and Father as the inverse of the theological order of Father, Son, and Holy Spirit.

Conclusion

Basil sees himself in *On Faith*—and I classified here also the creedal letters and a few passages of *On the Holy Spirit* and of *On Baptism*—as giving a simple exposition of the Trinity that is less open to misunderstanding, at least among fellow believers. In such confessions, the faith is presented holistically; it is not, as it were, lopsided because of the necessity of focusing on the mistake of an opponent. We see in these passages the essential elements of Basil's trinitarian faith: the incomprehensibility of God, the order among the three persons derived from their mutual relationships, and the grounding of faith in the baptism of triple immersion, which at once roots the faith in the liturgical practice of the church as well as in the Great Commission of the Lord and other passages of sacred Scripture.

5

The Trinity in Controversy

Against Eunomius and Eustathius

Just as certain features of Basil's trinitarian thought emerge in non-polemical contexts, so it happens when Basil engages in controverted argument over this central mystery. Most of the features that we now identify with the trinitarian thought of St. Basil emerge from the two great polemics in which he participated—namely, that with Eunomius of Cyzicus and that with Eustathius of Sebaste.

Before we turn to Basil's view of his opponents, however, we should consider their thought, however briefly, in its own right. Modern scholars have for a long time sought to understand ever more accurately what used to be called simply "Arianism." Over the years a number of different theological and historical categories have emerged, each in turn submitted to critical scrutiny that has revealed the strengths and weaknesses of the various possibilities. Thus, an important feature of the modern effort to understand the fourth century is a self-consciousness and caution in the use of categories, with a view toward finding the best categories—that is, the ones that will yield an accurate taxonomy of a complicated landscape and so produce genuine understanding. In an influential article, Joseph Lienhard recounted the various categories and offered two new ones. The choices are "Arian" and "Nicene"; "Alexandrian" and "Antiochene"; "Eusebian" and "Athanasian"; and Lienhard's own "mia-hypostatic" and "dyohypostatic."[1] We might add here those used by Richard Vaggione (but not only by him): "Nicene" and "non-Nicene."[2] Lienhard rightly criticizes the first three sets as either anachronistic or inaccurate, and that criticism would apply also to "Nicene and non-Nicene," for the Council of

Nicaea was not, historically speaking, the turning point of the controversy, though it became very significant from the middle of the fourth century on.

Most taxonomies assume two sides in the debate, but that too has come under scrutiny. At the conclusion of his study on mediation in Eusebius of Caesarea, Marcellus of Ancrya, and Athanasius of Alexandria, Jon Robertson criticizes Lienhard's categories of mia- and dyohypostatic because they obscure both the commonality between Eusebius and Marcellus (in Lienhard's taxonomy, they have little in common) and the difference in the theologies of Marcellus and Athanasius. According to Robertson, Eusebius subscribed to a theory of mediation that excluded the Son "from the identity of the one and only God"; Marcellus "desired to include the divine Word within the identity of the one and only God" but failed to recognize a Son eternally distinct from the Father and so restricted mediation to the man who was a visible image of the invisible God; and Athanasius posits a form of mediation that rests precisely on the Son's distinction from the Father while being nonetheless of one substance with him.[3] Thus, Robertson holds that Lienhard's two-category taxonomy—or, it would seem, any two-category taxonomy—both blurs the common ground between Eusebius and Marcellus and problematically aligns Marcellus and Athanasius.[4] On the level of theology, one can readily see Robertson's point, but on that of history, we might point out that Eusebius and Marcellus themselves posited no common ground in their respective theologies while Athanasius and Marcellus maintained a long friendship and ecclesial communion. Athanasius, that is, aligned himself with Marcellus, if not with the esoteric points of Marcellus's earlier trinitarian thought, and he did not think the alignment problematic.

How then should we understand Eunomius and Eustathius? Or what are the best categories that we can use to get a handle on what they say and why they say it? Perfect categories may prove ultimately elusive, but it remains true that the successive attempts to make sense of the controversy, as well as the scholarly criticism of such attempts, contribute to our understanding of fourth-century theology. I would like to add one more set of binary categories, drawn from Richard Vaggione and fine-tuned by John Behr, that I find very helpful for understanding Eunomius and Eustathius and other non-Nicenes. The non-Nicenes read scriptural texts concerning Christ in a "univocal" way, the Nicenes, in a "partitive" way. These are more than exegetical categories, for standing behind them is a theological world and a particular christology.

Eunomius's Theology

Vaggione's book on Eunomius is dedicated to an accurate and sympathetic understanding of him, and Vaggione repeatedly returns to the theme of interpretive "frameworks." We have to appreciate Eunomius's framework, his context, his theological "map," if we are to understand the particulars of his theology. The key to the non-Nicene framework can be seen in the question, "Who is speaking when Jesus speaks?" For the non-Nicenes, "if there was only one Christ there had to be only one voice, [and] if there were only one voice, there had to be only one subject."[5]

Thus, in the non-Nicene framework, the various biblical texts that apply to Christ mark out his history in the economy of salvation. Non-Nicenes, Vaggione writes, "viewed the theophanies of Christ, which culminated in the incarnation, as successive stages in a single journey, because it was the journey of a single entity from first to last."[6] The incarnation, then, is not a radically new stage in the life of the Son, and Old Testament texts need not be taken as prophetic of this radical new stage; rather, they can simply be applied to him. For the non-Nicenes, "the drama of redemption began, not at Bethlehem or in the Jordan, but with the great concomitant act of creation which marked the beginning of the contingent universe as a whole."[7]

John Behr puts the point this way:

> The issue between the Nicenes and the non-Nicenes is a matter of exegesis. Both sides took Scripture as speaking of Christ. The non-Nicenes, however, insisted on an absolutely univocal exegesis, which applied all scriptural affirmations in a unitary fashion to one subject, who thus turns out to be a demi-god, neither fully divine nor fully human—created but not as one of the creatures.[8]

This "univocal" exegesis of the non-Nicenes contrasts sharply with what Behr calls the "partitive" exegesis of the Nicenes. For the Nicenes, Behr writes, "Scripture speaks throughout of Christ, but the Christ of the kerygma, the crucified and exalted Lord, and speaks of him in a twofold fashion[;] . . . some things are said of him as divine and other things are said of him as human—yet referring to the same Christ throughout."[9]

The discernment of two fundamentally different interpretive frameworks, marked by two different ways of reading the scriptural texts that speak of the Son, helps to explain also what Vaggione calls "the almost total absence of communication and mind-numbing immobility of the argument."[10] Each side read the data of Scripture from within their own framework and responded to the other by repeating the data, so that "after more than a century of debate, we find the last participants repeating the arguments of the first . . . to equally uncomprehending ears."[11]

In addition to the divergent ways of reading Scripture, there is another fundamental feature of these interpretive frameworks. In each framework, there had to be posited a "break," a gap, or *diastēma*, in the line of beings from God the Father to lowest creature, "for unlike their pagan contemporaries these otherwise divided Christians were convinced that there was no continuum, no unbroken chain linking final shade to ultimate source. The opening words of Scripture had created a gap in the chain of being which no mere creature could cross."[12] So if all agree that there must be a gap or break, the question is where to put it. In short, in the non-Nicene framework, the gap is between the Father and the Son, and in the Nicene framework, it is between the Trinity and everything else.

So this is the framework in which Eunomius operated, one that employed a univocal reading of christological texts and that taught the incomparable greatness of God the Father. We can see both of these in his *Exposition of the Faith*. Eunomius wrote the *Exposition* in 383, at the direction of Emperor Theodosius. With the Council of Constantinople in 381, the Nicene faith became imperial law, and those who were anathematized were called to a conference in June 383 so that Theodosius might attempt an accommodation or reconsideration.[13] The conference failed, and Theodosius asked the various heretical groups for a written statement of faith. Eunomius's *Exposition of the Faith* is, essentially, a filled-out creed, in which we can observe both his univocal approach to the Scriptures and his placing of the gap between the Father and the Son.

In his confession, Eunomius does not immediately name God as Father. Rather, he confesses "the one and only true God" who is "beginninglessly, everlastingly, unendingly alone" (*Exp. of Faith* 2; 151, altered). This God is indeed alone, for "he has none to partake of his Godhead, none to divide his glory, none to inherit his authority with him, none to share the throne of his kingdom" (*Exp. of Faith* 2; 151).

As the "Almighty is the 'one and only God' [John 17:3], 'God of gods' [Ps. 50 [49] (50):1], 'King of kings and Lord of lords'" [1 Tim. 6:15], and so on (*Exp. of Faith* 2; 151), so Eunomius confesses the Son to be, in the language of the Scriptures, the "Son of God" (2 Cor. 1:19, etc.), "the Only-begotten God" (John 1:18), "the First-born of all creation" (Col. 1:15), and "the beginning of the works and ways of God" (Prov. 8:22). Eunomius does not leave these scriptural texts to stand without interpretation. The Son is "a genuine 'son,' so not unbegotten; genuinely 'begotten' before the ages, so not without an act of begetting prior to his own existence to be called 'Son'; 'born' before 'all creation,' so not uncreated . . . existing 'in the beginning,' so not without beginning" (*Exp. of Faith* 3; 153). Eunomius goes on to cite and explain many more texts, but all in the framework that preserves the incomparable superiority of the unbegotten and unoriginate God.

There is nonetheless an "exact likeness" between the begotten and the begetter:

> not as Father to Father (there are not two Fathers), nor yet as Son to Son (there are not two Sons), neither as Unbegotten to Unbegotten (only the Almighty is unbegotten and only the Only-begotten is begotten), but as son to father, the image and as the seal of the whole activity and power of the Almighty [Col.

1:15; John 6:27], the seal of the Father's deeds, words, and counsels. (*Exp. of Faith* 3; 155, altered)[14]

The Son is similar, then, not to the being of the Almighty but to his activity.[15]

In all of this, Eunomius's univocal reading of the Scriptures is already on display, but it is especially evident at the end of the clause on the Son, wherein Eunomius essentially gives a record, a history, of the Son's life in relation to the economy. He "overwhelmed the earth beneath the waters"; he punished the Sodomites and the Egyptians; he gave the law and spoke through the prophets; he recalled the disobedient; he "received the whole power of judgment"; he was born of a woman as a man for the salvation of men; he preached, was crucified, died, and rose; he sits at the right hand of the Father and will come again in judgment (*Exp. of Faith* 3; 155–57). There is no attempt here to distinguish the Son's activities as divine from his activities as human, no "partitive" exegesis; the incomparability of the Almighty and the lower status of the Son make partitive exegesis unnecessary.

Eunomius finishes his exposition of the faith with a clause on the Holy Spirit and one on the resurrection and the final judgment. His confession of the Spirit is little more than a string of biblical texts describing the activity of the Spirit, yet all understood in the non-Nicene framework that we described above. The Spirit is less than the Almighty and his Son, "being the first and most mighty work of the Only-begotten, the greatest and most beautiful," greater than all other creatures (*Exp. of Faith* 4; 157).

Within the non-Nicene framework, Eunomius articulated a particular—and very controversial—understanding of salvation. "Salvation," Lienhard writes, "is the most basic of all religious concepts, and every religious system offers some kind of salvation."[16] Eunomius's theory of salvation sets him apart not only from those theologians who shared his interpretive framework but also, and especially, from the Nicene theologians who thought his claims simply absurd. The ancient historian of the church Socrates writes that "Eunomius himself has the hardihood to utter . . . [that] 'God knows no more of his own substance than we do; nor is this more known to him, and less to us'" (*Eccl. Hist.* 4.7; 98). Socrates's reaction to this thought is, as well ours might be, to regard it an "absurd fallacy" of someone who is "utterly insensitive to his own folly" (*Eccl. Hist.* 4.7; 98).

Maurice Wiles and Richard Vaggione, however, present Eunomius in a more sympathetic light on the reasonable assumption that a theologian would not set out to be purposefully and obnoxiously blasphemous. Summing up his own argument, Wiles writes that one can perceive in Neo-Arian thought "a deeply felt religious and soteriological concern—how to affirm the true and transcendent God in such a way that we may know him and worship him as he really is."[17] Eunomius, then, did not claim to know everything that there is to know about God; rather, his point was that God made possible genuine knowledge of who he really is, knowledge of his substance. The Eunomians, Vaggione points out, claimed *exact* knowledge of God but not *complete* knowledge of him.[18]

For the Eunomians, the knowledge of God is not discursive and is not the product of human investigation or conceptualizing. Like God's self-knowledge, our knowledge of him is immediate. Alluding to Plato's theory that a name is a "tool," Vaggione explains:

> To say . . . that names are "tools" in that context is to say that, when they tell us what things are, they do so by putting us *in actual contact* with the essence. What is true in general is true also of God: to know God's Name is to acknowledge the presence in our minds of the Essence it represents. . . . To know the name is to gain "real" access to an intelligible reality that really exists independently of ourselves.[19]

Thus, for the Eunomians, there must be real knowledge of God or there is no salvation, and this knowledge of God, in order to be real, cannot be a human fabrication, the conclusion of an argument made by a discoursing human mind. Rather, knowledge of God is the knowledge of his name, and his name is "unbegotten." "When we say 'Unbegotten,'" Eunomius writes, "we do not imagine that we ought to honour God only in name, in conformity with human conceptualizing [*kat' epinoian*]; rather, in conformity with reality, we ought to repay him the debt which above all others is most due God: the confession that he is what he is" (*Apol.* 8; 41–43, altered).

While Vaggione highlights the Platonic background of the Eunomian theory, Mark DelCogliano locates this background in a more complex vision of the Eunomian theological project. DelCogliano does, indeed, locate philosophical sources in Eunomian theology, but he stresses that these sources are mediate.[20] Eunomius is operating within a Christian tradition primarily, though, of course, it is a tradition that itself bears philosophical influence. Moreover, DelCogliano shows that Eunomius did not first hold a general theory of names and then make sense of God's name according to it; rather, he set out to make sense of names applied to God and then later, in response to the criticism of St. Basil, justified his theology by articulating a general theory.[21]

Thus, Vaggione, Wiles, and DelCogliano make the traditional understanding that Eunomius was simply a logic-chopping rationalist and hardly a Christian at all completely untenable. This, of course, does not mean that Eunomius's understanding of Christianity and Christian salvation is above criticism. Because of their work, however, we are in a better position to see the real thrust of Basil's arguments against the Eunomians and the direction in which Basil takes the Christian tradition to which both he and Eunomius were heirs.

Eustathius's Theology

Basil's other great theological opponent was Eustathius of Sebaste, whom we have already met and whose role, both in the ascetic movement of the fourth century generally and in the life of Basil himself specifically, we have seen. Like Basil, Eustathius set himself against Eunomius, but, like Eunomius, Eustathius subscribed to a univocal reading of Scripture. The question remains, however: what precisely did Eustathius believe and why did he believe it?

On the surface, this question seems very difficult to answer. We know that Eustathius attended the synod of Ancyra that was called by Basil of Ancyra, the father of so-called Semi-Arianism, and that he signed that synod's letter. This means, then, that Eustathius was a non-Nicene, but one that recognized the problems with the doctrine of the Eunomians and tried to address them. We know too that Eustathius attended the Synod of Lampsacus in 364 and was part of an embassy sent to Rome to establish communion with Pope Liberius. Liberius refused to admit them on the grounds that they were "Arian" and rejected the Nicene Creed. Eustathius and company "replied that by change of sentiment they had acknowledged the truth . . . and avowed the Son to be in every way 'like the Father': moreover that they considered the terms 'like' (*homoios*) and *homoousios* to have precisely the same import" (*Eccl. Hist.* 4.12; 100–101). Liberius then demanded a written confession, and the embassy produced the synodal letter of Lampsacus, Smyrna, "and other places," in which they quoted the entire Nicene Creed (*Eccl. Hist.* 4.12). Thus, in 357 at Ancyra, Eustathius rejects Eunomius but also Nicaea, and in 364 he rejects Eunomius but embraces Nicaea. Eustathius reaffirmed his commitment to Nicaea in 372, as we have seen, so that Basil might repair his relationship with Theodotus. Suddenly in the same year, however, Eustathius renounced Nicaea and rejected the divinity of the Holy Spirit.

Basil himself finds the behavior of Eustathius very difficult to explain. He came to the simple conclusion that he was fickle in faith. He was a man like a cloud, "being borne according to the changes of the winds, now to one part now to another part of the air" (ep. 244.9; 3:469). Basil had written to another bishop, Patrophilus, who himself had been a mutual friend of both Basil and Eustathius. Patrophilus wrote Basil asking for an explanation of their falling out, and Basil laid out, again, the series of events that led to the rupture in their friendship. In the end, however, Basil could not explain Eustathius's actions, and this made them all the more painful for him. When Basil received Eustathius's letter breaking communion with him, he was "astounded at so unexpected and sudden a change" that he "was not even able to make reply" (ep. 244.4; 3:459). "For my heart was constrained," Basil confesses, "and my tongue failed, and my hand grew numb" (ep. 244.4; 3:459). Eustathius had deeply shaken Basil, who began to think that if his friendship with Eustathius had not been genuine, then none could be. Basil had turned over and over in his mind the events surrounding the ruin of their friendship but nonetheless failed to make sense of it. He writes, "Revolving these matters in my mind by myself, and turning them continually in my heart—or rather being overturned at heart by them, so did they sting and prick me through my recollection of them—I gave no answer to that letter, not keeping silence through disdain . . . , but through perplexity and helplessness and inability to say anything worthy of my grief" (ep. 244.4; 3:459–61). Thus, Basil could only conclude that Eustathius and his followers were shifty. First they followed Arius, then Hermogenes (Basil's predecessor thrice removed who attended and supported the Council of Nicaea), then Eusebius of Caesarea (Palestinian not Cappadocian). They set forth one creed after another, constantly changing their faith (ep. 244.9).

Eustathius's character aside, we do have a sense of the rationale that lay behind the Pneumatomachian faith that he last professed. Basil tells us in *On the Holy Spirit* that his opponents reject the divinity of the Holy Spirit on the grounds that they cannot find it in the Scriptures. The Spirit-fighters, writes Basil, "are like true debtors [who] cry out for proofs from the Scriptures and dismiss the non-scriptural witness of the fathers as worthless" (*On H. Sp.* 10.25; 56).[22] Or again, "They do not stop babbling up and down that to give glory with the Holy Spirit is unattested and non-scriptural, and the like" (*On H. Sp.* 27.68; 107).

While it is very easy to sympathize with Basil's assessment of Eustathius—and Basil may well be right—there is a more generous interpretation of Eustathius's doctrinal position. Vaggione has shown that "interpretive frameworks," explained above, were far more important than terminology.[23] The former could remain firm and the latter, plastic. Perhaps Eustathius, then, held the same interpretive framework throughout, the univocal one, even when he confessed the creed of Nicaea, though here he would be bending terms to the point of breaking, for *homoousios* seemed to be about the only term that the univocal approach could not comfortably apply to the Son. Even still, on this reading, Eustathius's rejection of the Nicene Creed in 372 is not from fickleness in doctrine but from a desire to confess more clearly the interpretive framework that he held all along.

We have another wonderful example of plasticity in terminology in Eusebius of Caesarea's interpretation of the Nicene Creed. He had refused to sign on to the statement of faith of the synod of Antioch (325), and the synodal letter condemns him along with Theodotus of Laodicea and Narcissus of Neronius as "individuals forgetting the Holy Scriptures and apostolic teachings, [who] by various turns attempted to escape notice and conceal their errors."[24] Out of brotherly love, however, Eusebius and the others were given a chance for repentance at Nicaea, and he took advantage of it. We know that he was very unhappy with the language of Nicaea, but Eusebius made it work by finding a way to interpret its language in his own theological framework, and he succeeded in escaping condemnation.

Nicaea's "from the *ousia* of the Father" and "*homoousios* with the Father" can be admitted on the grounds that they are not corporeally understood, "after the affections of bodies," but rather simply mean that the Son is from the Father.[25] Nicaea's "begotten not made" can be a very powerful expression of the Nicene framework, but Eusebius renders the phrase harmless when he said, "We accepted 'having been begotten and not made,' because they declared that 'made' was a common designation of the other creatures who came into existence through the Son and to whom the Son has no resemblance."[26] Eusebius, of course, here interprets Nicaea to be affirming that the Son is a unique creature.

If we can bring ourselves to accept Eusebius's interpretation so far, it becomes truly fantastic when he turns to Nicaea's anathemas. He agrees to the anathemas against those who say that the Son is "from nothing" and who say that "once he was not" on the grounds that such phrases are unscriptural.[27] It is Nicaea's last anathema that Eusebius seems to find the most difficult, and it is here that his interpretation, I think, ultimately fails. Nicaea had anathematized those who say "before he was begotten, he was not." Now, this anathema simply communicates in a very nontechnical and negative way what "*homoousios*" and "from the *ousia* of the Father" were intended to communicate technically and positively. Further "begotten not made" teaches the same truth. This anathema teaches the eternal generation of the Son; he was begotten and has no beginning. Eusebius does not take the phrase this way. He says, rather, "Still it did not appear outrageous to anathematize 'before he was begotten, he was not,' for the confession of all is that the Son of God was before the generation according to the flesh."[28]

The first sign that Eusebius is grossly and, indeed, outrageously misreading Nicaea is that he takes the council fathers to be refuting here a mistake that no one has made. If the confession of all is that the Son existed before he was incarnate—and truly this was universally confessed—then why would they bother to condemn those who deny it? That point aside, Eusebius's interpretation that the council here refers to the incarnation, the Son's generation according to the flesh, rather than to his divine generation is fanciful in the extreme. There is no reason to infer this, and every reason not to.

Let us return to Eustathius. Eusebius's handling of Nicaea well illustrates Vaggione's point that terms can remain plastic where the interpretive framework does not. It is very interesting that Eusebius was able to manage the technical terms and phrases far more successfully than he was able to handle an apparently redundant anathema. If Eusebius could read Nicaea with non-Nicene glasses, then so could Eustathius. But just as Eusebius's reading of Nicaea illustrated both his plasticity and his duplicity, so, we can assume, Eustathius too could not affirm Nicaea without some mental reservations and interpretive gymnastics.

More important than settling the matter of Eustathius's constancy (or lack thereof) between 357 and 372 is the fact that from 372 Eustathius unequivocally subscribed to a Pneumatomachian, or Macedonian, theology.[29] Eustathius's theology, then, is one among others. "It would be a mistake," R. P. C. Hanson writes, "to imagine that Macedonianism ever was a neatly defined doctrinal system, nor even that at any point it could be determined who was Macedonian and who was not."[30] There are, nevertheless, some teachings common to all Macedonians. Most basically and obviously, they all deny that the Holy Spirit is God, equal to the Father and the Son, and they all hold this by appeal to the scriptural argument that there is no biblical evidence for the position of their opponents and much for their own.

While Eustathius holds these two points, to be sure, we can fill out some of the finer points of his teaching from the particular arguments that Basil mentions in On the Holy Spirit. In addition to the charge that the divinity of the Spirit is unscriptural, Eustathius seems also to say that he is "different in nature" (On H. Sp. 10.24) and that he should not be numbered or ranked with the Father and the Son (On H. Sp. 17.41). This does not mean, for Eustathius, that the Spirit is to be numbered and ranked with creatures. Rather, "he is neither slave, they say, nor master, but freeman" (On H. Sp. 20.51; 87). Basil, of course, rejects these positions and argues against them from the Scriptures and sometimes reports the Eustathian response to his scriptural arguments. The Eustathian interpretation of particular passages, however, is less important than these mainline teachings that clearly reflect the subordinationist non-Nicene framework in which he operated.

Basil's Response to Eunomius and Eustathius

So this is what Eunomius and Eustathius held. How did Basil respond? In short, Basil responds in a twofold way: negatively, he criticizes the arguments and the scriptural interpretations of his opponents; and positively, he offers his own theological and scriptural views. Basil's criticisms of Eunomius and Eustathius are many and need not be enumerated here, but the chief objection to their respective views is that they compromise our access to God the Father and so ruin our very salvation. In his positive articulation of his own view and in contrast to both Eunomius and Eustathius, Basil uses what we may call, following Behr, a partitive exegetical framework. We can infer from Basil's use of this framework the set of truths that he wishes to protect.

There are, in fact, only a few texts wherein Basil employs partitive exegesis, and in all he makes the distinction between "theology" and "economy" to ground the exegesis.[31] Some texts refer to the Son or the Spirit "theologically" and some, "economically." Basil begins the second book of Against Eunomius with one of the "blasphemies" that Eunomius "unleash[ed] . . . against the only-begotten God" (Ag. Eun. 2.2)—namely, that the Son of God is "something made" (poiēma) (Apol. 12). Basil argues that the word is unscriptural and untraditional: neither the Scriptures nor the saints have applied the word to the Son. Basil explains that Acts 2:36 ("God has made [*epoiēsen*] him both Lord and Christ") is no exception to his rule. To say "God has made him" is very different from saying that he is "something made." In the case of creation, the Scriptures make the inference from "God made" to "something made," but in the case of the Son, the Scriptures do not make the same inference, and Basil sees meaning in this (*Ag. Eun.* 2.2). Here Eunomius has refused to listen to the silence of the Scriptures. In any case, Basil writes that "it was not the intention of the Apostle to communicate to us the subsistence [*hypostasis*] of the Only-Begotten before the ages"; Peter was not "talking about the very substance of God the Word, who *was in the beginning with God* [John 1:2], but about the one who *emptied himself in the form of a slave* [Phil. 2:7], became *similar in form to the body of our lowliness* [Phil. 3:21], and *was crucified through weakness*" [2 Cor. 13:4] (*Ag. Eun.* 2.3; 133). Basil goes on to say that Peter obviously does not intend to "teach us in the mode of theology, but hints at the reasons of the economy" (*Ag. Eun.* 2.3; 133).

A bit later in the same book of *Against Eunomius*, Basil again broaches the distinction between theology and economy, though this time mentioning by name only the former. The context here is Eunomius's argument that the Son did not eternally exist with God. Basil sums up Eunomius's train of thought:

> For God has begotten the Son either when [the Son] existed or when he did not exist. But if it occurred when he did not exist, no one should accuse me of audacity. But if it occurred when he did exist, this reasoning is not only the pinnacle of absurdity and blasphemy, but also utter silliness. For that which exists has no need of begetting. (*Ag. Eun.* 2.14; 148; *Apol.* 13.1–7)

Basil points out in response that Eunomius has transferred an argument that legitimately applies to animals to the subsistence of the Only-Begotten. Such a crude comparison provokes Basil's sarcastic rejoinder: how noble Eunomius "is for providing us with his *theology* of the begetting of the Only-Begotten!" (*Ag. Eun.* 2.14; 148, my emphasis).

Moving beyond sarcasm, Basil's substantive response to Eunomius's argument is an extended contemplation of John 1:1: "In the beginning was the Word, and the Word was with God, and the Word was God." Basil explains that "beginning" here is absolute and nonrelative, a synonym for "eternity," and "was" communicates the same (*Ag. Eun.* 2.14–15). Basil contrasts, as Origen did before him, the opening of John's Gospel with that of the other evangelists. Matthew, Basil writes, "explained the Son's begetting according to the flesh," and, similarly, Luke "approached the *theology* by going through the corporeal origins"; John, however, "apprehended the beginning itself and left behind all corporeal and temporal notions as lower than his *theology*" (*Ag. Eun.* 2.15; 150, my emphasis). Basil describes the first verse of John's Gospel as a "theology" that sketches a clear outline of the nature of the Son. Though in this passage Basil uses only one in the pair (theology and economy) of technical terms, it is clear that he nonetheless invokes the distinction: Matthew and Luke recount the Lord's *economic* beginning, John his *theological*. The openings of the various Gospels, then, are a simple example of partitive exegesis.

John Behr has called attention to still another example of partitive exegesis, that involves, as they all must, the distinction between theology and economy.[32] Amphilochius of Iconium had written Basil to ask a series of questions, one of which dealt with the passage in the Gospel where the Lord confesses ignorance of the day and the hour of the end. After pointing out that this passage is a favorite prooftext of the Eunomians, Basil offers essentially two different interpretations, one economic and one theological, though he does not name them as such.

"To one who examines intelligently," Basil writes, "the Lord often discourses with men from his human side [*apo tou anthrōpinou merous*] also" (ep. 236.1; 3:391). "Give me a drink" (John 4:7) is an example, and the ignorance of Christ would be another. Thus Basil says that "someone will not be carried beyond a conception consistent with piety who applies the ignorance to him who advanced in wisdom and grace with God and men" (ep. 236.1; 3:391, altered).[33] Out of context, this sentence may sound Nestorian. That is, it could mean that Basil predicates ignorance of the day and the hour of one person and knowledge of it of another person, as if he who advanced in wisdom and grace were someone other than the Son of God. When we look at the sentence in context, however, it is clear that Basil does not intend to identify two subjects, for the one who asked for a drink (and by implication, the one who confessed his ignorance of the day and the hour) "was not flesh without soul, but Godhead which had made use of flesh endowed with soul" (ep. 236.1; 3:391).

There is another interpretation. The Son who received the things of the body and of human knowledge economically also received theologically the things of God. In this case, Basil explains that the Son's confession of ignorance is a confession that the Father is the cause of his divine knowledge. Basil paraphrases the Gospel passage in this way: "Regarding the day or the hour no one knoweth, neither the angels of God, nay not even the Son would have known had not the Father known; for from the Father was knowledge given him from the beginning" (ep. 236.2; 3:395). The Father, for Basil, is always the first cause, but sometimes, so to speak, he causes theologically and other times he causes economically. The divine generation of the Son is the former, the incarnation is the latter.

The distinction between economy and theology illuminates also Basil's treatment of the Holy Spirit. The Spirit's role in the economy differs from that of the Son most obviously and most markedly in that he was not incarnate. This means, of course, that there can be no partitive exegesis for the Spirit as for the Son: it cannot be that some texts refer to his human nature (or to him in his human nature) and others to his divine, or, as Basil puts it, that sometimes the Lord speaks from his human side and other times, if we fill out Basil's thought, from his divine.

While biblical texts that speak of or about the Spirit cannot be handled in just the same way as those regarding the Son, Basil does find it very useful to employ the distinction between theology and economy in *On the Holy Spirit*. Some texts are theological and so refer to the Spirit's eternal relationship with the Father and the Son, while others are economic and denote, as Basil says, "the grace given to us" (*On H. Sp.* 27.68; 107).

Basil uses the distinction between theology and economy to defend his doxology: "Glory to the Father, with the Son, together with the Holy Spirit." "Why," Basil reports the question of his opponents, "why, . . . if the word 'in' is peculiarly suitable for the Spirit and is quite enough for our every thought about him—why, then, do you introduce this new word by saying 'with the Holy Spirit' instead of 'in the Holy Spirit'?" (*On H. Sp.* 26.65; 103–4). Basil responds that each phrase "contributes to true religion": "in," Basil offers, describes well "what concerns us," "the grace given to us" (*On H. Sp.* 27.68; 107), and "the grace that works in those who share it" (*On H. Sp.* 25.63; 102); "with" describes "the Spirit's communion with God," his dignity (*On H. Sp.* 27.68; 107), "his pretemporal existence," and "his unceasing abiding with the Father and the Son" in eternal union (*On H. Sp.* 25.63; 101–2).

While Basil does not here use technical language, we may. When we speak of the Spirit's actions on behalf of man's salvation, we speak *economically* and give glory to the Father, through the Son, *in* the Spirit. When we speak, however, of the Spirit's eternal communion with the Father and the Son and his nature and dignity, we speak *theologically* and give glory to the Father, with the Son, together with the Holy Spirit, or to the Father, and the Son, and the Holy Spirit.

In a couple of places in *On the Holy Spirit*, Basil does mention the words *economy* and *theology*, though not together. He takes Psalm 33 [32]:6 theologically: "The heavens were established by the Word of the Lord, and all their power, by the Spirit [breath] of his mouth." Basil explains that "the Word is with God in the beginning, and is God, and the Spirit of the mouth of God is 'the Spirit of truth, who proceeds from the Father' [John 15:26]" (*On H. Sp.* 16.38; 71). The psalmic image comes up again in a beautiful passage on the monarchy (*On H. Sp.* 18). The Spirit has communion in nature with the Father and the Son "because he is said to be from God, not as all things are from God, but insofar as he comes forth from God, not begottenly as the Son does, but as the breath of his mouth" (*On H. Sp.* 18.46; 81). After explaining that the text cannot be taken literally (God the Father has no bodily mouth), Basil writes that, "while the kinship is thus made clear, the manner of its existence remains unspeakable" (*On H. Sp.* 18.46; 81). We might recall here

Basil's sarcastic rejoinder to Eunomius—how gracious of Eunomius to supply us with a theology of the divine generation of the Son. Such an account,
whether of the Son's or the Spirit's origin or manner of existence, is impossible.
Scripture, that is, tells us *that* there is a theology, but it remains a mystery. Like
the Eunomians, the Spirit-fighters claim too much. "As for those who insist,"
writes Basil, "on saying that there is a sub-numeration into first, second, and
third, let them know that they have introduced the polytheism of the errant
Greeks into the undefiled *theology* of the Christians" (*On H. Sp.* 18.47; 83,
my emphasis). They end up with three gods.

The univocal approach of
Let us pause over the rhetorical power of this last point. The Spirit-fighters
are supposed to be the Christians who defer to the language of the Scriptures.
It is they who are scrupulous about not speaking and thinking in unbiblical
ways. They are moderate and humble in their theology, refusing to go beyond
the teaching of the Scriptures. When they order the Godhead into first, second,
and third rank, however, they are importing into Christian faith the worst
aspect of Greek thought: its polytheism. Basil charges them with supplying a
theology where the Scriptures remain silent, and the theology that they supply
comes from the most foreign and unbiblical of sources. It is Basil, accused
of saying too much and reading beyond the revelation of the Scriptures, who
respects both the Scriptures' teaching concerning the fact of the Trinity and
their silence concerning its unspeakable manner of existence.

The "accommodations" or "economies" [*oikonomiai*] that the Lord Jesus
has made for man are accomplished through the Spirit. That is to say, the
economic activity of the Son is also the economic activity of the Spirit. Basil
asserts that this is true whether one considers Old Testament accommodations
or New. The incarnation itself, the temptations, the miracles, the resurrection
from the dead, the second coming, and the final judgment—in short, the whole
economy—will be accomplished by the working of the Spirit (*On H. Sp.* 16.39).

In his first sermon on man, we have seen, Basil uses "theology" simply to
describe the Trinity: Father, Son, and Holy Spirit who are nonetheless one
God. Here he explains God's deliberation in Genesis 1:26, "Let us make man
[*anthrōpos*] in our image, after our likeness." "Let *us*," Basil explains, is a
reference to Father, Son, and Holy Spirit. But lest we be led to polytheism,
Genesis continues, "so *God created* man" (Gen. 1:27, my emphasis). "The
prelude to our creation," says Basil, "is true theology" (*Hex.* 10.4; 34).

The whole point of partitive exegesis and the theology-economy distinction that grounds it is that they open us to the truths about God (in himself
and in relation to us) communicated in Scripture. The univocal approach of
the Eunomians, in Basil's mind, both blinds them to the truth about the Son
and ruins his salvific work. The same applies to the Spirit. The Spirit-fighters
take economic texts univocally, without distinction, and so come away with a
distorted view of both the dignity and the work of the Holy Spirit. Basil addresses this Pneumatomachian hermeneutic in *On the Holy Spirit*. He reports

their objection that the Spirit is not divine because "he intercedes for us" (Rom. 8:26–27; *On H. Sp.* 19.50). Basil first points out that their logic would also apply to the Only-Begotten, and then asks,

> Surely it is not the case, then, that because the Spirit is in you—if indeed he is in you at all—or that because he teaches and guides us who have been blinded to choose what profits us, you should diminish the pious and lawful glory owed to him? (*On H. Sp.* 19.50; 86)

The Pneumatomachians have made the divine benefactor's love for man the occasion of ingratitude (*On H. Sp.* 19.50). Basil's argument here is little more than a reductio ad absurdum. He neither dwells on the problems with such a univocal reading nor offers an alternative approach.

We find a similar objection and response a bit later in *On the Holy Spirit*. Basil here gives the Pneumatomachian objection that the Spirit, the gift, cannot be exalted by the same honors as the Father who gave the gift (*On H. Sp.* 24.57). As in the last text, Basil's response is brief and rhetorical. So "the Holy Spirit is the gift of God," a gift of life, and freedom, and power. "Why," Basil asks, "is the Spirit so despised for this?" (*On H. Sp.* 24.57; 95). After all, the Father gave the Son also to men. In their folly the Spirit-fighters consider God's "excessive kindness as the road to blasphemy" (*On H. Sp.* 24.57; 95). Here again, the argument is largely rhetorical.

Eunomius thought that Basil's partitive exegesis was blasphemous. As he writes in his *Apology for the Apology*,

> If the Word that was in the beginning and was God be one, and he who "emptied himself" and "took the form of a servant" be another, and if God the Word, by whom are all things, be Lord, and this Jesus, who was crucified after all things had come into being, be Lord also, there are, according to this view, two Lords and Christs.[34]

Vaggione explains that "as far as Eunomius was concerned, this was blasphemy in the strict sense, for in his eyes Basil could only mean that there were *two* Christs, one human and the other divine."[35] Eunomius seems to assume that partitive exegesis necessarily leads to the supposition of two subjects in Christ. That is to say, if we use later categories, partitive exegesis must be "Nestorian."[36]

Vaggione makes no response on Basil's behalf to this charge (his book is about Eunomius rather than Basil).[37] We may ask, nonetheless—it is imperative that we ask—whether Eunomius's claim is right.[38] Did Basil deny in Christ a single subject? Was Basil a "Nestorian" before Nestorius?

Basil, of course, never addresses the question directly, but we do well to call to mind a couple of simple points: first, some of Basil's texts are ambivalent, open to a two-subject reading; second, others are not ambivalent and seem to allow only a one-subject interpretation. The particular piece of exegesis that Eunomius thought blasphemous seems to be open to either a one-subject or two-subject interpretation. On the one hand, Basil does say that in Acts 2:36, St. Peter was speaking not about the "very substance of God the Word, who *was in the beginning with God* [John 1:2], but about *the one [peri tou kenōsantos heauton]* who *emptied himself in the form of a slave*" [Phil. 2:7] (*Ag. Eun.* 2.3; 133). Thus God the Word, or the substance of God the Word, would be one subject, and the one who emptied himself would be another.[39] On the other hand, a few lines later Basil writes that St. Peter was speaking of "his rule and power over all, which the Father entrusted to him." Peter was not "describing his arrival at being" or the "original begetting of the Only-Begotten." Both texts refer to the same person. Eunomius has erroneously transferred the text "he made" from the Son's rule and power to his origin.

For an excellent example of a text that is patient only of a one-subject interpretation, we can look to *On the Holy Spirit*.[40] Basil here argues that the Son's care for men should not be taken as an indication of his weakness but of his power. Indeed the Son's role in creating and regulating the universe does not show his strength as much as his "join[ing] himself to death through the flesh without suffering, in order by his own suffering to give us freedom from suffering" (*On H. Sp.* 8.18; 47).

We find the same ambiguity in Gregory of Nyssa's defense of Basil: some texts are open to a two-subject reading, some to a one-subject reading. Consider the passage where Gregory turns the charge of being ashamed of the cross back on Eunomius. "Who, then," he asks, "is it who is ashamed of the cross? He who, even after the Passion, worships the Son equally with the Father, or he who even before the Passion insults him, not only by ranking him with the creation, but by maintaining that he is of passible nature, on the ground that he could not have come to experience his sufferings had he not had a nature capable of such sufferings?" (*Ag. Eun.* 5.3; 176). Gregory, then giving his own position, asserts that "even the body in which he underwent his Passion, by being mingled with the divine nature, was made by that commixture to be that which the assuming nature is" (*Ag. Eun.* 5.3; 176). Thus the Son suffered his passion in his body. Such a way of speaking indicates a single subject.

And yet sometimes Gregory's words are open to a two-subject interpretation. Speaking again of the Lord's passion, Gregory writes that "he who was highly exalted after his Passion was made Lord and Christ by his union with him who is verily Lord and Christ" (*Ag. Eun.* 5.5; 180); or "The blows belong to the servant in whom the Lord was, the honours to the Lord whom the servant compassed about, so that by reason of the contact and the union of natures the proper attributes of each belong to both, as the Lord receives the stripes of the servant, while the servant is glorified with the honour of the Lord; for this is why the cross is said to be the cross of the Lord of glory" (*Ag. Eun.* 5.5;

181). Gregory can speak of the human nature of Christ as if it were a subject separate from the Son, as if it were the human nature of a person other than the Son, the person of the "servant" united to him.

Basil's anti-Apollinarian polemic also sheds some light on the question of whether Basil posited one subject or two in Christ, for it indicates to what extent Basil does and does not take up the question of the person of Christ. In his treatment of this polemic, John Behr has called attention to a set of texts that are relevant to this question, although he does not take up our subject in just this way.[41]

The textbook definition of Apollinarianism is rather straightforward and neat: the denial to Christ of a human rational capacity. This means that Christ is made up of either divine Logos and flesh (*sarx*) or divine Logos, soul (*psychē*), and flesh (*sarx*). In any case, God the Word, consubstantial with the Father, serves as Christ's rational faculty. Basil, though, gives us not the textbook definition but something else. In fact, he seems hardly to mention at all that Apollinaris's Christ has no human rational faculty. For Basil, Apollinaris's errors are the following: Christ had a heavenly body rather than one from Mary; Christ had no *psychē*, the seat of anxiety and grief; the divine nature changes; and a kind of second Judaism or millenarianism involving too physical a view of the resurrected body (ep. 263.4). Only the second and third charges bear on the question at hand.

In epistle 260, to Bishop Optimus, Basil sums up the current positions on the incarnation of the Lord over which "men do not cease contending":

> Some [conclude] that he assumed a body, while others maintain that his advent was without body, and some [hold] that he had taken on a body capable of sensations [*pathēton*], while others held that he fulfilled through a sort of phantasy the functions which the body performs; and some say that his body was earthly, but others that it was heavenly; and some claim that his beginning was from eternity, but others that he had his beginning from Mary. (ep. 260.8; 4:71)

With the second and third pair of opposing positions, Basil has the Apollinarians in mind. In the next letter (261, to the people at Sozopolis), he explains the significance of the (alleged) Apollinarian belief in a heavenly body: in short, such a belief abolishes the saving dispensation of our Lord Jesus Christ, for it destroys our solidarity with Christ. He must be from Adam, as we are, in order to pay the price of death to save us (ep. 261.2).

Setting aside the question of the heavenly body, we can see that the other set of opposing positions (whether or not the Lord's body was capable of feeling, or *pathos*) is more relevant. Basil distinguishes three types of suffering, three types of *pathos*: the *pathos* proper to the flesh (e.g., division, diminution, or dissolution); the *pathos* proper to ensouled flesh (*sarx empsychos*) (e.g., weariness, pain, hunger, thirst, sleepiness); and the *pathos* proper to the soul that has made use of the body (*psyche sōmati kekrēmenē*) (e.g., grief, anxiety, and concern) (ep. 261.3). Basil sums up his position: the Lord "assumed our flesh along with its natural feelings, but he 'did no sin'" (ep. 261.3; 4:83; 1 Pet. 2:22). Basil sees two major problems with Apollinaris's denying a soul (*psyche*) to the Lord: first, he makes the incarnation fantastic and apparent rather then real and genuine; second, if there is no soul as the seat of *pathos*, then, by implication, the *pathē* of the Lord must be predicated of the divinity itself, and Apollinaris is forced to say, in contradiction to the Scriptures and all good sense, that the divine nature changes (ep. 261.3; ep. 262.1–2).

While I sympathize very much with our Basil in his rejection of Apollinarianism, this inference from the Lord lacking a soul to the divine nature changing, is not, I think, logically necessary. That is to say, Apollinaris need not predicate the Lord's *pathē* of the divine nature, for he could attribute them (as St. Cyril and the Council of Ephesus would teach) to the person of the Son and not to the divine nature. I point this out not to find fault with Basil, but to indicate the state of the question. Basil's argument here indicates that he has not made the distinctions that will be made in the next century, and there is no fault in that. This innocent lack of prescience helps to explain the looseness and ambivalence that we have seen in some of Basil's words. I would conclude that Eunomius's accusation of two Christs misses the mark, but that Basil's (and Gregory's) language lacks the precision that would make the charge ridiculous.

If Basil and Gregory are not so clearly prescient of the fifth-century distinction between person and nature, then neither are the Eunomians. The theology of Basil and Gregory of Nyssa, if I may put it so, pushes them in the direction of the fifth-century distinction; so much is evident in the texts that imply a single subject together with a nature shared with the Father and another shared with us. The theology of the Eunomians, however, does not even hint of the later distinction. For them, Christ is not only a single subject but a unique nature. Thus it would make no difference (as it would in the case of the Nicenes) if they treat the nature of the Son as the subject of his actions; indeed, their position seems to demand so much. For them, to posit two natures in Christ is to posit two subjects; they have no conception of a single subject with two natures.[42]

So far then, we have examined the theological positions of Eunomius and Eustathius, as well as Basil's response, the heart of which is the distinction between economy and theology, the attendant style of exegesis, and the truths that this distinction and this exegesis serve and protect. We have seen that the unknowability of God, the divine generation of the Son, and the spiration of the Spirit are examples of such truths. One more still is the radical distinction between God—Father, Son, and Holy Spirit—and creation.

Here we return once again to Vaggione and the question of the "break." He puts this question in an interesting way: "Where did the 'break' [*diastēma*] come?"[43] All Christian theologians, he argues, must posit a break, but the question is where to put it. This point, in fact, Vaggione reasonably holds, distinguished Christians from their pagan contemporaries. For Christians, there was not continuous change of being from the highest being to the lowest, for the first words of Genesis had created a gap, or break, unbridgeable by creatures.[44] Nicenes posit the break between the divine Triad on the one hand and all else on the other. The non-Nicenes, however, put it between the Father and the Son. For them, to put the break between the divine Triad and creation is to posit a break in Christ himself. We have seen that for them Christ cannot be composed of an uncreated and a created nature and remain a single Christ. Thus to put the break in Christ is to posit two Christs. According to the non-Nicenes, "the 'break' between contingent and non-contingent could only come as the final, mediating term of a hierarchy whose node was the mysterious dichotomy between Father and Son."[45]

The Nicenes and Basil, even before he would have called himself a Nicene, put the break between the Father, Son, and Holy Spirit on the one hand, and creatures on the other. A couple of examples that span Basil's theological career will suffice. In the third book of *Against Eunomius*, Basil's first theological work, he writes:

> It is said that there are two realities: divinity and creation, sovereignty and servitude, sanctifying power and sanctified power, that which has virtue by nature and that which achieves virtue by freewill. In which class shall we rank the Spirit? (*Ag. Eun.* 3.2; 187–88)[46]

Of course, Basil answers that the Spirit, as well as the Son, belongs on the side of divinity. From the mid- to late 370s we have a fantastic text from *On the Holy Spirit*. Basil here refutes the idea that the Spirit occupies a middle position between God and creature. The Spirit-fighters say that he is neither slave nor master but freeman. Such an expression agitates Basil. "O the clever stupidity," he exclaims, "O the pitiful boldness of those who say such things. What do I lament more, their stupidity or their blasphemy?" (*On H. Sp.* 20.51; 87). Basil goes on to say that these men have thought of God in too human a way, as if the differences of rank that obtain among men will obtain also with "the divine and unspeakable nature" (*On H. Sp.* 20.51; 87). This middle rank that they propose for the Spirit does not exist, so that if the Spirit "is created, he is clearly a slave along with everything else . . . but if he is above creation, he participates in the kingship" (*On H. Sp.* 20.51; 89).

Thus is Basil's main response to the Eunomians and the Eustathians. It is nothing short of a radically different vision of God and his relationship to the world, and a correspondingly different way of reading God's self-revelation in the Scriptures, especially as the revelation bears on Christ. In the course of responding to his opponents Basil made two other correlative contributions to theology that ought to be mentioned. In his polemic with the Eunomians he developed a theory of names that explains how human language is predicated not only of God but of anything whatever; and in his polemic with the Eustathians, he develops a theory of tradition.

A Theory of Names

Since Basil's theory of names is a response to Eunomius's, let us first outline the basics of Eunomius's theory.[47] The first thing to say is that Eunomius does not offer a general theory of names but, at least at first, only a theory of divine names. His chief concern is "how names operate when applied to God."[48]

We have seen already Eunomius's insistence that knowledge of God be exact and that our salvation, in his view, depends upon our knowing God as God knows himself. Another way to put this same point is that Eunomius eliminates the "notional level" or "mental space" between the name and its referent.[49] That is to say, for Eunomius a name predicated of God does not refer to an idea or a notion but rather to the divine substance itself. The names for God, especially "unbegotten," disclose God's substance, not some notion of him. If names of God referred to notions rather than to the divine substance, then we could not know God but only our own passing thoughts. Thus, for Eunomius to posit a notional mediation in our knowledge of God compromises that very knowledge and our salvation too.

There are two obvious consequences of Eunomius's theory that are indicated by Eunomius himself and stressed in the scholarly analysis of his thought. First, names predicated of God and creatures are homonyms; they have the same sound but cannot mean the same thing. Names predicated of God and creatures are equivocal. Second, all the different names predicated of God are really synonyms. Thus, Eunomius insists that any name applied to God is synonymous with "unbegotten" (*Apol.* 16–17).

Basil offers a very different view. In the first place, his theory of names is not limited to God but applies generally. Language does not work one way with God and a completely different way with creatures. Basil does not here think of God in a creaturely way or anthropomorphize him, for the names have to be purified of their terrestrial and corporeal connotations when they are used of celestial realities. Nonetheless, Basil emphatically rejects Eunomius's equivocal understanding of predication. DelCogliano explains that

> Basil's appeal to *purified* common usage is a rejection of Eunomius's equivocity. He agrees with Eunomius that "father" is not applied to God and men in the ordinary, corporeal sense of the term, but disagrees that the name is used equivocally. He therefore formulates a notion of fatherhood that results in a univocal use of "father" in divine and human contexts.[50]

Conceptual purification makes it possible for Basil to apply names to God and creatures in a fundamentally similar way; it enables his theory to be generalist rather than specific to God-talk.

The most important difference between Basil's and Eunomius's respective theories of names is that Basil posits the "notional level" and the "mental space" that Eunomius denies. This is to say that, for Basil, names refer above all to notions rather than things. A name does not grant immediate and exact access to a substance, whether God's or a creature's. Even though notions often have really existing referents and can reflect the truth about these things, the relationship between names and notions does not depend upon the notion having such a referent. Basil offers the example of the centaur or the chimaera (*Ag. Eun.* 1.6). They do not exist, and yet the name calls to mind a notion. When notions do correspond with really existing things, in Basil's theory they always designate properties of the substance rather than the substance itself. This is true of proper names (like "Peter" and "Paul"), absolute names (like "man"), and relative names (like "Father" and "Son") (*Ag. Eun.* 2.4).[51]

While there are some simple and universally applied principles at the foundation of Basil's theory of names, he articulates a number of distinctions to accommodate the complexity of human predication. There are basic notions and derived notions, and of the former, some are immediately present to the mind while others have to be purified.

We may illustrate Basil's distinctions so:

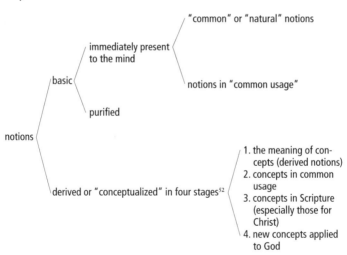

As an example of a basic common notion, Basil considers grain (*Ag. Eun.* 1.6). Everybody has a preconception of grain by which it is immediately recognized by the mind. Notions given in common usage are those of ordinary speech. Basil gives the example of generation. In common usage it designates both the passion whereby the begotten is begotten as well as the kinship between the begotten and the one who begets (*Ag. Eun.* 2.4). These mundane notions must be purified when they are used of God. Finally, beyond basic notions, there are derived notions, conceptualizations that are arrived at by the mind's working upon basic notions. Basil again gives the example of grain, though this time deriving further concepts from the basic notion. "The same grain," he writes, "can be called at one time 'fruit,' at another time 'seed,' and again at another time 'nourishment'" (*Ag. Eun.* 1.6; 98). Basil uses these distinctions to make sense of the full range of our theological predication, from basic ideas commonly thought of God to the names of Christ in the Scriptures, to those concepts like "unbegotten" that are of human derivation.

So Basil's polemic with Eunomius inspired a general theory of how human language is predicated of both God and everything else, a theory that takes early pagan and Christian theories of naming as a point of departure but develops them in original ways.[53] This theory of names fits perfectly with Basil's larger view of man, the Bible, and creation that we have explored in earlier chapters. Material creation bears a similarity to God, the things of God, and the salvation of man. God has invested the created order with meaning, from the posture of the human body, to the behavior of animals, to the constitution of plants. With his theory of names, Basil extends the similarity from the things themselves to human language about things. Thus, for Basil, "names common to God and created beings are [not] homonymous; rather there is a strong connection between the use of words in divine and mundane contexts," and every name has a notion truly predicated of divine and mundane objects.[54]

There is more. Creation and the Bible are books that yield their meaning only when the reader engages them and reasons upon them. So also words predicated of earthly objects cannot simply be applied with all earthly connotations to divine objects. Rather, they must be reasoned upon. The reader thinks about the meanings of a word—*father*, for example—in its mundane context and must adjust it—purify it—for application to God. It is left to us to figure out "how all the names for God, which have been handed down by scripture and tradition, can be used in a way that is appropriate for God."[55]

Tradition

At the beginning of *On the Holy Spirit*, Basil explains why he is writing the work: some have charged him with liturgical innovation—in the ancient church, no small accusation—for worshiping God with the doxology ("Glory to the Father, with [*meta*] the Son, with [*syn*] the Holy Spirit") (*On H. Sp.* 1.3).[56] His opponents attack it as unscriptural, and Basil must mount a defense. "They do not stop babbling up and down," Basil writes, "that to give glory with the Holy Spirit is unattested and non-scriptural, and the like" (*On H. Sp.* 27.68;

107). "They cry out for proofs from the Scriptures," he writes in another place, "and dismiss the non-scriptural witness of the fathers as worthless" (*On H. Sp.* 10.25; 56). Against "this 'Puritan' or 'Protestant,' so to speak, mentality of Eustathius, this acute 'biblicism,'"[57] Basil argues that the Scriptures cannot be rightly understood apart from apostolic and patristic tradition, and in this case the tradition is liturgical.

This fourth-century *sola scriptura* is the context for Basil's well-known distinction between tradition and Scripture in *On the Holy Spirit* 27.66. Here he differentiates *dogma* from *kērygma*, the latter designating what the church publicly proclaims, the former, what it reserves for the initiated. Of the *kērygmata* and *dogmata* "that are guarded in the church, we hold some from the teaching of the Scriptures, and others we have received in mystery as the teachings of the tradition of the apostles" (*On H. Sp.* 27.66; 104). In other words, the deposit would be made up of scriptural *kērygmata* and scriptural *dogmata* as well as nonscriptural *kērygmata* and *dogmata*. On this reading the *kērygmata* are the bare words and the *dogmata* comprise the right understanding of these words. The Scriptures are public, but the knowledge whereby they are properly understood is reserved to the initiated. This is why the Scriptures are obscure: obscurity conceals the *dogmata*, the right understanding of its teaching, lest it be despised for being familiar.[58] There are also, as de Mendieta has indicated, kerygmatic and dogmatic nonscriptural traditions; things publicly known whose real meaning is not.

> We all look to the East [Basil writes] when we are praying (*kērygma*). But few of us know that we are seeking after our own old country, the Paradise, which *God planted in Eden, in the East* (*dogma*). It is in the standing posture that we are offering our prayers, on the first day of the week (namely on Sunday or Lord's day) (*kērygma*). But the reason of this (posture) we do not know, at least not all of us (*dogma*). (*On H. Sp.* 27.66)[59]

Basil offers more examples, but the point is clear from the parenthetical comments that de Mendieta inserts into his translation: nonscriptural tradition contains both *kērygma* and *dogma*.

This would be plain enough, were it not for the fact that other texts yield a different picture wherein *dogma* is one and the same with nonscriptural tradition. All of the things that de Mendieta has identified as kerygmatic nonscriptural tradition are, says Basil, transmitted in fact by nonscriptural and mystical tradition; they are not public. Along these lines, the distinction between *kērygma* and *dogma* seems to be the same as that between Scripture and tradition. Thus, Scripture would not contain *dogmata* and tradition would not contain *kērygmata*. A single example stands against this construal of the distinction between *dogma* and *kērygma*. In *On the Holy Spirit* 27.66, explaining why we stand for prayer on Sunday, Basil writes that we so stand because

Sunday "seems somehow to be an image of the age to come. On account of this, although it is the beginning of days, Moses names it not 'first' but 'one.' For it is written, 'There was evening, and there was morning, one day' (Gen. 1:15), as if the same one often repeated" (*On H. Sp.* 27.66; 106). All of the examples of *dogmata* except this one just mentioned are tied to the liturgy. There is, nevertheless, a tension in Basil's use of *dogma* and *kērygma*, and we can see it in his letters.[60] In epistle 125, the confession of faith for Eustathius of Sebaste, he says that the creed of Nicaea contains saving *dogma* (ep. 125.1; 2:265). In epistle 90, however, Basil exhorts, "Let us also pronounce with boldness that good *kērygma* of the Fathers, which overwhelms the accursed heresy of Arius, and builds the churches on the sound doctrine, wherein the Son is confessed to be *homoousios* with the Father" (ep. 90.2; 2:127, altered). Obviously, he is talking about the creed of Nicaea.

In spite of these difficulties, Basil very clearly asserts that *dogmata* are communicated secretly or "mystically" and are understood only by the initiated or by an elite, not by all. The nature of this secrecy and the identity of the elite are related. R. P. C. Hanson thinks that Basil's nonscriptural tradition is secret and esoteric and thus that the elite who possess them are very much like the Gnostics.[61] Basil has turned Christianity into "a mystery religion or an ecclesiastical freemasonry" so that he could invest his doxological customs and, hence, his theology of the Spirit with greater authority.[62] Hanson sees Basil as breaking from his own earlier thinking about tradition and from Athanasius and his predecessors. Georges Florovsky sees it differently. He eloquently stresses the liturgical and mystical nature of the transmission rather than its secrecy.[63] Thus, the "'silent' and 'mystical' tradition, 'which has not been made public,' is not an esoteric doctrine, reserved for some particular elite. The 'elite' was the Church."[64] Basil, then, though using peculiar language, has not broken with early fathers in his thinking about tradition but has perpetuated their insight that Scripture cannot be understood apart from the rule of faith, which contained the "credal core" of the Scriptures and epitomized them.[65] De Mendieta proposes a position between Florovsky's and Hanson's. He agrees with Hanson that tradition is secret and not "mystical," but he thinks that this secrecy does not make Basil into a Gnostic.[66] De Mendieta distinguishes three levels of *dogma*, each of which is understood by a particular group. The baptized know customs, but not all know what the customs mean. Beyond these two levels are a theologically trained monastic elite who can understand the more profound *dogmata*.[67]

Who, then, is right? When we look at the crucial text (*On H. Sp.* 27.66) and the examples that Basil gives, we can make the following judgments. Florovsky is right to emphasize the liturgical character of the tradition, but of course not all of the baptized will understand all of the *dogmata*. De Mendieta is right to make distinctions here; some *dogmata* are more profound than others, and some require more education and illumination. Gribomont accentuates

Basil's debt here to Origen's homily 5 on Numbers, where he "combines the allusions to the *disciplina arcana*, where initiation involves all the baptized, and those with a superior knowledge, where the initiated are fewer and the doctrinal formulation less definite."[68] As did Origen, Basil sees the spiritual life as having stages.[69]

In addition, Hanson's argument that Basil deviated from his own earlier views and from the larger tradition does not persuade. In *Against Eunomius*, the argument runs that Basil, like Athanasius, "thinks that Scripture is doctrinally sufficient," for he refuses Eunomius's technical language precisely because the words cannot be found in the Scriptures.[70] Basil, then, in his letters uses tradition more flexibly, largely through his realization of the importance of the Nicene Creed.[71] Finally, in *On the Holy Spirit*, Basil forsakes the sufficiency of the Scriptures interpreted by tradition and posits the necessity of a secret, extra-scriptural, apostolic tradition. There are a couple of problems with this view of Basil's devolution. First of all, while he refuses Eunomius's nonscriptural technical language, he uses his own. His reprimand of Eunomius is not evidence of a kind of thoroughgoing biblicism that would reject the use of words not found in the Scripture. Eunomius's words are unscriptural more because they contradict the meaning of Scripture than because they cannot materially be found there. Moreover, Basil sees his opponents in *On the Holy Spirit* as contradicting Scripture and himself as following it (*On H. Sp.* 10.24). Hanson writes that Basil was motivated to make his innovations because "he could not meet Eustathius's demand for a full documentation from Scripture of his doctrine of the Holy Spirit."[72] It is rather that Eustathius could not see the force and meaning, the *dogma*, of the many scriptural proofs that Basil offered, precisely because he rejected the liturgical tradition in which the meaning of the Scriptures became patent. And this rejection itself was rather unscriptural. Basil would never have conceded that Eustathius was truer to the Scriptures than he; rather, Eustathius had the words of Scripture but not their sense.

Hanson also accuses Basil of falsely, but not necessarily intentionally, calling his doxology apostolic.[73] He invented a "legend of apostolic origin for rite and custom" that was not justified by the Scriptures, and in his hands "tradition, instead of being left as the word to describe doctrinal development and exploration in continuity with the original Gospel, becomes an historical fiction."[74] Basil's statement in fact is quite strong. After tracing his doxology in patristic authors as far back as Irenaeus and Clement (*On H. Sp.* 29.72), he affirms that it has been welcomed by all the churches "from the time when the Gospel was proclaimed" (*On H. Sp.* 29.75; 116). What, then, does Basil mean when he says that his doxology is apostolic? Jean Gribomont answers this well.[75] First of all, Basil maintains that it is apostolic—that is, consistent with the wishes and practice of the apostles—to accept nonscriptural traditions, for Paul commends the Corinthians and the Thessalonians to do so (1 Cor. 11:2; 2 Thess. 2:15). Second, Gribomont points out that Basil is not naive. He has shown, for example, in his canonical letters to Amphilochius, that he is "very knowledgeable of the variety and flexibility of customs."[76] Basil "loves to join in one voice 'the Apostles and Fathers'"; thus he expresses the continuity so important to tradition and his vision of the church's unity in history.[77] "Apostolic" means consistent with the teaching of the apostles preserved in the fathers.

Basil realized that his opponents had focused too narrowly on the authority of the Scriptures. Their demand for explicit scriptural proof for all teachings compromised the integrity of the faith. He tersely summarizes the consequences of their logic: "Let them teach us not to baptize as we have received, or not to believe as we have been baptized, or not to give glory as we have believed" (*On H. Sp.* 27.68; 107). As did fathers before him, Basil learned that the Scriptures do not interpret themselves, and, as they did, he thinks that the rule of faith enshrined in the liturgy has a special place here. In the end he realized that the problem of authority in the church is not a simple one, and tradition itself can be quite complex and varied. It is not as though the Scriptures are obscure but tradition patent. William Tieck has worked out the Basilian view of authentic tradition. Authentic tradition must be of long usage, universal ecclesial recognition, and most important of all, "bearing a sense in accord with piety and true faith."[78] This is to say that authentic tradition must be consistent with apostolic (in the broad sense) liturgy and worship.

Just as Basil's theory of names fits in well with his larger theological vision, so does his theory of tradition. The two books that the Lord has given man, Scripture and creation, are not self-interpreting: man must engage them with a pure heart in the presence of the Spirit. In polemic with the Spirit-fighters, Basil realized that there is another necessary help to open the meaning of the Scriptures to its readers: the tradition of the church, especially the liturgical tradition but also the creedal tradition that springs from it. Thus, tradition is, as it were, a pair of glasses, apostolic glasses, that the reader wears when trying to discern the teaching that the Lord wishes to communicate in the Bible. Basil saw that when he read the Scriptures while "wearing" the liturgical tradition, he saw more clearly what they were teaching about the Spirit from both a theological and economic point of view.

Conclusion

Our investigation of Basil's "simple" proclamations of his faith yielded a sense of what for him are its most basic truths about our knowledge of God, the saving knowledge to which God has led us through the book of Scripture. God is Father, Son, and Holy Spirit, a consubstantial Trinity among whom there obtains a particular order, and that order is manifest to us in the manner of our salvation: we are baptized into the Spirit, and then the Son, and then the Father.

Basil's polemic works provide a deep theological background to these truths, reveal the limitations of his thought, and offer us a glimpse into his creativity as a theologian. *Against Eunomius* and *On the Holy Spirit* show us that, though Basil, Eunomius, and Eustathius could profess a common baptismal creed, there existed between them a doctrinal and theological chasm. Basil understands the Scriptures to reveal a Son and Spirit equal in dignity to the Father, and this scriptural revelation encourages—indeed, requires—him to read the Bible in a particular way. In the language that we have been using in this chapter, when one puts the break, or the gap, between the Trinity and the world, one must in turn read some scriptural texts as referring to the activity of the Son and the Spirit in the economy and others as referring to the Son and the Spirit in theology, so to speak. The consubstantiality of the Son and the Spirit ground and require partitive exegesis. If, with Eunomius and Eustathius, we put the gap, or break, between the Father and the Son, then we will have not only a very different way of reading the biblical text but we will also derive from the text a different revelation, a different message about who God is and how he saves us. If we put the break between the Father and the Son, there is no reason to employ a partitive reading instead of a univocal reading of particular texts. These same distinctions showed us the limitations of Basil's theology. To put it unfairly, he is not perfectly prescient of the later doctrinal tradition. As we saw, some of this partitive exegesis was open to a two-subject, or a Nestorianizing, interpretation. These limitations are balanced by the flashes of brilliance that Basil showed in developing a general but subtle theory of names and a defense of the role of tradition in understanding the Scriptures. We could see these as two foundations of a Christian epistemology.

6

Heavenly *Politeia*

The Basics of Christian Discipleship

The disarray in which the church found itself in the 360s played a role in Basil's conversion to the ascetic life. He contrasted the discord in the church with the harmony that he saw "in other arts and branches of knowledge" while he was studying in Athens (*On Judg.* 1; 77). This unhappy juxtaposition set Basil wondering about its cause, and he leaned this way and that until he found illumination in the verse of Judges, "In those days there was no king in Israel" (Judg. 21:25). Leaders in the church had ceased to acknowledge God as King, "each deserting the teaching of our Lord Jesus Christ and arbitrarily claiming the right to arguments and definitions of his own" (*On Judg.* 1; 78). In short, they sought to rule rather than to be ruled, and so cast the church headlong into internal strife.

Basil realized that the church is what it ought to be when it reflects and imitates the order that obtains among the Father, Son, and Holy Spirit. The Lord Jesus came not to do his own will but the will of him who sent him (John 6:38); he does nothing of himself (John 8:28), and himself receives a commandment from the Father (John 12:49). The Spirit likewise speaks nothing of himself but what he hears (John 16:13). This being so, Basil asks, "how is it not much more necessary that the whole Church of God should strive earnestly to keep the unity of the Spirit in the bond of peace?" (*On Judg.* 4; 81). In this way the church will fulfill the charter for the Christian community found in Acts 4:32, "Now the company of those who believed were of one heart and soul, and no one said that any of the things which he possessed was his own, but they had everything in common." For Basil, Christians achieve this unity above all by living a life faithful to the precepts of the gospel. "If those who obey one command and have one king," he writes, "are characterized by good order and agreement, then all discord and division is a sign that there is no one to rule" (*On Judg.* 2; 78–79).

In a word, the problem with the church as Basil saw it in the 360s—the source of division and discord—was sin. Christians, and Christian leaders in particular, simply were not living life according to the gospel: the church was experiencing a crisis of holiness. Ironically, even the church's traditional practice of penance, designed to restore lost holiness, had become, in practice at least, part of the problem and not part of the solution. Many of the fathers speak of the great triad of death-dealing sins (*hamartiai pros thanaton* [1 John 5:16]; or *mortifera*): apostasy or idolatry, adultery, and murder. The penitential ritual of the church dealt with only these grave sins, lesser ones being left to less drastic means for forgiveness—almsgiving, for example, or the "Our Father." Basil alludes to these major sins and their corresponding penitential rite when he decries the "perverted tradition" that has emerged in the church whereby some sins are avoided and others virtually condoned. "Bad custom," he says, "has led us astray," for we feign "violent indignation against some [sins], such as murder and adultery and so forth," but judge "others not deserving even bare rebuke" (*On Judg.* 7; 86). Basil, of course, did not reject the custom of second penance (baptism being the first penance). Indeed, as a bishop, he administered it and advised a younger contemporary, Amphilocius of Iconium, on the administration of it in the so-called Canonical Epistles. The canons dealing with second penance grew in number and subtlety to match the complexity of the situations they were meant to address. So, for example, the reconciliation of different schismatics and heretics differed according to circumstances such as the validity of their baptism (ep. 188.1). Second marriage after the death of a spouse receives a lesser penance than third (ep. 188.4). There is a difference between beating someone accidentally to death and murder (ep. 188.8). And so on. In spite of all the gradations and distinctions, however useful they were, Basil saw that the system of second penance should not be a source of complacency. The fact that it dealt only with serious sins (in all their complexity of circumstance) could not be used to excuse or justify smaller ones. These small sins, Basil holds, are really a serious matter. Clarke noted that when Basil criticizes the system of second penance, he has in mind here not so much "the existing penitential discipline . . . , but the moral outlook formed by it."[1]

Even among the death-dealing sins, Basil distinguishes according to greater and lesser gravity, but in *On Judgment* he wishes to stress that all sin without distinction is displeasing to God. Indeed he brings to this point a slew of biblical prooftexts. God will punish all disobedience without distinction. "I find," Basil writes, "when I take up the divine Scriptures, in the Old and New Testaments, that disobedience towards God is plainly judged to lie not in the multitude of sins nor their magnitude, but in mere transgression of any one command, and that there is a common judgment of God against all disobedience" (*On Judg.*

4; 81). The church, he implies, must not use the traditional distinction among sins or the customary penitential rite as a cover to engage in all manner of divisive disobedience. The only way out of the present crisis is for all in the church to follow more faithfully the teaching of the Lord.

Doctrinal division was also rooted in sin. It was a universal assumption in the early church—and Basil is no exception—that mistakes in doctrine are rooted in malice and vice. He singles out for mention the Eunomians.

> What was most horrible of all, [Basil writes,] I saw its [the church's] leaders differing so much from one another in sentiment and opinion, and so hostile to the commandments of our Lord Jesus Christ, and so mercilessly rending the Church of God, and unsparingly agitating his flock, that now, if ever, when the Anomoeans had sprung up, was fulfilled the saying: "From among your own selves shall men arise, speaking perverse things, to draw away the disciples after them" [Acts 20:30]. (*On Judg.* 1; 77)

People like the Eunomians and the Spirit-fighters, Basil thought, know better. They know both that their teaching is out of line with the gospel and that they are destroying not only the faith and salvation of individual souls but also tearing asunder the bonds of communion in the church. The only explanation for such behavior, as Basil sees it, is extreme malice. This, as we have seen, is why Basil is dumbfounded by the betrayal of Eustathius of Sebaste. Here is a man who was a dear friend and teacher, an ascetic respected for his own personal holiness. He turned against the Holy Spirit and against Basil, and Basil simply has no explanation for it.

Nowadays we are inclined to disagree with the ancient assumption of guilt and ill will in doctrinal deviants. At the very least, we rightly realize that such matters are extremely complicated and that the simple assumption of guilt (or innocence) cannot do the situation justice. As our last chapter indicated, there is ample reason to think that Eunomius, for one, saw himself as preserving the ancient teachings of Christianity, not destroying them. Moreover, he saw his own teaching as making salvation accessible rather than compromising it. In any case, we need not decide the question of Eunomius's guilt or innocence. It remains true that Basil himself discerned sin and disobedience to be the cause of the sorry state of the church at the time. It is also true, I believe, that if more had in fact lived lives more faithful to the precepts of the Lord, the church, in spite of inevitable differences over the meaning of a doctrine, would not have fallen to such a state as to throw Basil into "profound darkness" (*On Judg.* 2; 78).

Once Basil had diagnosed the problem and its source, he set about the solution. Above all, the solution meant his own renewed dedication to living an evangelical life. This is the "conversion" about which we have spoken earlier. Basil determined to obey all the commandments; he was baptized and embraced a life of earnest and zealous discipleship. From the beginning, this was a communal affair. At first the circle was small, for it included only Gregory of Nazianzus and perhaps the members of Basil's family who had already embraced the ascetic life, but it quickly grew. Once he moved from Pontus to Caesarea and accepted ordination to the presbyterate, he began to gain a wider following. Between 358 and 365 Basil went from fellow ascetic with friends and family to leader and advisor of a more or less formal group of ascetics. His counsel to observe all the commandments remained a constant theme.

As in *On the Judgment of God*, Basil insists in the *Longer Rules* that one must keep all the commandments. We cannot be content with the keeping of some and not others, for it is impossible to keep them piecemeal. As Basil says, "According to the sound meaning of the word [Scripture] the commandments are so interdependent that if one is broken, the others are of necessity broken too" (*Lg. Rul.* prol. 2; 155). From this vantage point, there is no room for mediocrity in the Christian life, and it is an all-or-nothing proposition. Having described the importance of keeping all the commandments and marshaling a number of scriptural proofs to that effect, Basil reports the obvious objection: "In that case, someone will say, is it no use that the great number of Christians who do not keep all the commandments, keep some of them?" (*Lg. Rul.* prol. 3; 156). Really, he leaves the question unanswered, but he does not compromise the point; instead he offers another apostolic proof. If Peter, as good as he was, would have had no part with the Lord if he had not let his feet be washed, if he would have had no part with the Lord for this one fault, how can we? We can guess what Basil might say had he offered a direct answer to the question: "Of course it is better for the multitude to keep more rather than fewer of the commandments, for the more they keep, the closer they are to salvation, and the fewer they keep, the further they are from it; *nevertheless* all must be kept to avoid the wrath of God."

So there is no room for mediocrity when it comes to the number of commandments kept, but there is when it comes to the disposition with which one keeps them, for Basil sees three different dispositions that lay behind and motivate the life of obedience to commandments. In short, one could keep them in the manner of a slave, a hireling, or a son. Slaves keep commandments out of fear of punishment, hirelings for the reward that they will achieve, and sons, out of love. In any case, all the commandments are kept, and those who transgress commandments "neither serve God as Father, nor believe in him as promising great things, nor submit to him as master" (*Lg. Rul.* prol. 4; 157).

"Good Teacher, What Must I Do to Inherit Eternal Life?" (Mark 10:17)

With his insistence on the keeping of all the commandments, Basil seems to make no distinction in the commands of the Lord and, therefore, no distinctions in kinds of discipleship. Indeed, at first glance Basil seems to teach a universalist understanding of Christian asceticism. Basil's failure to distinguish two types of discipleship calls to mind the athletic Christianity of Pelagius. Commenting on Pelagius's *Letter to Demetrias*, Peter Brown writes:

> This message was simple and terrifying: "since perfection is possible for man, it is obligatory." Pelagius never doubted for a moment that perfection was obligatory; his God was, above all, a God who commanded unquestioning obedience. He had made men to execute his commands; and He would condemn to hell-fire anyone who failed to perform a single one of them.[2]

When one turns to the Gospels to discern the fundamentals of Christian discipleship, a crucial question quickly emerges. Does everything Jesus commands apply to everyone? Is there a single standard of Christian discipleship, or can distinctions be made? The Lord seems to have made the distinction that Basil seems not to have made. The prominent Jesus scholar Dale Allison has offered new insights on the old thesis that Jesus did, in fact, teach to two different audiences with a different set of rules for each. Allison, of course, does not present Jesus as anachronistically teaching fourth-century (and later) distinctions about lay and religious life—his approach is strictly and self-consciously historical. He does, however, present a very convincing explanation of the evidence that the Lord did in fact distinguish between an inner circle of followers who were expected to participate in the missionary and itinerant preaching of the gospel and those who received the gospel and lived it but without becoming missionaries themselves.[3]

From very early on, Christian theologians and bishops picked up on and developed the distinction in audiences. Allison offers examples from the *Didache*, Tertullian, Origen, Eusebius of Caesarea, Augustine, and Gregory the Great.[4] Basil does not seem to fit with this tradition. Moreover, it is important to point out that those who wonder about distinctions may not be motivated simply by the desire to live by a lower, less demanding standard of discipleship, though such motivation is surely there in the fourth century.

Thus, when we come to ask what Basil thought about our life in Christ, we must first determine the scope and parameters of this life. That is to say, did Basil make the distinction that the Lord made? Once we answer this question, we can then turn to the matter of the benefits and obligations that Christ confers upon his disciples. So then, first, is there one form of discipleship or two?

In Basilian scholarship, this question coincides with that of the audience of Basil's early ascetic writings. Did he write the Small Asceticon, the *Morals*, and epistle 22, for example, to outline the demands of the Christian life in general or was he outlining the way of life peculiar to consecrated ascetics and not ordinary Christians?

Anna Silvas sees Jean Gribomont and Paul Fedwick as "revisionists" on this question, as they advocate an "anti-monastic" reading especially of the Small Asceticon, the name given to an early form of Basil rules—a sort of freeze-frame, if you will, of Basil's ascetic thought in the 360s, frozen, as it were, in the Latin translation made by Rufinus. Basil continued to edit his ascetic writings throughout the rest of his life, and so the early stages of his thought have not been preserved in Greek as such but subsumed into the later, more mature editions.[5] Silvas acknowledges the legitimacy of striving to avoid an anachronistic reading of Basil's ascetic works that would project later developments onto earlier texts, but such a concern, she writes, "becomes overriding to the point of distortion when it obscures any evidence that in the Small Asceticon Basil is dealing with distinct ordered cenobitic communities."[6] Indeed, she suspects "an animus against any sign of latter-day 'religious life'" as the true source of this concern turned prejudice.[7]

The revisionist reading of the Ascetica attempts to make sense of the fact that Basil calls all Christians to ascetic living. Fedwick holds that the Ascetica could be interpreted to favor organized monastic communities, but that they can also help us to understand the church of the baptized living in the world.[8] He argues that the "ideal of ascetic perfection was intended for all Christians," and that only later did Basil envision "a difference in the status of Christians living in the world and cenobites."[9] Thus, the revisionist approach seeks to explain a prominent feature of Basil's thought: the universality of the ascetic call, but it does so by downplaying the properly monastic features of especially the Small Asceticon.

The problem with the revisionist approach, Silvas persuasively demonstrates, is that it fails to account for the clear evidence even in the Small Asceticon of the formal aspects of the dedicated ascetic life. The community of the Small Asceticon, she points out, is a brotherhood (*hē adelphotēs*)[10] with separate communities of men and women (*Reg. Bas.* 7.7) who are tested before acceptance into the community (*Reg. Bas.* 7.7 and 31–33) and, upon acceptance, embrace poverty (*Reg. Bas.* 5 and 29), obedience under a superior (*Reg. Bas.* 15.Q, referring to the male superior; and 198.Q, to the female), and a habit of dress (*Reg. Bas.* 11). Silvas comments that all such features of the Basilian community make it clear that Basil was not "benignly offering 'advice' to an *ad hoc* party of lay-enthusiasts who might be considered free to come and go and do what they please."[11]

While Silvas acknowledges the fact that the revisionists are trying to explain the universality of the ascetic call, she rightly rejects the revisionist position that the Small Asceticon reflects a sort of universal asceticism in the sense of an ascetic Christian life open to all, precisely insofar as it lacks those elements that formally set some apart from others. On the universality of the call, Silvas writes that "the rationale for the existence of dedicated ascetic communities is derived from no other source than that vocation proposed to *all* the baptized—it is never couched in any other way."[12] Basil knows no distinction between precepts and counsels, between those commandments that all must fulfill and those for the overachievers who strive for perfection, Silvas adds, and the Small Asceticon addresses itself to "Christians." One is reminded here of epistle 22, wherein Basil outlines in some detail the life pleasing to God. Such a life is profoundly ascetic and bears the features of a nascent organized religious life. Most important here, though, the constant refrain throughout the letter is "the Christian ought."

> The Christian ought to think thoughts worthy of his heavenly vocation. (ep. 22.1; 1:131)

> The Christian ought not to speak in a light vein. (ep. 22.1; 1:131)

> The Christian should not grumble, either at the scarcity of his necessities or at the labour of his tasks, for those charged with authority in these matters have final decision over each thing. (ep. 22.2; 1:133)

> The Christian should not be ostentatious in clothing or sandals, for all this is idle boasting. (ep. 22.2; 1:135)

> The Christian should not turn from one work to another without the approval of those assigned for the regulation of such matters. (ep. 22.2; 1:135–37)

So Basil sees the organized ascetic life as the proper Christian life and the truest evangelical discipleship. This is unexceptional in a way, for he is simply following herein the teaching of St. Paul who said, "To the unmarried and the widows I say that it is well for them to remain single as I do" (1 Cor. 7:8). Basil, of course, is typical of fourth-century thinkers in considering celibacy as the quintessential discipleship.

Perhaps the most famous example of this is St. Augustine's account of his conversion in *The Confessions*. Augustine had intellectually come to embrace Christianity but had not yet been able to renounce sexual intimacy with his concubine. At his mother's behest, he left her and was betrothed to a girl of higher social standing. Augustine, however, was disappointed with himself that he was not able to live a celibate life, and when he heard Ponticianus's story of the life of Antony and the two soldiers who abandoned life in the world upon hearing of Antony's great holiness, he was "vehemently stirred up" in the "intimate chamber of the heart" (*Conf.* 8.8.19; 146). Then, of course, Augustine ran into the garden, heard the childlike voice of God commanding him to pick up and read, lighted upon Romans 13:13, and was flooded with the grace to live as a celibate and undergo baptism. "The effect of your converting me to yourself," Augustine confesses to God, "was that I did not now seek a wife and had no ambition for success in this world" (*Conf.* 8.12.30; 153–54). Augustine's conversion experience in the garden was not a conversion to Catholic Christianity, for he was already convinced of that. It was a conversion to a life of celibacy—but not just celibacy. Augustine had been moved to give his life entirely to God.

Basil's understanding of the superiority of the ascetic life differs from Augustine's, however, in at least one very important respect: the latter holds, both in principle and in name, the distinction between evangelical counsels and precepts, while the former does not. That is to say, Augustine takes certain commandments of the Lord to apply only to consecrated ascetics and others to all the baptized. "Virginity," he writes, "is a counsel, not a command."[13] To marry is not to disobey God, and so to merit a punishment.[14] Obedience to the commands of the Lord bears on eternal life and death, while acceptance of the advice of St. Paul bears on glory. The virgins will enjoy a higher level of heavenly glory than the married who kept the commandments. "Think of that special place in his house," Augustine writes, "whatever it is, far better than the one for the sons and daughters. . . . Believing in this and hoping for it and cherishing it, you will have the power, not to avoid marriage because it is prohibited, but to fly beyond it because it is allowed."[15]

Basil and Augustine both treat the story of the young rich man but take it differently. In *On Faith and Works*, against those who wished to dispense with pre-baptismal moral catechesis, Augustine says: "Let them recall what the Lord himself answered when the rich man asked him what good things he should do to obtain eternal life."[16] When the rich man indicated that he had kept the commandments specified by the Lord, "the Lord added also the commandment of perfection: that, having sold everything he owned and given alms to the poor, he would have treasure in heaven."[17] Augustine is clear that someone who keeps the Decalogue but not the "command of perfection" is able to love both God and his neighbor. Basil, however, makes no distinction in the commandments of the Lord. For example, when Jesus tells the young rich man, who had kept all the commandments from youth, "You lack one thing; go, sell what you have, and give to the poor, and you will have treasure in heaven; and come, follow me" (Mark 10:21), Basil takes this command to apply to all Christians. While Augustine sees in the story of Jesus and the young rich man a distinction between two forms of the Christian life—one in which eternal life follows upon the keeping of the commandments and another in which perfection follows upon poverty, and, we might add, celibacy—our Basil treats the same text in his *On Baptism*, but to make a different point. Basil notices that the Lord "bade the young man [to] sell his goods and give to the poor before he said to him: 'Come, follow me'" (*On Bap.* 1.1; 341). Thus, for Basil, one cannot truly be a disciple, a follower of the Lord, without selling all of one's possessions and giving to the poor. Indeed, the young rich man's keeping of all the commandments availed him nothing, "for he had not yet received pardon for his sins, you see, nor had he been cleansed by the blood of our Lord Jesus Christ, but he was in the service of the Devil and under the domination of sin dwelling within him" (*On Bap.* 1.1; 341–42). The young man's inability or refusal to sell his possessions indicates, for Basil, a deadly attachment to the things of this world. Genuine discipleship comes only when we "renounce not only the world and its concupiscences, but also the just claims we have on one another, and even our life itself, whenever any of these things distract us from the whole-hearted and immediate submission we owe to God" (*On Bap.* 1.1; 347). Basil makes the same point describing the newness of life that follows upon baptism.

Moreover, we have seen that Basil insists repeatedly that we cannot be saved unless we keep all the commandments without exception. The obvious implication of all this is that apparently only those who live the formal ascetic life can be saved. Here we see the eternal significance of the revisionist thesis. Now, perhaps, in spite of its flaws, the revisionist hypothesis acquires a sense of urgency. If there were "informal groups of lay-enthusiasts," then the way of salvation has a universal rather than a narrow scope. If Basil's Ascetica embrace laymen as well as formal religious, then the former have a way of salvation along with the latter. If, however, the Ascetica are addressed only to formal ascetics, then the salvation of the lay-enthusiasts may be in jeopardy. Fedwick and Gribomont, it must be said, do not seem to be motivated by an agenda to open wide the narrow doors of salvation; they are striving to make sense of the evidence.

In this context we can treat another, related criticism that Silvas offers against the revisionist theory. Fedwick had maintained that Basilian texts responding to the ascetic extremism of the Eustathians are confined to the later Great Asceticon and absent in the early Small Asceticon. Silvas demonstrates that "Basil was well aware of hyperascetic tendencies in general and of Gangra's censures of ascetic excesses in particular," even in the Small Asceticon.[18] She offers a summary of positions that Basil and the anti-extremist synod of bishops at Gangra hold in common:[19] both opposed ascetic individualism and self-pleasing (Gangra, pref.; *Reg. Bas.* 3, 12, 30, 80, 133, and 181); both opposed the ascetic rejection of local institutional authorities (Gangra, pref. 5, can. 6–7; *Reg. Bas.* 31.4); both observed a distinction in male and female dress (Gangra, pref. 7, can. 13, 17; *Reg. Bas.* 143.2); both opposed the breakup of families under the pretext of asceticism (Gangra, can. 14–16; *Reg. Bas.* 7.4); both opposed the hyperascetic attitude toward dress (Gangra, pref. 4, can. 12; *Reg. Bas.* 144), food (Gangra, pref. 9, can. 2; *Reg. Bas.* 181), and work (Gangra, can. 7, which condemns the ascetic appropriation of tithes; *Reg. Bas.* 127); and, finally, both oppose spiritual elitism (Gangra, can. 19–20; *Reg. Bas.* 124, 168).

Even more than adopting much of Gangra's teaching, Basil even discourages in very strong terms the ascetic way of life that he himself had attempted in the 350s. "It was precisely Basil's intention," Silvas writes, not to further the lifestyle of the lay-enthusiasts but to win them over to "the cenobitic life properly so called—a sober, disciplined, doctrinally coherent and well-grounded form of community life": in short, Basil wanted them to make the transition that he himself had made.[20] In the Small Asceticon he enumerates the advantages of the cenobitic life: we have need of each other for the procurement of the necessities of life; the common life better provides for the recognition and correction of faults; the community can fulfill all the commandments simultaneously while a solitary cannot; the community can receive all the charisms while an individual cannot; and, most important, the common life provides the opportunity for humble love of others (*Reg. Bas.* 3).

The implication is that one cannot truly be a disciple of Jesus, one cannot keep all his commands and so be pleasing to the Father, unless one lives an organized and formal ascetic life. The revisionist attempt to salvage salvation at least for "lay-enthusiasts" has utterly failed. One, I think, can only agree with Silvas's criticisms of the revisionists, for she clearly demonstrates that they have misread the Small Asceticon. Silvas, however, overestimates the agreement between Basil and Gangra.

Another way to put the problem is that Basil seems to contradict Gangra and its rejection of ascetic extremism in two important respects. First, Gangra had rejected virginity based upon a reviling of marriage together with the idea that "those in the married state have no hope with God" (Gangra, pref. 1; 487): "If anyone finds fault with marriage, reviling and finding fault with her who sleeps with her husband, though she is a believer and pious, as if she were unable to enter the Kingdom, let him be anathema" (Gangra, can. 1; 490; also can. 9–10, 14). Second, the bishops at Gangra include in their list of hyperascetic errors that the Eustathians "condemn the rich who do not forsake all their possessions, as having no hope with God" (Gangra, pref. 14; 489).

Let us take up the second point first and briefly. Basil seems very clearly to contradict the bishops of Gangra. What we have just seen Basil say in *On Baptism* about the young rich man he had said repeatedly. There is no such thing as a rich disciple.

Regarding marriage, Basil, it must be said, nowhere affirms what Gangra condemns—namely, that the married have no hope of salvation. Even still, he does not seem to adopt as positive a view of marriage as the bishops of Gangra who "honour the reverent cohabitation of marriage" (Gangra, concluding exhortation; 493). Basil's view of marriage is more pessimistic.

It is for him, as for St. Paul, a distraction, and in order to grasp the profound significance of this fact, we must call to mind the importance in Basil's conception of the Christian life of remembering God and keeping the mind focused on him. Just as the skill of the potter cannot accomplish the work of the blacksmith, and the art of the flautist that of the athlete, so the person attached to the things of this world cannot achieve the state of pleasing God.

"The discipline," writes Basil, "of being well pleasing to God in accordance with the gospel of Christ, is achieved through withdrawal from the cares of the world and by entire estrangement from distractions" (*Lg. Rul.* 5.1; 174). When our mind is not distracted and instead focused on God—when we "bear about the holy thought of God stamped in our souls" (*Lg. Rul.* 5.2; 175)—our mind naturally rises to the love of him. Mindfulness of God both engenders the keeping of God's commandments and, in turn, is itself nourished and deepened by the same observance. "In our striving," Basil writes, "to work exactly according to God's will, we shall be joined to God through memory," and we shall thus abide in the love of Christ, who, by keeping his Father's commands, abides in his love (*Lg. Rul.* 5.3; 176).

Distraction, then, is very serious and risks salvation, for in distraction something else, some created good, is placed before God. Thus true discipleship demands that we renounce not only our possessions—this we have seen—but also the "kinship of the flesh" and "the worldly life" (*Lg. Rul.* 5.2; 175). Basil quotes the Lord: "Everyone of you who does not renounce all that is his own, cannot be my disciple" (Luke 14:33; *Lg. Rul.* 5.2). The Lord bids us to take up our cross and follow him (Matt. 16:24), and he demands exclusivity: "If anyone comes to me and does not hate his father and mother and wife and children and brothers and sisters, yes, and his own life too, he cannot be my disciple" (Luke 14:26, cited twice in *Lg. Rul.* 8.1–2).

We see a splendid, if extreme, example of the distracting power of marriage in Basil's treatment of the money-loving wife, "who stirs up the love of luxury and inflames the craving for pleasure, spurring on fruitless pursuits" (*Hom. Rich* 4; 47). Basil goes on to describe in vivid detail the destructive effects that money-loving wives and their complicit husbands have on the household and society. Indeed, the extreme opulence of the rich provides a context that tempers the severity of Basil's interpretation of the demands of the gospel. He writes of pearls, emeralds, sapphires, gold, porphyry, sea silk, extravagant jewelry, silver-encrusted furniture, and ivory-inlaid beds and couches (*Hom. Rich* 4). "How can anyone care for the soul," Basil asks, "while catering to the whims of a greedy wife?" (*Hom. Rich* 4; 48). And, of course, the greedy wives cannot look after their own souls either, as "they occupy themselves . . . day and night" with the procurement of precious stones and metals" (*Hom. Rich* 4; 47). One can only agree with St. Basil that the attachment to such wealth and its increase would make such a husband and wife less mindful of God and the gospel.

The trouble with marriage, then, is that it belongs to this world of distractions rather than to the next world of heavenly remembrance of God. What Basil says about second marriage in a letter to Diodore he would equally apply to first marriage. It belongs, in the words of St. Paul, to the "form of this world [that] is passing away" (1 Cor. 7:31; ep. 160.4). "Time has grown very short," and those who have wives should "live as though they had none" (1 Cor. 7:29).

Basil says that he laughs at anybody who would mention by way of rejoinder the procreative purpose of marriage, for such a person "does not distinguish the times of the promulgations of the law" (ep. 160.4; 2:409). Marriage, then, can be good, but it belongs to the old dispensation rather than to the new. Paul, Basil says, "contrasted [the] preoccupations [of marriage] with the cares which are focused on God, as if the two were inconsistent with each other" (*Lg. Rul.* 5.1; 174, citing 1 Cor. 7:32–33).

Even though marriage is out of place in the new dispensation, Basil acknowledges that the apostle allows "what pertains to marriage and deem[s] it worthy of blessing" (*Lg. Rul.* 5.1; 174). We might say that though Christian marriage belongs to the old dispensation, it looks forward to the new, to the "short time," the time of the complete renunciation of the evils and goods of this world, making possible total dedication to God. Marriage looks forward to renunciation in that it is, as Basil says, "relief from fornication" (ep. 160.4; 2:409).[21] One is reminded of St. Paul's "it is better to marry than to be aflame with passion" (1 Cor. 7:9).[22]

First marriage and second marriage (what Basil calls "bigamy," marriage after the death of one's spouse) stand, as it were, on the threshold of the new dispensation, for they can be and should be the occasion for the married to grow in virtue to the point at which they can renounce the bonds of the flesh and so become ever more mindful of God. Even though Basil sees even second marriage as a "relief from fornication," it is nonetheless very much frowned upon. Indeed, a "bigamist" was to do penance for one or two years (ep. 188.4). "Trigamists" and worse, "polygamists," serve penance for proportionately longer times and such people are not said to have a "marriage" at all. Rather, Basil says, they are said to have "polygamy, or . . . restricted fornication [*porneian kekolasmenēn*]" (ep. 188.4; 3:25).

An ascetic discourse in the Basilian circle, but probably not written by Basil, nonetheless reflects his thoughts on the married. "Do the Gospels apply, do you think," he asks, "to the married?" (*On Renunc.* 2; 61, altered). Of course, they do apply, and all will have to give an account at the end. The married man, however, receives a concession or an accommodation. He will be pardoned "for his lack of continence and his desire for and intercourse with woman" (*On Renunc.* 2; 61). Even still, this accommodation cannot become for the married man a source of complacency. "Beware of slackness," Basil admonishes, "you who have chosen to live with a woman" (*On Renunc.* 2; 62). The married man does not have permission to embrace the world. Indeed, in some respects he has chosen the more difficult path by deciding to "dwell in the midst of snares and the might of the rebel powers" (*On Renunc.* 2; 62). Living in the trenches, he must expect a fight, and fight he must in order to attain the victory of salvation.

In sum, we can say that Basil offers a more qualified view of marriage than the Council of Gangra. He does not condemn the married to damnation, but neither is he willing, without qualification, to "honour the reverent cohabitation of marriage" (Gangra, concluding exhortation; 493). With St. Paul, Basil preserves a balanced tension concerning marriage: it can help one on the way to citizenship in heaven in spite of distracting one from the remembrance of God. Without marriage, most would suffer a more severe—indeed, an adulterous—attachment to created goods and a truly damning forgetfulness of God. Basil was certainly not a hyperascetic in the sense of condemning out of hand the ordinary life of lay Christians. Nevertheless, he clearly affirms that all Christians must be moving in the direction of the formal ascetic life in order to be a true disciple, pleasing to God. One of the beautiful features of St. Basil's understanding of Christian discipleship is the clear recognition of the fact that heavenly citizenship is a reality toward which one progresses by steps. Indeed, Basil's whole understanding of not only the church but also the formal ascetic community is premised on the assumption that different people are at different stages in the spiritual life and the crucial function of life in common is mutual advancement toward the heavenly kingdom through a sharing of the gifts of the Spirit.

Basil came to the realization of the necessity of the more formal ascetic life over time. Rousseau comments that eventually Basil "felt the ascetic life was developing in such a way that its boundaries needed more careful definition."[23] The moving force behind the separate organization of the ascetics was the need to foster and protect both the human effort to please God as well as human communion: "Authentic community," writes Rousseau, "was a product of the individual's genuine love for God, [and] for that reason . . . the experience of community life could not remain haphazard."[24] Another related factor in the growth toward organized community life is obedience. If the love of God secured the authenticity of horizontal community, then obedience to a superior promoted the love of God and delivered the ascetic from self-deception and self-will. Thus, far from inhibiting or crushing the spirit of Basil's asceticism, the movement toward formality and institutionalization guaranteed the ascetic progress that the community had so far made, and opened up further possibilities for growth. Silvas very much agrees with this assessment; only she is very clear that this development in Basil's thought had already taken place by the early 360s when Rufinus translated Basil's ascetic writings into Latin, thus fixing the form of the so-called Small Asceticon (while in Greek Basil continued to write and to edit what he had written, thus giving us the Great Asceticon). So she rejects the attempt of Fedwick and Gribomont to locate a lay asceticism in the Ascetica.

Basil has left us with works that reflect his thought in its various stages. We have early works and later ones addressed to any serious Christian, and early and later works addressed to an increasingly demarcated group of ascetics. As I have indicated, we are left with the final impression that earnest Christians who are not consecrated ascetics are on the way to being such. In spite of this line of continuity we can nonetheless identify features that are, on the one hand, distinctive of any serious-minded Christian and the larger Christian community, and, on the other hand, those that are distinctive of formal ascetic communities. To answer directly the question with which we began this chapter, Basil does, in fact, make a distinction in the Lord's disciples, a distinction that we now call "lay" and "religious," but, for Basil, the former is ordered to the latter and discipleship demands that the former progress toward the latter.

Basil gives us, we might say, not two ways of life but one way of life that has two stages. He differs very much here from someone like Eusebius of Caesarea, according to whom Christ gave two ways.

> The one is above nature, and beyond common human living; it admits not marriage, childbearing, property, the possessions of wealth, but is wholly and permanently separate from the common customary life of humanity.[25]

The second way is "more humble" and "more human," for it allows procreation, and serving in public office and in the military. "It allows," Eusebius says, people "to have minds for farming, for trade, and the other more secular interests as well as for religion."[26] It is for this second, secular group that there are specific times of retreat and days set aside for the practice of religion. Basil thinks of things very differently, for he mixes Eusebius's two ways. First, Basil's "lay" are less secular than Eusebius's: they must strive to approximate the "religious" life and ever progress toward it. Eusebius could countenance a rich disciple, while Basil did not. Second, Basil's "religious" are more secular than Eusebius's. Basil's monks are often engaged in what Eusebius associates with the secular world, namely, farming and trades of various sorts. Basil seems far more reluctant than Eusebius to admit two different forms of discipleship, and when he does admit the difference, the distance between the one form and the other does not seem so great.

As a bishop, Basil cared not only for a group of ascetics well on their way in the pursuit of a heavenly life but also for ordinary people in the world. That is to say, he acknowledged and dealt with the fact of which ascetic extremists were in denial: the church is mixed. As Basil put it, "In this great house of the church not only are there vessels of every kind, gold and silver and wood and earthenware [2 Tim. 2:20], but also skills of all kinds" (*Hom. Attend* 4; 97–98). In at least two fundamental ways Basil recognizes a mixed church. First, the church is composed of saints and sinners: people who are more or less zealous in their Christian living. Second—and often these two ways overlap—the church is made up of people who are more or less involved in the secular order that is passing away. Marriage is the obvious example, but Basil mentions that "the house of God, which is the church of the living God [1 Tim. 3:15] has hunters, travelers, architects, builders, farmers, shepherds, athletes, soldiers" (*Hom. Attend* 4; 98). While it is true that Basil's monks were engaged in various sorts of work, and work, of course, that would only find a place in this secular order, there can be no question of a monk being an athlete or a soldier.

Our good bishop, moreover, reached out to all in his congregation: the unbaptized, the baptized who had fallen into serious sin, the advanced ascetics, and the ascetics who fell from their heavenly commitment, and to those in his congregation who were more involved in secular pursuits. In the text just quoted, for example, Basil draws out a connection between each of the secular pursuits and the Christian life. Hunters are to capture their prey with the Word of truth and to bring to the savior the sinfully savage and wild. Travelers are admonished not to stray from the path; architects, to lay the firm foundation of faith; builders, to use only the fine materials of gold, silver, and precious stones; shepherds, to find the lost, bind the broken, and heal the diseased; soldiers, to wage war against the devil; athletes, to strive lawfully as Paul did (*Hom. Attend* 4). There is a scriptural text behind every profession, and Basil is able to find Christian relevance in each because a prophet, or the psalmist, or Paul, or Jesus first did so.

Basil on Christian Discipleship

We begin our treatment of Basil's view of discipleship with the Christians who refused it. One of the sad and well-known facts of the fourth century is that so many Christians remained on the fringes of life in the church. They refused to enroll for baptism and so kept the Christian mysteries at a convenient but dangerous distance. The most obvious reason why so many put off baptism was a crass calculation. One had a better chance at salvation by reserving baptism for the remission of sins committed in the course of life rather than by receiving baptism early in life and risking serious sin later. The ancient church did know a remedy for serious post-baptismal sin, as we mentioned at the outset of this book, but it could be received only once and involved lengthy and difficult penances.

While Augustine, like so many, postponed baptism as a wager against chastity, the silver lining in this dark custom is that for all—for both those who sinned seriously before baptism and those who did not—baptism was an important matter. It was no custom or religious practice that was so deeply ingrained in the culture that one received it without much reflection or preparation. Baptism was not something one just did or had done; it was a choice, solemn and serious. Basil, like Augustine, postponed baptism, but not as a concession to the power of sin. We have every indication that Basil and his family were very earnest in their practice of the faith, and still baptism was postponed. Unlike Augustine, Basil was expected not to sin;

like Augustine, Basil's baptism was associated with his decision to embrace a profoundly ascetic Christian life that entailed both celibacy and some sort of poverty.

Like every other fourth-century bishop, Basil had to grapple with this growing pastoral problem of increasing numbers of unbaptized Christians in his congregation, and he tried any number of arguments to persuade them to embrace the full Christian life. There is no wrong time to attain salvation (*Protr. Bap.* 1); baptism is free and painless, and the yoke of Christ is sweet and light, adorning the neck rather than hurting it (*Protr. Bap.* 1); no one knows how long he will live, and death may come suddenly (*Protr. Bap.* 5); and finally, there is the escape of eternal punishment in hell. For how wretched is the one who says,

> unhappy me, not to have washed away my stains, but to be thus besmirched with sins! I would now be with the angels, I would now be enjoying heavenly blessings. Oh! Wicked decisions of mine! I am tormented for eternity for a temporary enjoyment of sin. . . . God's judgment is just; I was called and I did not listen; I was instructed and I did not attend; I was warned, and I made light of it. (*Protr. Bap.* 8; 86–87)

Basil acknowledges the reason for the delay by speaking in the person of his audience: "I will receive baptism when I finally cease from sin" (*Protr. Bap.* 5; 82). He tried to persuade them not only that such a way of thinking and acting made no sense when one compared the goods that come with baptism to the harm that sin brings but also that they had fallen for the trick of the enemy who suggests that we "sin today and be just tomorrow" and says, "today is mine, tomorrow, God's" (*Protr. Bap.* 6; 84). The power of the devil's tactic is its subtlety. He does not advise us to leave God completely, to put him off forever, but only to put him off for a day, but in such a way that he accomplishes the same effect, for tomorrow is the next today (which the devil claims for himself), and God ever gets only tomorrow (*Protr. Bap.* 6). God foils the devil's stratagem when, through the psalmist, whom Basil quotes, he says, "If today you hear my voice" (Ps. 100 [99]:8).

In his homily *To the Rich*, Basil again turns to the young rich man who, like the unbaptized, inquires about the life of discipleship but does not commit. Basil offers a wonderful metaphor for the rich in his congregation, and it applies just as well to the unbaptized. They are like a "traveler who hastens to arrive at a famous city, but then stops short and lodges in one of the inns just outside the city walls" (*Hom. Rich* 3; 46). Both the rich and the unbaptized deprive themselves "of beholding the sights of the city" (*Hom. Rich* 3; 46), the first because they will not extend baptismal discipline to their possessions and baptismal love to the poor, and the second because they will not embrace the discipline of baptism at all.

Toward the end of his protreptic on baptism Basil concedes, at least implicitly, a measure of sympathy if not legitimacy to the procrastination of the unbaptized, for he acknowledges what they well know, that the Christian life that they keep putting off is difficult. Basil urges them to enroll for baptism but compares their enrollment to the enlisting of a soldier or the registration of a competitive athlete. "Come over to me," he pleads with his congregation, "transfer yourself totally to the Lord. Give in your name, be enrolled in the Church" (*Protr. Bap.* 7; 84). Basil urges them to undergo baptismal instruction and to "learn the constitution of the Gospels: vigilance of the eyes, control of the tongue, mastery of the body, humility of mind, purity of thought, and an end to anger"—but he admits that it is hard (*Protr. Bap.* 7; 84). One must struggle not only to acquire the baptismal life but also to keep it. "When," he asks, "is goodness easy?" (*Protr. Bap.* 7; 84). One cannot win without running, and victory cannot be had without effort and sweat. Nevertheless, the tribulations and trials of Christian discipleship are the only reasonable choice for the unbaptized, for these difficulties cannot compare with the good that comes through them.

We turn, then, to Basil's understanding of Christian discipleship, which, of course, he develops through a consistent engagement of the biblical text. One of his favorite descriptions of Christian discipleship is the saying of the Lord, "If any man would come after me, let him deny himself and take up his cross and follow me" (Matt. 16:24). Basil paraphrases this text to mean "let him become my disciple" (*On Bap.* 1.1; 343). This saying of the Lord expresses a twofold movement that is foundational to Basil's interpretation of discipleship: first comes freedom from sin and the breaking off of worldly attachment, and then comes discipleship.

Repentance and renunciation is the first step. Basil opens his *Morals* with these words: "That those who believe in the Lord must first repent, according to the preaching of John and our Lord Jesus Christ himself" (*Mor.* 1.1; 101). The baptism of John is, as it were, a halfway house, for it brings us to the point of renunciation of sin and even forgiveness of sins, but it does not establish in us the new life that Jesus's baptism does. Basil goes so far as to say that John's baptism grants "access at once to the grace of God and his Christ" (*On Bap.* 1.2; 355). John's baptism, baptism in water, is taken up into the first of the two movements of Jesus's baptism, which is baptism in the Spirit and fire. Baptism into Christ is first baptism into his death. Drawing on Romans 5, Basil writes that "we were buried . . . with him through baptism into death, knowing . . . that our old man was crucified with him, that the body of sin might be done away, that we should no longer be in bondage to sin" (*Mor.* 80.22; 130). This is what it means to be born of water. To be born of the Spirit, which we will consider soon, is to rise with Christ, to become "that very thing of which [we were] born," (*Mor.* 80.22; 130), for "that which is born of the Spirit is spirit" (John 3:6; *Mor.* 80.22; 130).

Renunciation, however, involves not only dying to sin but also dying to legitimate goods that one might enjoy. One who, Basil says, "has entangled himself in the affairs of this world, or who is solicitous even for the necessities of this life" (*On Bap.* 1.1; 341) cannot serve the Lord. One should not go to court even for necessary clothes, and one should not avenge oneself (*Mor.* 49.1–2). "The just claims that we have on one another, and, even our life itself" must be renounced if they distract us from "the whole-hearted and immediate submission we owe to God" (*On Bap.* 1.1; 347). Love of neighbor, too, demands that we not seek our own good, "but the good of the loved one for the benefit of his soul and body" (*Mor.* 80.22; 130).

We have already seen one striking example of renunciation in Basil's understanding of Christian discipleship: the renunciation of material possessions, and this renunciation could be either that which concerns a sinful attachment to the goods of this world or a matter of a "just claim." Renunciation of possessions applies to all and not just the extravagantly wealthy. While Basil applies this evangelical command to those with thousands of silver- and bronze-plated carriages pulled by multitudes of horses who themselves have silver and gold spangled bridles, he applies it also to those who seek to provide for the future needs of their children in the form of an inheritance. "Was the command found in the Gospel, 'if you wish to be perfect, sell your possessions and give the money to the poor,' not written for the married?" (*Hom. Rich* 7; 54; Matt. 19:21). God will provide for the children. One should first provide for one's own soul by giving away bodily riches rather than provide for the body and the children and thus leave one's soul orphaned.[27]

Basil's view of the renunciation of goods rests upon two important principles, one economic and one theological. The theological principle is that there is no private property and no right to private property in authentic Christian discipleship. The goods of this world belong to everyone. Basil articulates this point most forcefully in a sermon delivered in the great famine of 369. "Resolve," he admonishes his congregation, "to treat the things in your possession as belonging to others" (*Hom. Barns* 2; 61). He goes so far as to say that the greedy are robbers and thieves, for they "take for themselves what rightly belongs to everyone" (*Hom. Barns* 7; 69). The rich, writes Basil, are like someone who comes first to the theater and then prevents everyone else from attending, so that "one person alone enjoys what is offered for the benefit of all in common" (*Hom. Barns* 7; 69).

Those, then, who have been given an abundance of material possessions are not the owners of these goods but the stewards of them. "It befits those who possess sound judgment," Basil writes, "to recognize that they have received wealth as a stewardship, and not for their own enjoyment" (*Hom. Rich* 3; 46). But if this is so, if the goods of the world are meant for all, why did God not distribute them equally? Why are there wealthy and poor in the first place? "Why else," Basil answers, "but so that [the rich] might receive the reward of benevolence and faithful stewardship, while the poor are honored for patient endurance in their struggles?" (*Hom. Barns* 7; 69). God wishes to teach the rich generosity, and the poor, patience.

In addition to this theological principle—the earth's goods were given to everyone—there is an economic one that illuminates Basil's understanding of wealth. Basil himself puts it very simply: "Wealth left idle is of no use to anyone" (*Hom. Barns* 5; 66). This was true in the fourth century, but, of course, it changed as economies developed and matured. Indeed, the growth of economies and the emergence of the fruitfulness of money coincides with the growth of the church's understanding of usury. As economies became ever more complex, so the prohibition on taking interest on money became ever more qualified. For Basil, however, the matter is very straightforward: the prohibition on usury is absolute. He has no conception of interest on a loan that could be an appropriate compensation for the loaner, who is sacrificing the fruitfulness of his money by loaning it, and a wise investment for the borrower who could use the borrowed money to generate enough wealth not only to pay back the loan with interest but also to provide better for himself and his own. For Basil, if you are in a position to loan, it is because you have been selfish and greedy, withholding for yourself what you should have given freely, and if you are so poor that you have need of a loan, then you have no hope of paying it back and should not seek it in the first place (*Hom. Usury* 1 and 3). The only appropriate loan is a gift on which God pays the interest. Basil quotes the proverb, "He who is kind to the poor lends to the LORD" (Prov. 19:17). And God pays back in a currency vastly superior to money.

The theological ground, if not also the economic, of Basil's view of goods and wealth inevitably yields the impression that he is a socialist. It is more accurate to say that he is an "eschatological commune-ist": the earth's goods are for all and to be held in common by all in anticipation of the eschaton. Basil's understanding of wealth and ownership ultimately derive not from this-worldly concerns about equality and social justice, but from the end. Very simply, Christian discipleship is both a return to paradise and a forecast of the eschaton; in the end, there is no private property, and so, according to Basil's view of discipleship, there should be none now. Thus Basil's view of property approximates his view of marriage and diet. We did not eat meat in paradise and will not, it seems, eat at all in the end; so the Christian, especially the ascetic, eats only vegetables, and even then only as much as is necessary to sustain the body until it no longer needs any physical nourishment. Likewise with marriage: it should be avoided altogether if possible, for the time is short, and we are neither married nor given in marriage in the end. If one must marry, at least let it be only once so that marriage may be made a pathway to the eschaton rather than away from it.

It is very important, for an accurate understanding of Basil's view of property, to recognize that he conceives of no role for human government.

His acceptance of support for his charitable endeavors from Emperor Valens does not represent a principled place for government, for Basil's commune-ism is not political. It does not result from human governments redistributing equally what nature or chance has distributed unequally. Rather, it results from Christian charity and Christian discipleship. The holding of all things in common is the necessary outcome of Christians loving one another and by that love redistributing equally for the good of all what God had purposefully distributed unequally for the good of all. Christians, Basil repeatedly claims with St. Paul, inhabit a heavenly kingdom and have citizenship in heaven. Human government, so far from being the instrument of "eschatological commune-ism," itself belongs to the world that is passing. Basil indicates as much in an incisive passage from *On the Holy Spirit*. In the course of refuting the Spirit-fighters' assertion that the Spirit is like neither master nor slave but free man—an impossible middle nature—Basil argues that the various stations in life wherein one exercises authority over another do not belong to nature. War, poverty, and lack of intelligence lead to some exercising rule over others. Basil does not directly say that there would be no human government had there been no fall, or that there will be none in the end, but he does say "the things of heaven do not rule over each other, since they are devoid of greed and all are subject to God, giving him both the fear that is owed to him as master and the glory that belongs to him as maker" (*On H. Sp.* 20.51; 88).

The fact that Basil is not really a socialist in no way rationalizes his view of property or accommodates it to our modern-day sensibilities or weaknesses. His message still strikes our ears with challenging severity, for the truth re-mains that, for Basil, discipleship necessarily entails evangelical poverty. "One should be poor, not rich, according to the word of the Lord" (*Mor.* 48.3; 113).

We can sum up Basil's understanding of baptismal renunciation by revisit-ing the theme with which we began this chapter: the rule of God. So many problems emerged in the church when her members rejected the rule of God and chose instead to rule themselves. One's renunciation of created goods and the sinful abuse of them is the renunciation of power over oneself. In baptismal renunciation one dies to the power of wealth, sexual desire, and passion, and embraces instead the rule of God. What does the rule of God bring? What is the new life of discipleship that follows the death of renunciation? To these questions we now turn.

To be ruled by God and by his commandments makes one like unto him. We have seen Basil say that baptism in the Spirit makes us like that into which we were baptized: it makes us Spirit (*Mor.* 80.22). And when we follow God's commands, we follow the example of the Son who came not to do his own will but the will of him who sent him (John 6:38). Baptism not only makes us like the persons of the Son and the Spirit; it also recalls us "to our original glory as the image of God" (*On Bap.* 1.2; 358).

The doctrine of the gospel molds us like wax and forms the inner man, renewing him "unto knowledge according to the image of him that created him" (*On Bap.* 1.2; 359; Col. 3:10). Basil cites the same text in his extended and beautiful answer in the *Morals* to his question "What is the mark of a Christian?" (*Mor.* 80.22).

The new life that baptism gives is, moreover, the justice of Christ. By his death, the Lord delivered us from "death in sin," reunited us to God, and made us able to please him. This, Basil writes, is "a free gift of justice" (*On Bap.* 1.2; 373). Basil contrasts the justice of Christ with "justice according to the Law." Submission to the justice of God, the justice that comes by faith in Christ, is submission to "the rule for pleasing God laid down by our Lord Jesus Christ" (*On Bap.* 2.8; 413). This justice, Basil asserts, is superior to the justice of the law and human conceptions of justice, for they have, as St. Paul says, zeal without knowledge (*On Bap.* 1.2; Rom. 10:2). It is this superior justice that calls the Christian away from the law courts and forbids the avenging of injury (*Mor.* 49.1–2). The law of Moses permits revenge for an offense committed against us, but the law of Christ does not (*On Bap.* 1.2). Christian justice calls one "not to seek one's own good, but the good of the loved one for the benefit of his soul and body" (*Mor.* 80.22; 130). The Christian gives to the needy "over and above what the law requires" (*On Bap.* 1.2; 364).

Basil takes this to be the meaning of St. Paul's exhortation that we be dead to the law. Being dead to it does not mean one is free not to keep the moral standard that it imposes; rather, being dead to the law means that one keeps a stricter moral standard still. Being dead to the law means renouncing the law's protection of one's own property and person just as the Lord did. The law is for the world—the *saeculum*—and it governs and orders life in this world with a corresponding justice. The justice of Christ belongs to the next world, to heaven, and the Christian in this world lives in the justice of the next. "Not only should we not endeavor to increase our possessions and to acquire greater gains, as do men of the world," we are not surprised to hear Basil say, "but we should not even lay claim to the property which has already been acquired and is our own" (*On Bap.* 1.2; 364).

When we live according to the justice of Christ, we acquire not only an external resemblance to the Lord Jesus and his manner of living, we also receive an interior newness of life in Christ. Basil masterfully pieces together some of his favorite and oft-cited Pauline texts to make this point.

If we, dying thus in a likeness of his death and being buried with Christ [Rom. 6:5], walk in the newness of life, we do not experience the corruption of death and our burial is only in semblance, as a planting of seed. By mortifying ourselves with regard to what is forbidden and in manifesting the faith that "worketh by charity" [Gal. 5:6], we are made worthy to share the hope of the Apostle and to say with him: "But our conversation is in heaven, from whence also we look for the Saviour, the Lord Jesus Christ, who will reform the body of our lowness, make like to the body of his glory according to the operation whereby also he is able to subdue all things unto himself" [Phil. 3:20–21]. (*On Bap.* 1.2; 366–67)

"Conversation" here translates *politeuma*, which, Bauer and others note, often "denotes a colony of foreigners or relocated veterans."[28] Indeed, to be a Christian is, for Basil, to be a citizen of heaven and thus a foreigner in this world. The heavenly *politeuma* is ruled by Christ and those who live there conduct their lives according to Christian justice: faith that works by charity.

For Basil, our new life in Christ, that of Christian justice, is profoundly sacramental. I mentioned baptism in the first chapter as having a place in his progress as a theologian as well as a practitioner of the Christian life. Most of what we have been describing so far here has been derived from Basil's work *On Baptism* and only confirms our first impression. Baptism has the power to change us, and much of *On Baptism* is simply Basil's lengthy exposition of this change: in baptism we become spiritual "in mind, word, and deed" (*Mor.* 20.2; 107). Though the sacrament is very important, faith is never far from it in Basil's thought, and he posits a close relationship between the two. "Those who *believe* in the Lord," Basil exhorts, "must be baptized" (*Mor.* 20.1; 107, my emphasis).

The debate with the Spirit-fighters was the occasion for Basil to articulate most clearly the relationship between faith and baptism.[29] Baptism cannot save unless faith in the Father, Son, and Holy Spirit accompanies it. Basil argues that it is faith that makes us Christians and the grace of baptism that saves us. We must "guard at every moment the confession which we set down" at our baptism (*On H. Sp.* 10.26; 56). A baptism void of this confession is invalid and benefits no one; baptism without the tripartite confession does not lead to light or to divine knowledge (*On H. Sp.* 10.26). On the relationship between faith and baptism, Basil writes that they "are two ways of salvation that are naturally united with each other and indivisible. While faith is perfected by baptism, baptism is established by faith, and each is carried out by the same names" (*On H. Sp.* 12.28; 59). Or again, "The confession that brings salvation comes first and there follows baptism which seals our assent" (*On H. Sp.* 12.28; 59).

Indeed, Basil binds very closely baptism, salvation, and faith. Faith is the beginning of salvation, for it is the beginning of knowledge of God as Father, Son, and Holy Spirit. But faith must be confirmed by baptism. Saving knowledge only comes with the death of the life of the flesh, which the water of baptism accomplishes, and only with the new life given by the Spirit in baptism (*On H. Sp.* 15.35).

It has been said that, generally speaking, baptism is the sacrament that got the most attention in the patristic age, while the Eucharist comes into focus in the Middle Ages. Basil's treatment of the two follows this rule: he treats the

Eucharist in shorter compass than baptism. Two themes stand out in his treatment of the Eucharist: worthiness to receive it and the importance of memory (*Mor.* 21.1–3; 80.22).[30] In fact, the theme of memory remained a constant bedrock in Basil's own experience of and thinking about the Christian life. On the first theme, Basil several times cites or alludes to 1 Corinthians 11:29, "For any one who eats and drinks without discerning the body eats and drinks judgment upon himself."[31] We must, writes Basil, have a "consideration of the manner in which participation in the body and blood of Christ is granted" (*Mor.* 21.2; 108); otherwise, we are not benefited but condemned. What, then, is the considered manner of reception? Here we move to the second dominant theme: when we receive the body and blood of the Lord, we must be mindful of, we must remember, his obedience unto death.

Basil's understanding of the Eucharist is colored through and through by the Lord's command: "Do this in remembrance of me" (Luke 22:19). Our Lord's words at the Last Supper are "useful to us," Basil says, because "they help us, when eating and drinking, always to remember him who died for us and rose again" (*On Bap.* 1.3; 388). This mindfulness is so important because if we have it, "we are certain to learn how to follow before God and his Christ" the teaching of St. Paul who commends us to live and die for him who lived and died for us (*On Bap.* 1.3; 388; 2 Cor. 5:14–15). Augustine Holmes expresses well the power of memory:

> For Basil this memory is not a mere storehouse of recollection, nor is it concerned with a theory of knowledge as in Plato. More psychological than metaphysical, it is none the less a faculty of great power and is the means of gaining love towards God, the very apex of Basil's spirituality. Memory of God's wonders leads to love, which leads to the practice of the commandments, which in turn preserves the memory and love.[32]

This dynamism, from memory to love, is evident in the *Longer Rules* 2. Basil here is explaining at length the fact that love of God is natural to man; it only needs to be sparked into flame. He offers a couple of examples to make his point. First, we all by nature love beauty (*Lg. Rul.* 2.1). Second, we all by nature love someone who has done good for us. Basil then lists at length the great benefactions the Lord has provided for us: the wonders of creation; the creation of man himself; the help of the law after our fall into sin; the incarnation, suffering, and death of the Lord, and his bestowal on us not only of life but also of "the dignity of his divinity" and "the gift of eternity" and eternal rest (*Lg. Rul.* 2.3–4; 170). Basil quotes the psalmist: "What return, therefore, shall we make to the Lord for all that he has given to us?" (Ps. 116 [115]:12; *Lg. Rul.* 2.4; 171). The return is love. The divine benefactions are "reminders implanted in our souls that ever stir up the divine yearning" (*Lg. Rul.* 2.4; 171). Rufinus takes this yearning into Latin as *amorem Dei*, "love of God."

We are well beyond the Eucharist and into a theme with which we can fittingly conclude this treatment of Christian discipleship—a theme of broad and enduring significance, for it ties together the development in Basil's own thinking over the years: to be a disciple of Christ is to remember God. Memory of God unifies both historically and theologically: historically in that it is the common denominator in the stages of Basil's own ascetic journey, and theologically in that it brings together all of the themes to which we have so far attended—Basil's theological anthropology, his view of Scripture and the world, and his understanding both of the economy of salvation and of Christian discipleship.

In Basil's first awakening, colored profoundly by his philosophical training and aspirations, he decided to live a life more mindful of God. In epistle 2, to Gregory of Nazianzus, we saw that Basil had retired to his Pontic retreat in order to live a life of prayer and withdrawal from the world. Both withdrawal and prayer, however, are ordered toward the communion with God that one enjoys by remembering him: "The indwelling of God is this—to hold God ever in memory, his shrine established within us" (ep. 2.4; 1:17). The goal of the ascetic life thus conceived is both positive and negative. Negatively, through withdrawal, one prevents earthly cares and passions from interrupting the continuous memory of God (ep. 2.4); positively, by prayer, the reading of Scripture, and the singing of psalms, one cultivates mindfulness of him. Augustine Holmes describes the shift from Basil's early thought and experience to his later, the shift from epistle 2 to the *Rules*, as a transposition of memory and its opposite, forgetting, from the "ontological plane" to the "moral plane."[33] We might add that memory has a sacramental plane, as our treatment of the Eucharist shows, as well as a liturgical one. Holmes points out the similarities between a section of the anaphora of St. Basil that "recounts the history of God's dealings with his human creation" and *Longer Rules* 2, alluded to above.[34]

In spite of the complexities surrounding the authenticity of the Liturgy of St. Basil, Holmes submits that there must be a direct connection between these two texts (see chart on p. 124). He surmises that in the *Rules* Basil was recalling the liturgy.[37] If this is correct, Holmes rightly highlights the consequent fact that this parallel points to "the ecclesial and corporate nature of the type of life he was building up among the ascetics."[38]

Conclusion

Thus memory has a role in prayer, liturgy, and the sacraments. It also has a place in Basil's understanding of Scripture itself and the very created world. We treated Scripture and creation earlier and can sum up the fruit of that investigation thus: the whole point of Scripture and the creatures of the world is to make man remember God and to keep him in memory. In his homily against anger, Basil explains that in Scripture we have a great help in avoiding the passion of anger, for it recounts for us the lives of blessed men, especially that of the Lord Jesus. "Remembering the examples of blessed men" checks "the frantic and passion-stricken movement of the soul" (*Hom. Anger* 5; 88). Scripture is a psychologist, or, as Basil calls it, "a physician for our souls" (*Hom. Attend* 4; 97).[39]

To be a disciple of Christ, then, is both to forget and to remember. We must forget the things of this world, including possessions and marriage, so that we can remember the Triune God and his economy for our salvation. For if we remember, we will love, and if we love, we will keep the commandments, all the commandments, of Christ.

> We ought to guard our hearts with all watchfulness so that we never cast aside the thought of God or defile the memory of his wonders with the phantasms of vanities, but bear about the holy thought of God stamped in our souls like an indelible seal through constant and pure memory. For in this way love for God ascends within us both stirring to the work of the commandments of God and, in turn, being preserved by them constant and unfailing. (*Lg. Rul.* 5.2; 175)

Thus, we abide in the love of Jesus as he abides in the love of the Father (John 15:10).

Comparison of the Anaphora and the *Rules*

Anaphora of St. Basil	*Longer Rules 2.3–4*
	Let us then pass over in silence the risings of the sun, the circuits of the moon, the varying temperatures of the air, the changes of the seasons, the water descending from the clouds or springing forth from the earth, the sea itself, the whole earth and what grows in it, the inhabitants of the waters, the tribes of the air, the myriad varieties of animals, everything in fact that is ordered to the service of our life. But that supreme benefit we could not neglect even if we wished. To be silent about it is absolutely impossible for anyone with a sound mind and reasoning power; but to speak of it worthily is still more impossible.
Having made man, in taking dust from the earth, and having honoured him with your image, you had placed him in the Paradise of delight, promising him immortality of life and eternal good things in the observance of your commandments. But when he disobeyed you, the true God who created him, and was led astray by the deception of the serpent and was put to death by his own transgressions, you cast him out in your righteous judgement, O God, from paradise into this world and you caused him to return to the earth from which he was taken, providing for him the salvation of regeneration in your Christ himself. For you did not totally reject your creature, which you made, O Good One, nor did you forget the work of your hands, but you visited him in manifold ways because of your tender mercy, you sent him the prophets, you wrought wonders through your saints who were pleasing to you in each generation, you have spoken to us through the mouth of your servants the prophets announcing beforehand the salvation to come, you have given us the law to help us, you appointed angels as guardians.	For God made man in his own image and likeness, made him worthy of knowledge of himself (i.e., God), adorned him with knowledge beyond all other creatures, allowed him to luxuriate in the inconceivable beauties of Paradise and made him ruler of all earthly things. Then when he had been deceived by the serpent and fallen into sin, and through sin into death and all it entails, God did not reject him; but first gave him a law as a help, set angels to guard and care for him, sent prophets to reprove vice and teach virtue, frustrated the impulses by threats, stirred up eagerness for good by promises, made clear in advance the end of virtue and vice by the frequent example of many persons who served as a warning for others, and, in addition to these and others like them, he did not turn away from those persisting in disobedience. For we were not neglected by the goodness of the Master, nor even did we hinder his love for us, even though we had insulted our Benefactor by callous indifference to his gifts.
But when the fullness of time came you spoke to us in your Son himself, through whom you had also created the ages, he who is the splendour of your glory and the form of your substance, and upholding all things by the word of your power, did not count equality with you, O God and Father, a thing to be grasped, but being God before the ages he was seen on earth and lived among men, and having taken flesh from a holy Virgin, he emptied himself taking the form of a servant.[35]	On the contrary, we were called back from death and made alive again by our Lord Jesus Christ himself. In him even the manner of the benefit given is a great wonder: "Being in the form of God, he did not count equality with God a thing to be grasped, but emptied himself, taking the form of a servant" [Phil. 2:6–7].[36]

7

The Monastic Life

From Commandments to Community

Monasticism is the most authentic form of Christian discipleship. As Basil sees it, if we would let the Lord's grace have its way with us, if we would follow our baptism to its end and keep all the commandments, we would end up in the monastic life. Indeed, Basil's word (*eisagomenoi*) for candidates seeking to enter the monastic community is also the word for catechumens, indicating a "link between the ascetic life and baptism."[1] Basil's "monks"—as they would later be called and as we call them—"were simply," Robert Taft writes, "Christians taking the whole business seriously."[2] The monastic life, then, differs from the life of ordinary discipleship not in essence but in intensity. But what does this most intense Christian life look like in Basil's thought and practice?

One of the most fascinating features of the fourth-century church is that we get to observe monasticism in its various stages of development, from devoted and pious family to highly organized monastery, from informal household virginity to ritually consecrated virginity. Indeed we have seen this progress in Basil's own life and family largely through Gregory of Nyssa's *Life of Macrina*. Here, however, we look at Basil's monastic thought in its more mature, its more or less final, form.[3]

Life Apart and Life in Common

The necessary condition for any sort of organized monastic life is the state of being set apart and withdrawn from ordinary intercourse in the world and

even among ordinary Christians. Thus Basil advises that "retirement to a secluded dwelling is of great assistance in keeping the soul from distractions"
(*Lg. Rul.* 6.1; 178). At first sight, he seems merely to *recommend* seclusion
or retirement rather than to insist upon it. Further, the recommendation is
softened by the fact that withdrawal is said to "help" rather than to be "necessary." Basil's soft language here seems to support a spiritual interpretation or
a metaphorical reading of separation: what really matters is that one's heart
is withdrawn, not so much whether one is physically set apart. Basil's early
ascetic experience seems to confirm this line of thought. We have seen that
when Basil first retired to his Pontic retreat to lead a life devoted to God, he
was physically secluded but struggled to be spiritually so. "I have indeed left
my life in the city," he wrote, "as giving rise to countless evils, but I have not
yet been able to leave myself behind. . . . We carry our indwelling disorders
about with us, and . . . consequently we have derived no great benefit from
our present solitude" (ep. 2.1; 1:7–9). Thus Basil introduces a gap between
physical and spiritual withdrawal from the world, and his own experience
taught him that the spiritual withdrawal need not follow the physical, so
that one can be physically set apart from the world and yet spiritually, in the
heart, attached to it. We may be inclined to draw the conclusion that since
spiritual separation need not follow on physical, then physical separation is
not necessary at all and that one may be spiritually detached from this world
while physically immersed in it.

This line of thinking, I believe, is foreign to the basic thrust of Basil's ascetic
thought. Basil's spirituality generally tends against a spiritualization of the
gospel and certainly against rationalizations of it. It is not enough, for example,
to be interiorly detached from one's possessions; one must give them away or,
at least, truly consecrate them to God. The Lord "did not instruct us to throw
away possessions as evil and flee them, but to administer them" (*Sh. Rul.* 92;
323). Basil does not interpret the "poor *in spirit*" of Matthew's Gospel (5:3)
as a qualification of the disposition by which one might retain possessions
and still have the heart, the spirit, of poverty. Rather, the poor in spirit are
"those who become poor for no other cause but for that teaching of the Lord"
commanded to sell all and give to the poor (Matt. 19:21; *Sh. Rul.* 205; 384).

It is not enough, to give another example, to be interiorly detached from
sexual intercourse with one's spouse, one must progress toward continence
(hence the negative attitude toward bigamy). So also, it is not enough that
one withdraw internally; one must in some way be physically separate from
the many. "To deny oneself is to forget everything to do with one's former
way of life and to withdraw from one's own will" (*Lg. Rul.* 6.1; 179). But if
this interior movement is not followed by actually separating oneself from
evildoers, then "to emend and correct oneself while continuing in the same
habits and former way of life is very difficult, if I do not say entirely impossible" (*Reg. Bas.* 2.102; 179).

In all cases, the interior movement is the heart of the matter, but the exterior movement is the sign of the genuine presence and authenticity of the interior—if you really are interiorly detached from your possessions, you will give them away; if truly detached from sexual pleasure, you will not marry again upon the death of your spouse; if truly undistracted and withdrawn from the world, you will not associate with sinners.

To live apart is not necessarily to live alone. Indeed, Basil's ascetic theology is justly famous for his insistence upon the necessity of life in common. So one must live secluded, apart from the world, but in community with others who are likewise withdrawn from the world. When Basil is asked whether it is better to live the solitary life or the common, he responds directly: "I observe that a life spent in company with those of the same mind is of greater advantage in many ways" (*Lg. Rul.* 7.1; 180–81). He then enumerates the reasons for his position. First, by divine design and ordination, the common life is necessary for the provision of bodily needs (*Lg. Rul.* 7.1). Second, Christ's command to love makes the common life necessary (*Lg. Rul.* 7.1). Third, the common life makes possible the fraternal correction that is necessary for progress in the Christian life. Fourth, the community, taken as a whole, can fulfill all the Lord's commandments, while the individual cannot fulfill them all by himself. Here Basil's argument rests upon a corporate personality attributed to the community. In the common life, "all of us have been gathered up in the one hope to which we were called (Eph. 4:4) [and] we are one body having Christ as head and we are members of the other (Rom. 12:5)" (*Lg. Rul.* 7.2; 182). Thus, only the corporate Christians, the members acting as one, can simultaneously visit the sick, for example, welcome the stranger, feed the hungry, clothe the naked, rejoice with the joyful, and weep with the weeping.[4]

The final argument that Basil gives for the superiority of the common life also draws on the corporate personality of the Christian ascetic community: no single person can receive all the spiritual charisms (*Lg. Rul.* 7.2). Not only can no single person receive all the charisms but also the charisms are given for the benefit of others. The solitary buries the charism given him just as the servant who "received the one talent went and dug in the ground and hid his master's money" (Matt. 25:18; *Lg. Rul.* 7.2). In the common life, however, "each enjoys his own gift, even as he multiplies it by sharing it, and reaps the fruit of others' gifts, as if they were his own" (*Lg. Rul.* 7.2; 183–84).

These texts raise two important issues in Basil's ascetic thought: charisms and the significance of the community's corporate personality. The first we will mention and then treat later; the second, we will dwell on for a bit. What, concretely, was Basil thinking of when he mentioned the charisms of the community? Or, if we frame the question a bit differently, how did Basil apply 1 Corinthians 12 to his monastic community? "To one is given through the Spirit the utterance of wisdom, and to another the utterance of knowledge according to the same Spirit, to another faith by the same Spirit, to another gifts of healing by the one Spirit, to another the working of miracles, to another prophecy, to another the ability to distinguish spirits, to another various kinds of tongues, to another the interpretation of tongues" (1 Cor. 12:8–10). In the *Longer Rules* 7.2, concerning the corporate reception of charisms, Basil does not give any examples of charisms aside from those mentioned in his quotation from 1 Corinthians 12:8. We will see later that the chief spiritual charism that God has given to some in the Basilian community is the gift of leading others in the pursuit of holiness.

Now we move to the question of the corporate personality. To put it bluntly, Basil does not allow the corporate fulfilling of the dominical commands to the broader church as he does to the monastic community. In particular, we could not argue that the Christian community as a whole follows the Lord's commands because, even though not all keep all the commands—such as that to give away one's possessions—at least some keep it, and so the whole keeps it. Implicit in Basil's thought here is a distinction: some commands must be kept by everyone in the community (whether one thinks of the broader church or the monastery), while other commands need only be kept by some. Or, better put, for some dominical commands, when some Christians keep them, the whole keeps them; they can be kept corporately. Other dominical commands, however, bind every single Christian; they cannot be kept corporately but must be kept singly. It would be absurd, for example, to argue that only some members of the community need live chastely or only some members of the community keep holy the Sabbath, on the specious grounds that when some keep these commands, the whole keeps them. We have considered Basil's understanding of the command to be poor at great length in the last chapter. Suffice it here to say that the command to be poor, is, for him, the sort of command that must be kept singly and is not the sort of command that may be kept by the whole in being kept by some: the command to be poor cannot be fulfilled by the corporate personality. So, for Basil, the commands concerning hospitality, care of the sick, the consolation of mourners, and work can only be kept corporately, while the Ten Commandments and the commands to be poor and celibate must be kept singly.[5]

Of course, the community that corporately keeps the commands of the Lord is the body of Christ. Thus, for Basil, it is the monastic community and not the wider church that is most properly called the body of Christ. This point is of a piece with the basic principle of Basil's view of Christian discipleship. Just as there is a single form of discipleship whose most intense expression is monastic, and lesser forms only approximate it, so there is a single Christian community that is purely the body of Christ in its monastic form, and other forms of Christian community only approximate this body of Christ.

On a few occasions, Basil applies the words of Romans 12:5—"so we, though many, are one body in Christ, and individually members one of another"—and 1 Corinthians 12:27—"Now you are the body of Christ and individually members of it"—to the monastic community. For example, having just argued that the common life is required for the fulfillment of all the Lord's commands, Basil, alluding to Romans 12:5, says, "We are one body having Christ as head" (*Lg. Rul.* 7.2; 182). The common life is a "dispensation" pleasing to God, in which we are "fitted together through our harmony into the solidarity of one body in the Holy Spirit" (*Lg. Rul.* 7.2; 182). If we live alone, we cannot be members to one another or the subjects of the head, Christ (*Lg. Rul.* 7.2). Or again, in the monastic community, "There will be a decent and well-ordered way of life in which the principle of the *members of the body* is observed" (*Lg. Rul.* 24; 225; 1 Cor. 12:27).[6]

The fact that Basil calls the wider church the body of Christ does not stand against the point that the monastic community is most properly so called (*On Judg.* 3; *Mor.* 50.1, 80.4). Two points are especially important here. First, to say that the monastery is the body of Christ does not imply, for Basil, that the wider church cannot also be the body, but less intensively. Second, the claim that the monastery is most properly the body of Christ in no way drives a wedge between monks and bishops or asceticism and the sacraments, for, as we shall see, Basil's view of the ascetic community has a significant place for bishops and priests as well as baptism and the Eucharist. We do well, moreover, to remember that *On Judgment* and the *Morals* do not conceive the ideal Christian as a member of a fully mature and organized monastic community. Basil has not yet come to the point of seeing a monk in community as the perfect disciple. Though in these early works the ideal Christian is not a monk, the ideal Christian is deeply ascetic. Just so, the body of Christ here is the cohort of Christians living a disciplined and ascetically minded life, if not a fully monastic one.

So far, then, we have it that the most intense form of Christian discipleship is the common life separate from the world. To live withdrawn from the world of distractions and temptations sets the life of the monastic community apart from the larger world as well as the church. Moreover, the monastic community itself observed various kinds of separation. Candidates for the community were separate for a time from the fully fledged members; adults lived apart from children, men from women, boys from girls, guests and the sick from members of the community. Such separations, of course, are ordered to the good of each group. The spiritual and physical needs of mature ascetics, for example, differ from those of children. "With regard to sleeping and rising," Basil counsels, "the time of meals and their quantity and quality, let a particular program and manner of life suitable for children be arranged separately" (*Lg. Rul.* 15.2; 202).

From these various separations within the community and the ways in which Basil speaks of them, we can infer that a monastic community comprised several separate houses. A single monastic community, Silvas writes, "comprised at least five or six separate 'houses': a house each for men, women, boys, girls, and a 'hospice' for the sick, short- or long-term guests, and those candidates described as still 'outside'" (Silvas, 201n246).[7] The separations, visibly manifest in the housing arrangements, were not absolute, for the members of the various houses came together for liturgy and prayer, and some of the more mature members served as guides to the less experienced, as in the case of the ascetics whose job it was to oversee the children (*Lg. Rul.* 15.2).

These various housing arrangements are a wonderful example of how living the gospel authentically necessarily requires a high degree of organization and formality in the community. The commandments concerning sexual continence require the separation of women from men, and yet Basil has already indicated that they must have some kind of life in common. Or again, the gospel requires those who would live it *both* to separate from those who are not living it *and* to correct and encourage those who are not; it is necessary both to live apart from nonmembers and to evangelize these same, and thus to have contact with them. In short, the gospel requires separation from the world but forbids the abandonment of those who remain in it, whether sinners, travelers, orphans, sick, or poor. Thus, the monastic community must remain in various ways engaged with the world from which it has withdrawn. The various houses, the rules governing interaction of those who live in them, and the rules that prescribe common acts among them serve to protect the common life of the fully initiated, especially the two major ranks of fully initiated men and fully initiated women, as well as to foster a common life, as it were, across all the ranks.

Admission

If the ascetic life involves life apart and life in common, the next and obvious question is, how do I get in? Indeed, the very next theme that Basil treats in the *Longer Rules*—after a consideration of renunciation, which is really of a piece with withdrawal from the world (*Lg. Rul.* 9)—is admission to the community (*Lg. Rul.* 10–15). How does one enter this life? The first thing to be said is that the admission policy is one of qualified universalism. The Lord invited all to embrace the monastic life, all "to take on his easy yoke and the burden of his commandments that lightens us up to heaven" (*Lg. Rul.* 10.1; 193; Matt. 11:30). Accordingly, Basil offers guidance for the acceptance into the community of a wide range of people. Those of both high and low social rank, rich and poor, are welcome, as are slaves (*Lg. Rul.* 11), married men and women (*Lg. Rul.* 12), and children, whether those still under the authority of parents or orphans (*Lg. Rul.* 15).

While in principle all are welcome, Basil found it necessary to make a number of qualifications. Most obviously, those who would enter must have reached a certain level of Christian virtue. Of course, they will have to have given away their possessions, and to have done so in a responsible way. Here Basil introduces an important qualification of Christian poverty. The point of giving away one's possessions is not merely one's own detachment from them, but also to help the poor and the needy. Thus, the candidate "must realize that it is not without peril either to relinquish [his property] to his relatives or to administer it simply through anyone at all" (*Lg. Rul.* 9.1; 191). There is a choice: one may relinquish one's property responsibly or administer it well, either personally or through another. For Basil, the administration of what has been dedicated to the Lord is just as good as its relinquishment. This, in fact, is what Basil and his family seem to have done with their great wealth: it was not so much given away as "consecrated to the Lord" and administered with care and piety for the sake of the ascetic community and the poor (*Lg. Rul.* 9.1; 191).[8]

Besides poverty, there are other qualifications of the universal invitation. Candidates must be of a stable and virtuous character. Those who have recently turned to the Christian life must be tested and proved (*Lg. Rul.* 10.2). All must have acquired sufficient progress in self-control (*to enkrateuesthai*), a virtue that Basil treats extensively.[9] Self-control, very obviously, is not the distinguishing mark of monks, for it is basic to the non-monastic form of the Christian life too. In fact, self-control is a "meta-virtue," as it were, for it is "an intrinsic element of all the virtues," as Silvas puts it. The interconnectedness of all the commandments—"it is impossible to accomplish one in isolation from another"—is, Basil says, "especially the case with self-control," for around it all are linked "as in a circular dance" (*Lg. Rul.* 16.3; 208).

While monks do not have a monopoly on the virtue, they will live it more intensely than ordinary Christians. We have seen these levels of self-control, these variations in intensity in Basil's understanding of Christian marriage: the bigamist has more self-control than the trigamist; the consecrated widow or widower, more than the bigamist; the consecrated virgin more than the person who marries at all. Thus, it is not self-control itself but its intensity that marks Basil's monks.

Before we turn to the particular form of self-control to which Basil calls monks, let us consider some important features of the virtue, regardless of its intensity in one group of Christians or another. First, and most significantly, is that the presence of self-control leads to theophany, and its absence to idolatry. The example of the saints illustrates the theophanic propensity of self-control. Basil lists, together with the Lord, a number of outstanding biblical models of self-control and its fruit in their lives. Moses persevered in fasting and prayer and heard the words of God "as one speaks with one's own friend" (*Lg. Rul.* 16.2; 206; Exod. 33:11). Of Elijah, Basil says that he "was counted worthy of the vision of God after spending a like space of time in self-control (abstaining from food)" (*Lg. Rul.* 16.2; 206; 1 Kings 19:8–18). Daniel attained to the vision of wonders by fasting (Dan. 10:2–3). And "the

Lord himself inaugurated his manifestation" by means of self-control (*Lg. Rul.* 16.2; 207; Matt. 3:4).

Basil offers a definition of self-control: "a taking away of sin, a weaning from passions, a *mortifying of the body* (cf. Rom. 8:13; Col. 3:5) *with its* natural *passions and cravings* (Gal. 5:24); it is the beginning of spiritual life, the sponsor of eternal blessings and extinguishes in itself the sting of pleasure" (*Lg. Rul.* 17.2; 210).[10] Man's natural yearning for God, so important for Basil's anthropology, is implicit here. Self-control frees the soul to rise to God by loosening its moorings in this world and its attachment to the goods of this world. It is the natural inclination that makes the taking away of sin to be theophanic. Basil's definition also contains the root of intemperate idolatry: pleasure. Pleasure draws us to sin; "by it every soul is dragged to death as with a fish-hook" (*Lg. Rul.* 17.2; 210). St. Paul provides the link for Basil between pleasure and idolatry, "for to serve pleasures is nothing else than *to make a god of one's own stomach* (*Lg. Rul.* 19.1; 214; Phil. 3:19). Pleasure leads one to eat beyond what is necessary, which, in turn, hinders one's ability to keep the commandments. Pleasure converts food from sustenance of the body into a weapon against it. It is difficult to be mindful of God while in a gluttonous stupor.

Basil often couples pleasure and vainglory, for to seek pleasure is truly futile and accomplishes nothing. Equally useless are expensive luxuries and the extravagant table, even set for a guest. If the guest is a Christian brother, he will be comforted as if at home, by the frugal and familiar table; if he is not a brother, then such a table will be a lesson to him of Christian poverty and an "example of sufficiency in eating" (*Lg. Rul.* 20.2; 216). Basil says that he groans over the wealthy because they have squandered their lives on vanity by making gods of their pleasures (*Lg. Rul.* 20.2). Thus, for Basil, there are no simple pleasures, only destructive ones, and just as self-control removes the earthly obstacles to the vision of God, so intemperance ultimately makes gods of these obstacles.

Anyone who would enter Basil's community, then, must be possessed of a certain measure of self-control. Taking sexual continence for granted, he spends most of his time in the *Rules* treating self-control in regard to food. His monastic legislation here, however, remains flexible, according to the varying needs of the various members. The young and the old, the sick and the well, those with strenuous occupations and those with light, have different dietary needs. All, however, have the benefit of hearing the Scriptures read at mealtime to forestall any undue attachment to food (*Sh. Rul.* 180).

Those who join Basil's monastic circle adopt the distinctive dress that indicates to all their profession. This "habit," which Basil calls simply "Christian dress," is, he says, a "pedagogue for the weaker," for it serves as a reminder to the one who wears it of the expectations that all will have of his behavior (*Lg. Rul.* 22.3; 222). One must act as one dresses, lest one's behavior contradict "the whole orientation of his life," and he be rebuked by all (*Lg. Rul.* 22.3; 222). Though the dress of the professed (a single tunic [*Lg. Rul.* 23]) was distinctive, it was also simple, cheap, and sufficient to meet the needs of the body. The same principle applies to footwear: "whatever is simple, readily obtained, in keeping with our goal, and sufficient for use" (*Lg. Rul.* 22.3; 223). Basil also calls for the wearing of a belt, both in imitation of the saints[11] and as a matter of practicality: the belt prevents the tunic from interference with work and makes it more efficient in keeping one warm (*Lg. Rul.* 23).

While the qualifications mentioned so far apply to all, the circumstances of slaves, the married, and children call for special consideration. With slaves, Basil follows the example of Paul: unlike the extreme Eustathians condemned at Gangra, Basil urges that "slaves still under the yoke who take refuge in the communities should be cautioned and restored to their masters in a better state of mind" (*Lg. Rul.* 11; 195–96).

While Basil here clearly accommodates ancient society and culture, as did Paul, there are clear limits to his toleration of the institution of slavery: Basil will not suffer a slave to be subject to a "base master," who forces the slave "to transgress the commandment of the true Master, our Lord Jesus Christ" (*Lg. Rul.* 11; 196). In such a case he counsels that the slave disobey the master and be prepared to suffer the consequences, or that the community accept him against the wishes (and the legal right) of the master and itself suffer whatever trouble may come.

Basil treats the obligations of the married similarly: when there is a conflict between the demands of one's spouse and those of the Lord, the latter take priority, "for nothing should be preferred to obedience to God" (*Lg. Rul.* 12; 197).[12] Basil is not unconcerned with consent of the spouses, as, again, he purports to follow Paul. In this case, however, he seems to place a meaning on Paul's words that is opposite of what Paul intended. Basil advises the married who wish to become ascetics in his community (or one of the communities under his direction) to get the consent of their spouses, but in the absence of that consent, the one party should nevertheless join the community, for, again, it is better to obey God than men. He says the same thing in the *Morals*: "A husband must not separate from a wife, nor a wife from a husband, unless one party be taken in adultery or be hindered as regards godliness" (*Mor.* 73.1; 125).

Thus Basil cites 1 Corinthians 7:4—the husband does not rule over his own body but the wife does—to ground his advice to obtain consent, but, in the end, he would deny to the objecting spouse the "conjugal rights" that each owes the other (1 Cor. 7:3). Basil also cites 1 Corinthians 7:5 when he says that married candidates should be "questioned whether they are doing this *with mutual consent*" (*Lg. Rul.* 12; 197). St. Paul, however, is not speaking about the married becoming consecrated and permanent celibates in a monastic community but about periodic abstinence: "Do not refuse one another except perhaps by agreement for a season, that you may devote yourselves to prayer; but then come together again, lest Satan tempt you through lack of self-control" (1 Cor. 7:5).

Basil's concern for the mind of the master and for the consent of the spouse have more to do with their own conversion than with a requirement to obtain their permission for the slave or the married person to follow the command of the gospel. Paul had written to Philemon that he was sending Onesimus back to him because he preferred to do nothing without Philemon's consent. Paul, however, specifies that he is asking Philemon's consent for Philemon's sake: "that your goodness might not be by compulsion but of your own free will" (Philem. 14). Likewise, Basil instructs a married person to obtain the consent of the spouse so that the spouse too may be given the opportunity to follow the command of the Lord. He says that he has known many cases wherein by prayer and fasting "the goal of living a life of chastity has been attained, since as a result of bodily necessity the Lord often leads the obstinate to concur in the right decision" (*Lg. Rul.* 12; 197–98). Basil seems to be indicating here that the forced celibacy on the part of the spouse who is abandoned by the other entering the monastery together with the prayer and fasting (presumably, of the monastic community and its newest married member) often leads the unwilling spouse to consent to what has already happened. Even still, with Silvas, we must acknowledge here Basil's ambiguity. She reports the conflicting interpretations of Garnier (the Maurist editor of the Greek text), and Clarke: the former interprets Basil to mean "that admittance of a married candidate whose spouse was unwilling was only conditional, dependent on the permission of the other spouse forthcoming before profession" (Silvas, 198n232); the latter takes the admittance to be unconditioned by the refusal of the spouse.[13] Silvas seems to lean toward Garnier's view, for Clarke's would imply Basil's contradiction of the Council of Gangra, and Silvas sees Basil's teaching to be basically in line with that of Gangra. I argued in the last chapter that Silvas may well overestimate the agreement between Basil and the bishops of Gangra; regardless, we simply do not have enough evidence to adjudicate with any finality these interpretations. It is remarkable—and inconsistent with the counsel of others fathers—that Basil would even provisionally allow a married person to join the community against the expressed wishes of the spouse.

The final group of candidates that require special treatment is children, whose right to enter the monastery was guaranteed by our Lord, who commanded the children to come to him (Mark 10:14), and St. Paul, who instructs children to learn the Scriptures and embrace the Lord's discipline (2 Tim. 3:15; Eph. 6:4). Children live apart from the fully initiated brethren, boys apart from girls. "They should be brought up in all love," Basil says, "as the common children of the community" (*Lg. Rul.* 15.1; 201). Children and elders live apart for the good of both, that the elders not be disturbed by the children's lessons, and that the children be protected from the occasion for either scandal or pride at the conduct of the elders (*Lg. Rul.* 15.1). Nevertheless they are not separate at all times, for they come together for the prescribed prayer times, again, for the good of both: "Children are usually stirred by the zeal of the more perfect, and their guides too receive no small help in their prayers from the children" (*Lg. Rul.* 15.2; 202).

Children are to be educated, and the program of learning that Basil calls for fits perfectly with his anthropology. The course of study is based on the Christian Scriptures rather than pagan myths. The children would learn biblical "histories of wonderful deeds" and "maxims from Proverbs," and they were to be rewarded for remembering what they were taught (*Lg. Rul.* 15.3; 203). The point is to habituate the mind to God and the things of God. Being able to remember God, the children will acquire the habit of avoiding distraction; as they grow, "reason will suggest what is useful, habit will lend facility to right action" (*Lg. Rul.* 15.4; 203).

The education of the children could also involve the learning of a craft. I will take up the role of labor in Basil's monastic thought later. Suffice it to say here that Basil allows "any of the children [who] seem fitted to learn" to spend their days with the teachers of the craft (so long as they eat and reside with their companions), for some crafts require training from childhood (*Lg. Rul.* 15.4; 204).

Only once the children are educated to the point of maturity will they be given the opportunity to profess virginity and join the full-fledged members. Their consecration should be public and in the presence of the local bishop. Basil seems to have in mind here no profound ritual signification of the relationship between the virgin and the larger ecclesial community represented by the bishop. Rather, the point is to protect the community against any charge of impropriety, taking liberties with the young or compelling them to celibacy. The community's good name is also protected in the event that the professed later reneges on his or her consecration and leaves the community. We can see very clearly from the Eustathians that the falling of consecrated virgins from virtue and their subsequent expulsion from the monastic community with its attendant scandal and tumult could easily cause tensions between the monastic community and the local episcopal authority. Silvas observes that Basil transfers a custom of female virgins to males also and thus "acts firmly to bring the ascetic impulse within the ambit of the Church" (Silvas, 203n253).

The Manner of Our Life Together

Longer Rules 24 marks an important change in Basil's treatment of the monastic life: we move, essentially, from matters of admission to the way of life of the monks. The monks ask Basil, "We would next like to learn about the manner of our life together" (*Lg. Rul.* 24.Q; 224).

The whole manner and way of life in Basil's monasteries is structured around a single basic relationship: the seniors or elders and, for lack of a better word, the subordinates. As Basil says, "There are two general orders: those who are entrusted with leadership and those whose part is to accede and obey" (*Sh. Rul.* 235; 401). The point is really a very simple one, though it gets worked out in myriad concrete and complex ways: those more experienced in the spiritual life, those further on the path to holiness, have the ability, the obligation, and the need to lead the less experienced into deeper communion with God. The primary way, moreover, whereby the senior ascetics fulfill this obligation and need is through the giving of counsel, what Basil so often calls the "charism of the word."

The "charism of the word" is, of course, St. Paul's phrase, for in 1 Corinthians he speaks of the "varieties of gifts [*diaireseis*]" (1 Cor. 12:4), the "word of wisdom [*logos sophias*]," and the "word of knowledge [*logos gnōseōs*]" (1 Cor. 12:8).[14] St. Paul is very emphatic that these gifts come from the Spirit, and this means, for St. Basil, that the relationship of authority created by the charism of the word manifests God's intention for the basic structure of that human community that most effectively secures the salvation of men. We might put the matter emphatically by saying that God himself creates the monastic community by inspiring some with words of wisdom and knowledge and others to listen to and obey these words.

The basic relationship of authority created by God's gift of a word explains the very existence of the Small and Great Ascetica. Basil is the experienced Christian whose advice in matters of holiness, virtue, sin, and the interpretation of Scripture is sought out by others. Indeed, we can think of the Ascetica as nothing but a collection of such questions and Basil's answers to them, a collection of "words." In the prologue of the *Longer Rules*, Basil urges those who seek his counsel, "Let us pray for one another, that we, for our part, may *give to* our fellow servants *their portion of food in due time* (Luke 12:42) and that you, for your part, may receive the word like the good earth and bring forth a mature and manifold fruit in righteousness" (*Lg. Rul.* prol. 1; 153). It is easy to see why Silvas, for her translation of the Ascetica, chose the titles, "The Longer Responses" and "The Shorter Responses" instead of the more traditional "Rules" that I have been using. "Responses" is a more accurate description of the original setting of the work, while "Rules" accents the authority that the responses carried: Basil's responses were rules of Christian life to the ascetics to whom they were given.

What sorts of questions arose in the monastic life? Sometimes the questions are of a practical nature, as we have seen. Who should be admitted to the community? How should they be admitted? What should the monks wear? Should a monk who is tired from work get more to eat than others (*Sh. Rul.* 135)? How should one deal with monks who are late for dinner (*Sh. Rul.* 136)? Should the monastery school educate the children of seculars (*Sh. Rul.* 292)? And so on.

Still other questions are of a more theological or scriptural nature. Often Basil is asked the meaning of a particular word or verse, or the difference between two scriptural words that appear to be synonymous. What, for example, is the difference between reviling and slander (Rom. 1:30; 1 Cor. 5:11; *Sh. Rul.* 24–25)? What is the difference between bitterness, wrath, and anger (*Sh. Rul.* 55)? "What is *the bank* in which the Lord says, *you ought to have put your money?*" (Matt. 25:27; *Sh. Rul.* 254). And so on.

These first two sorts of questions are very important for the common life of ascetic Christians and make the charism of the word necessary. It is the questions on the spiritual life, however, that drive to the center of the charism's purpose and role, for these questions and answers bear directly on the monks' efforts to grow in holiness. Basil, for example, offers counsel on how to conquer a number of spiritual maladies: lack of compunction for sin (*Sh. Rul.* 16); uncertainty over whether one's sins have been forgiven (*Sh. Rul.* 12, 296); desire to eat when one should not (*Sh. Rul.* 17, 126); distraction (*Sh. Rul.* 21, 201–2); anger (*Sh. Rul.* 29); base desire (*Sh. Rul.* 30); unwanted sleepiness (*Sh. Rul.* 32); pride (*Sh. Rul.* 35); loss of zeal (*Sh. Rul.* 37); the failure of the mind to think good thoughts (*Sh. Rul.* 80); and repeated fall into the same sins (*Sh. Rul.* 289). So very often Basil offers a single remedy to such spiritual problems—namely, the presence of God to the mind. We must remember that "God who tries hearts and inmost parts" (Ps. 7:10) is present (*Sh. Rul.* 21; 286). Basil quotes the same verse when he offers a word on how to attain undistracted prayer: "through being fully persuaded that God is before one's eyes; for if when someone sees a ruler or officer and converses with him, he keeps his eyes intent, then how much more does one who prays to God keep his mind intent on him who *searches hearts and inmost parts*" (Ps. 7:10; *Sh. Rul.* 201; 383).

Thus, those "entrusted with the charism of the word . . . have the capacity *to speak* and to listen *with knowledge* (cf. 2 Tim. 2:15; Heb. 5:13) in a way that builds up the faith" (*Lg. Rul.* 32.2; 234). Basil compares those with the charism of the word to physicians and stewards of bread. Not just anyone can "use the knife on the sick" but only he who has acquired the skill (*Lg. Rul.* 45.2; 258). And not just anyone is entrusted with the distribution of the bread (*Lg. Rul.* 45.2). Just so, not just anyone can "leap in with a cure through the word" or judiciously and carefully dispense spiritual food (*Lg. Rul.* 45.2; 258–59). Basil draws out the former analogy still further. Just as in physical life "we endure cuttings and cauterizations and the taking of bitter drugs for the cure of the body," so also in the spiritual life, "we must accept the cutting effects of the word that exposes and the bitter drugs of penalties for the cure of the soul" (*Lg. Rul.* 55.3; 266). Those senior members of the community who dispense the charism of the word must have, then, a physician's freedom to apply whatever remedy, however mild or severe, to the soul being treated or a steward's freedom to distribute food according to the different needs of those who are eating.

The charism of the word, given by God to the elders of the community, points to an interesting truth about the place of the Scriptures in the economy of salvation. On the one hand, and to use the words of Newman, "The Scripture statements are sanctions as well as informants in the inquiry; they begin and they do not exhaust. . . . [Scripture] begins a series of developments which it does not finish."[15] It is patently obvious that the Scriptures raise all manner of unanswered questions about the living out of the gospel. If I may again borrow the words of Newman, "Great questions exist in the subject-matter of which Scripture treats, which Scripture does not solve; questions too so real, so practical, that they must be answered, and, unless we suppose a new revelation, answered by means of the revelation which we have, that is, by development."[16] We might put it harshly thus: the very condition of the charism of the word is the insufficiency of the Scriptures, and they are insufficient in two basic respects—namely, in that they call for explanation on subjects that they do treat and in that they simply do not address certain subjects.

On the other hand, the charism of the word cannot, for Basil, be exercised apart from the Scriptures. One of the qualifications for becoming a senior member of the community is deep knowledge of Scripture. Those who are "entrusted with the leadership and care of the many," Basil writes, "ought to know and learn everything by heart, that [they] may teach the whole of God's will and show to each his duties" (*Sh. Rul.* 235; 401). Basil, moreover, is highly critical of the idea that a word comes ultimately from a man rather than from God and his Scriptures. He was asked whether it is permissible for a person to say "whatever he thinks good, without the testimonies of the God-inspired Scriptures" (*Sh. Rul.* 1.Q; 273). Basil's answer is a firm and lengthy "no." In imitation of the Lord, who pointed not to himself but to the Father, the person with the charism of the word must ever realize that the source of his authority is God and not himself. On those matters wherein there is a commandment of the Lord, the elder must be faithful to it (hence the importance of his having memorized the Scripture); and on those matters that the Scriptures pass over in silence, we must do what "builds up our neighbors and not whatever we please" (*Sh. Rul.* 1; 275). Thus, Basil points out, the charism of the word can never be the occasion for self-aggrandizement but always involves subjection to and service of others. Here he preserves for his monastic community a truly Christian understanding of authority whose whole point is not to lord it over others, but, Basil says, to "*dispense our words with judgment* (Ps. 112 [111]:5) that we withdraw (men) from sin and lead (them) to God" (*Sh. Rul.* 245; 406).

While the charism of the word is the senior members' most important exercise of leadership and their most serious duty—to neglect it is to be a "murderer of souls" (*Sh. Rul.* 45; 298)—there were other ways in which the elders exercised leadership in the community. The *Rules* mention often in passing a number of offices that would be carried out by an elder member. There is one who distributes the bread (*Lg. Rul.* 45; *Sh. Rul.* 100), one designated as an arbitrator to settle disputes in the community (*Lg. Rul.* 49), one who wakens the brothers for prayer (*Sh. Rul.* 43), one who has stewardship of the clothes (*Sh. Rul.* 87, 91) and of the storeroom (*Sh. Rul.* 148, 156), and the one entrusted with the oversight of the workers (*Sh. Rul.* 141–42, 145). All of these tasks had to be carried out with charity and wisdom for the proper functioning and good order of the community. These different offices, or, rather, the skills to execute them, are charisms, just like the charism of the word. They are the gifts of God to individuals that are to be applied to the benefit and advantage of the many (*Sh. Rul.* 253).

The monastic community is not ultimately governed by a council of elders but by a single presider, and Basil spends a fair amount of time outlining his (or her, for the sisters had a presider too) primary duties and requisite disposition.[17] The presider certainly has the charism of the word, but his exercise of the charism seems to differ from the other elders' in that Basil stresses the presider's obligation to rebuke the monks. He is charged to watch over all in the love of Christ (*Sh. Rul.* 19), but in such a way that he must give an account for each to God (*Lg. Rul.* 25.1–2). The presider must be free to be honest. His obligation to speak the truth to sinners cannot be compromised by a desire for human honors or a desire not to give offense (*Lg. Rul.* 25.2). Even still, he must be kind and compassionate, applying the remedies of sin "with all compassion and in just proportion" (*Lg. Rul.* 43.2; 255–56). He cannot rebuke in anger: "Let him show kindness towards the sinner," Basil counsels, "while reserving his displeasure of the evil done" (*Lg. Rul.* 50; 262). Like a doctor, he must battle not the patient but the disease (*Lg. Rul.* 51; *Sh. Rul.* 99). The presider thus has the authority and obligation to punish the sinners under his care. He should punish vainglory with practices of humility, idle speech with silence, excessive sleep with prayer vigils, laziness with hard work, overeating with fasting, and murmuring with isolation (*Lg. Rul.* 51). Even still, punishment cannot be levied in any mechanical way, for the presider must take into account the age of the sinner, the condition and disposition of his soul, and "the particular character of the sin" (*Sh. Rul.* 106; 331; *Sh. Rul.* 81–82).

As to the disposition that the presider ought to have, Basil stresses service and humility. "The care of many means the service of many" (*Lg. Rul.* 30; 232). The presider is to be "an accurate copy" of the humble Christ (*Lg. Rul.* 43.2; 255).

> If the definition of Christianity is this: the imitation of Christ in the measure of the Incarnation according to the duty of each one's calling, then those who are entrusted with the guidance of the many should through their own mediation spur on those who are still weaker to becoming like Christ (*Lg. Rul.* 43.1; 255).

What a beautiful and compact—and truly Basilian—expression of Christian authority! Be a Christian and help others, by example and word, to be

Christians. In addition to humility, the presider, we have already said, must have compassion; he must also be intelligent and prudent (*Lg. Rul.* 35.1, 43.2). Basil thinks that it is a rare person who has all these qualities (*Lg. Rul.* 35.1), and he is surely right in this. The presider is a father (*Sh. Rul.* 99), a doctor of the soul and spiritual life, a nurse (*Sh. Rul.* 98), the eye of the body (*Lg. Rul.* 35.1), a master of the Scriptures—and humble too.

We must add two further points about the presider, and these comport very well with Basil's vision of the office. First, the presider cannot attain this office by himself; rather, he is "chosen by the eminent in the other communities" (*Lg. Rul.* 43.2; 256). This is very much in keeping with the mutual subjection that is, for Basil, the hallmark of Christian common life. To make oneself presider would be to exalt oneself over others and to seek one's own will rather than the service of the community. Even after the presider is chosen, he "never acts alone," for all is to be done with counsel (*Lg. Rul.* 48; Sir. 32:19).[18] The second point is that the presider himself is not above correction, for the senior members of the community have the duty to correct the presider "if he is ever suspected of some error" (*Lg. Rul.* 27.228).

This is the first part of the basic relationship that forms the very structure and informs the whole way of life of Basil's monastic communities. Having considered the first of the two general orders (the leaders), let us turn to the second correlative order (the led). There are two activities at the heart of this second order, both of which correspond to the charism of authority: confession and obedience. Confession is necessary for the obvious reason that the elders must know the spiritual state, for good or ill, of the monks if they are to offer an appropriate word of counsel.[19]

> It is necessary that everyone in a subordinate position who intends to show any progress worthy of the name be found steadfast in the life according to the commandments of our Lord Jesus Christ, not keep any movement of his soul concealed in himself or utter an untested word, but lay bare the secrets of the heart to those entrusted among the brothers with the compassionate and sympathetic care of the weak. (*Lg. Rul.* 26; 227)

In another text, Basil alludes to Matthew's text on fraternal correction to ground the practice of confession in a dominical command. Matthew does not mention the sinner's confession of his own sin but others' reporting his sin, while Basil refers to both: whether by oneself or by others, "every sin must be brought before the one who presides" (*Lg. Rul.* 46; 259).

Just as with those in authority, so also with subordinates, Basil provides protections against self-will. The presider cannot attain his position by himself, and all the senior members are strictly beholden to the Scriptures. Likewise, a subordinate, even if he is convinced that his life is pleasing to God, cannot keep his thoughts to himself but must "lay his thoughts before others"

(*Sh. Rul.* 227.Q; 396). Thus he will avoid the curse: "Woe to those who are wise in their own eyes" (Isa. 5:21). The judgment that one's life is pleasing to God is not to be made by oneself. Confession is, then, not only the occasion for correction but also for confirmation (*Sh. Rul.* 227).

Although in one passage Basil implies that the fruit of confession is the forgiveness of sins,[20] this monastic confession had not yet developed into the sacrament of confession.[21] Silvas surmises that Basil considered it "fitting and desirable that any worthy *presbyter* ('elder') or male superior of a community be a priest" (Silvas, 431n764; *Sh. Rul.* 288). Basil himself and his brother Peter are excellent examples.[22] Thus, often confession was to a priest, though it was not the sacrament it later came to be.

If we think of the later form of confession as the convergence of earlier practices (confession of faults, remedial penances, and sacramental absolution) and their replacement of the public "second penance" of early centuries, then, Silvas interestingly points out, we may see the beginning of this convergence in Basil's thought and practice (Silvas, 432n764). The development that Silvas tentatively attributes to Basil is the requirement that ascetic confession be made to a priest-presbyter, rather than simply to an elder in the community.[23] Whatever Basil's role in the development of sacramental confession, we can certainly say with Silvas that "he would have concurred with the later idea in the West that priest-presbyters *should* be 'soul-doctors,' i.e., capable of authoritative spiritual guidance—that their office was singularly suited to it—but not that they could be assumed to be so simply *ex officio*," for they must possess the requisite spiritual and moral qualities as well as what Basil calls the charism of the word (Silvas, 432n764; her emphasis).

Having laid bare one's mind and having heard a word of counsel, whether a confirmation of virtue or a remedy for sin, the subordinate must do what the elder has advised. Indeed, the subordinate, Basil says, must obey "in the same disposition in which a little child overcome by hunger obeys the nurse who invites it to partake (of her breasts)" (*Sh. Rul.* 166; 363). To follow the counsel is to eat bread in imitation of the Lord whose food was to do the will of the Father (*Sh. Rul.* 166; John 4:34).

Even though Basil calls for obedience to the elders and the presider, he does not make too much of superiors, for his "doctrine of obedience," Holmes writes, "is based more on the scriptural commandments and the needs of the community than on the special position of the superior."[24] The authority of the seniors, moreover, is not absolute, and Basil makes provision for their counsel to be challenged. If a subordinate thinks that a particular counsel is actually contrary to the Scriptures, he should oppose the presider openly or in private (*Lg. Rul.* 47). If he is too timid to do this himself, others may do it for him. Thus, "if the command [of the presider] is contrary to Scripture he may deliver both himself and his brothers from harm, but if it is shown to be in accord with the word that fits the case then he may free himself from vain and perilous doubts" (*Lg. Rul.* 47; 260).

The consequences of disobedience are severe. Persistent disobedience merits a sharp rebuke before the whole community (*Lg. Rul.* 28.1). In the event that even this does not reform the disobedient monk, he must be excommunicated, cut "away from the body as a corrupted and wholly useless member," lest his miserable disease spread to others (*Lg. Rul.* 28.1; 229).[25]

While the practice of confession and the social structures that make it possible give the monastic community its basic form, the stuff of everyday life for the monks was work and prayer.[26] It is no surprise that, for Basil, work must be done because the Lord has commanded it (*Lg. Rul.* 37.1): Jesus says that the laborer is worthy of his food (Matt. 10:10), and Paul commands that we work so that we can give to the needy (Eph. 4:28). The monk does not get to choose his own craft, lest he fall into pleasing himself or choose a particular craft for the wrong reasons—because it is easy or because he can bring glory to himself through it; rather, the elders will decide how he can best serve the community in his work (*Lg. Rul.* 41.1). There was a wide range of possibilities here. In general, Basil advises the undertaking of those crafts that serve the peace of the community, whose materials are convenient to obtain, whose products are easy to sell, and that do not require "unsuitable or harmful meetings with men or women" (*Lg. Rul.* 38; 248). Beyond this general principle, Basil mentions in particular weaving, leatherwork, building, carpentry, copper-work, and farming (*Lg. Rul.* 38).

It is very important to Basil that the monks work with the right disposition. Each must bear in mind that he works not for himself but to fulfill the needs of others according to the command of the Lord (*Lg. Rul.* 42.1). There can be no pretensions to self-sufficiency but rather a keen awareness of dependency upon God. Work must be done with God ever in mind. "If in every undertaking we ask God to prosper our work," Basil counsels, "and we return thanks to him who gave the capacity for work, . . . we keep the goal of being well pleasing to him" (*Lg. Rul.* 37.3; 245). Margaret Murphy sums up these themes very well when she says that work "is to be a service carefully, zealously, and reverently rendered to God, an act of thanksgiving to Him who bestowed both the power to work and the means to accomplish it, a prayer of praise, a song of melody rising from the lips of him whose hands toil in the interests of charity, whose heart is engaged in the loving contemplation of God."[27]

Work in the monastery was the occasion for significant social intercourse. The apprenticeship of children to workers to learn a trade was an exception to their usual separation (*Lg. Rul.* 15.4). The buying and selling of crafts provided an opportunity for the members of one community to interact with those of other communities as well as with seculars. Sometimes it was necessary for the workers to travel to trading fairs (*Lg. Rul.* 39). Here, however, just as in other dealings wherein the monks forgo the benefits of separation,

Basil stipulates certain practices and forbids others, all with a view toward limiting the exposure of the monks to what would harm their way of life: the monks are not to travel alone, they are to stay in the same lodging, and they are to pray psalms while traveling (*Lg. Rul.* 39).[28] Only monks in good standing may participate in the social life that work opens. Indeed, the community must reject the work of a disobedient monk as if it were a blemished sacrifice (*Lg. Rul.* 29).

The Lord and the apostle Paul commanded not only work but also prayer. And just as work overcame in some ways the otherwise necessary separations within the community, so also in prayer the entire community—men, women, children, full members, and candidates—worshiped as one. The community came together for prayer seven or eight times a day to sing psalms and read the Scriptures.[29] Even though Basil calls for change and variety in psalms and readings—for "when there is monotony, the soul wearies more readily and becomes a prey to distraction" but is refreshed and made vigilant by change and variety—it seems very clear that certain psalms were sung at particular hours (*Lg. Rul.* 37.3–5). Here are the hours of the community's prayer life in the form of a chart.

Orthos/Matins/Lauds (dawn, or perhaps just before)	Psalm 5:3, "O Lord, in the morning thou dost hear my voice; in the morning I prepare a sacrifice for thee, and watch."
Terce (the third hour)	Psalm 51 [50]:10–12, "Create in me a clean heart, O God, and put a new and right spirit within me."
Sext (noon, the sixth hour)	Psalm 91 [90]:5–6, "You will not fear the terror of the night, nor the arrow that flies by day, nor the pestilence that stalks in darkness, nor the destruction that wastes at noonday."
None (the ninth hour)	
Vespers (evening prayer)	
Compline (night prayer)	Psalm 91 [90]:5–6, "You will not fear the terror of the night, nor the arrow that flies by day, nor the pestilence that stalks in darkness, nor the destruction that wastes at noonday."
Midnight prayer	

Each prayer time "has its own special reminder of benefits received from God" (*Lg. Rul.* 37.3; 245). In Lauds, the soul's first movements are dedicated to God, and God is put before work and the other activities of the day. Prayer at midday protects the mind from slumber, and evening prayer is the occasion for thanksgiving and the examination of conscience. Basil exhorts:

> Let us give thanks for what has been given us during the day and for what we have done well, whether voluntary or involuntary, or an inadvertent fault in

word or deed or in the heart itself, making atonement for all things through prayer. For the review of past deeds is a great help against falling into the like again. (*Lg. Rul.* 37.4; 246)

It does not seem that this examination would be the occasion for confession to an elder, for the whole community is present, and confession was not public. Nevertheless this "review of past deeds" would certainly be propaedeutic to confession, whenever it occurred. At night prayer, the monks ask that their rest be without offense and free from fantasies (*Lg. Rul.* 37.5). All in all, the purpose of prayer is to turn the mind to God who is present so that it may rise to him according to its natural inclination.

The *Longer* and *Shorter Rules* do not much stress the reception of the Eucharist as part of the prayer life of the monks. It is obvious, nevertheless, that the community attended the Eucharist, for Basil is asked about the worthy reception of the Eucharist in one question (*Sh. Rul.* 309.Q), and whether or not the offering should take place in an ordinary house (*Sh. Rul.* 310.Q).[30] We might mention, in addition, that Basil makes reception of the Eucharist one of the necessary marks of a Christian in the *Morals* (21.1; 80.22). His fullest treatment of communion, however, is found in epistle 93 wherein he says that "to take communion every day, that is to say, to partake of the holy body and blood of Christ, is good and beneficial, . . . [but] we . . . take communion four times each week—on Sunday, on Wednesday, on Friday, and on Saturday—and on the other days only when there is a commemoration of a saint" (ep. 93.1; 2:145).[31]

Conclusion

Thus it is, in sum, that Basil's simple baptismal aspiration became a complex and well-ordered way of life in common. Over the years he realized evermore the implications of keeping the commands of the Lord. To keep the Lord's commands is to live a life set apart and yet with others. This in turn requires a set of complex rules governing admission to the community and the interaction of the various groups that are set apart. To keep the Lord's commands, the spiritually advanced must help the weak, and the weak must confess to and obey them. Finally, to keep the Lord's commands, all must work and pray with a single-minded focus on God, who will in turn provide for the needs of those who are living in common. In this way the monks, both elders and subordinates, will be ever more profoundly conformed to the humble Christ, "who was not ashamed of ministering to his own servants, but was willing to wait on the earth and clay that he has made and fashioned into man" (*Lg. Rul.* 43.2; 255).[32]

We began this treatment of Basil's asceticism with the point that for him there is one Christian life: there is no proper "lay" spirituality in contrast to a "religious" one. The theological root of this is that Basil holds a deeply realized eschatology—we might say a too-realized eschatology. In this he has something in common with the ascetic extremists from whom he distanced himself. Extreme asceticism fails to reckon with an intermediate stage in the Christian dispensation between the first and second advent of the Lord. These ascetics demanded that all Christians live according to the eschaton, wherein there is no marriage, no slavery, no gender subordination, no rich and poor, no bishops exercising authority, and no killing of animals to eat them. In this view of the Christian life, there is no room for a genuine living of the gospel in the secular order but only a replacement of the secular order with the eschatological. This, of course, is nothing short of revolutionary, both for the church and the state.

While our Basil clearly did not teach an eschatology that was nearly so realized, his views of property and marriage indicate his eschatological leanings.

8

Tradition and Creativity

Theology and Asceticism

Basil appreciated that he stood in a long line of Christian teachers and saints. Indeed, he felt the pain of being accused of breaking with this tradition, for the Spirit-fighters had charged him with liturgical and theological innovation. The catalog of fathers at the end of *On the Holy Spirit* is one of the more well-known and obvious places wherein Basil self-consciously draws on the thought and work of earlier Christian thinkers. He calls to his side of the argument Clement of Rome, Irenaeus, Dionysius of Rome, Dionysius of Alexandria, Origen, Eusebius of Caesarea, Julius Africanus, Athenogenes, Gregory the Wonder-Worker, Firmilian of Caesarea, and Meletius of Antioch (*On H. Sp.* 29.72–74). Basil's concluding comment on his catalog of fathers is an important clue to his overarching attitude toward the great Christians of the past. "What has been said," he writes, "is a sufficient defense for reasonable men: we accept a word, so beloved and agreeable to the saints, and confirmed by custom so long that it is shown to be authorized by the churches from the time when the Gospel was proclaimed until the present. Most of all it is pious and holy in its meaning" (*On H. Sp.* 29.75; 116). Basil deeply values custom, especially long custom, but he values more a meaning that is pious and holy—that is, meaning that truly accords with God's revelation in the Scriptures.

Basil felt an absolute obligation to be faithful to the Scriptures. When it came to his other sources, however, he was freer. Mark DelCogliano, who has much studied Basil's use of theological (and philosophical) sources, describes well Basil's practice:

His use of the tradition is always critical, selective, and creative. What he deemed archaic he jettisoned, what he considered valuable he preserved, what he thought incomplete he supplemented, what he judged insufficient he revised. And if at times the tradition was silent where he did not want it to be, Basil did not shy away from innovating according to his own lights. So in many of his writings we encounter a blend of retrieval and innovation as he makes the tradition of the fathers his own.[1]

DelCogliano here writes of Basil's theological sources, but his words describe equally well Basil's attitude toward his ascetic sources. Our present concern, then, is to offer, after a brief word on tradition, some examples that illustrate Basil's approach to the theological and ascetic tradition that he inherited. We will, at the same time, fill out the picture that has so far emerged of both his theology and his spirituality.

On Tradition

We tend to think of the history of dogma after the manner of a relay race. Indeed, the last century's foremost authority on tradition, Yves Congar, wrote that "an equally good simile [for tradition] would be that of the relay race, where the runners, at spaced intervals, pass an object from one to the other, a baton, for example, or a torch."[2] On this model, the Lord passed the baton to the apostles; the apostles to Clement of Rome, Polycarp, and Ignatius of Antioch; these to Justin Martyr and Irenaeus; and so on down to Athanasius, who handed the baton to Basil of Caesarea and the other Cappadocians.

This view of tradition was reinforced for centuries by false attributions. Famously we have the spurious letters of Ignatius of Antioch that draw a direct connection between him and the teaching of Chalcedon, and there is the well-known body of Clementine literature. The fourth century, too, abounds in spurious works and the false attributions to Basil and to Athanasius of works that blurred the distinctive concerns and characteristics of their respective theologies. For example, the fourth oration against the Arians, now known to be spurious, makes Athanasius more like-minded with the enemies of Marcellus of Ancrya (such as Basil) than he actually was. Or consider Basil's spurious epistle 8. It clearly and unequivocally confesses that the Holy Spirit is God and *homoousios* with the Father.[3] Again, there are the spurious fourth and fifth books of Basil's *Against Eunomius* that may have been written by Didymus the Blind, and whose effect was to make Basil closer to Athanasius, for there seem to be connections between *Against Eunomius* books four and five and Athanasius's *Letters to Serapion*.

I do not mean to imply that this tradition, made too neat by spurious works, is all loss, a regrettable nuisance to scholars and an ancient roadblock thrown in the way of our genuine knowledge of the Christian past. On the contrary, such works offer something very important. Put in its most positive formulation, we can see many of the false attributions and spurious works as their authors' guidance in the interpretation of the key figures of the tradition. The spurious Ignatian letters, for example, direct us to read Ignatius in such a way that he is prescient of Chalcedon.[4] Or again, it is as if the author of Athanasius's fourth oration against the Arians is advising us, "Do not take in the wrong way the friendship and ecclesial communion between Athanasius and Marcellus: the former did not make the latter's mistake."

John Henry Newman has a wonderful way of interpreting the dubious side of tradition. In his University Sermon 15, on "The Theory of Developments in Religious Doctrine," Newman explains the value of fables and "mythical representations": the former are "economies or accommodations, being truths and principles cast into that form in which they will be most vividly recognized," while the latter "may be considered [as] facts or narratives, untrue, but like the truth, intended to bring out the action of some principle, point of character, and the like."[5] Newman comments on the spurious tradition that St. Ignatius was the child whom Jesus took into his arms. Although the tradition is unfounded, "it realizes to us his special relation to Christ and his Apostles."[6] These sorts of traditions Newman calls "the spontaneous produce of religious feeling under imperfect knowledge."[7] He eloquently and provocatively sums up this most positive approach to historically suspect tradition:

> If the alleged facts did not occur, they ought to have occurred (if I may so speak); they are such as might have occurred, and would have occurred, under circumstances; they belong to the parties to whom they are attributed, potentially, if not actually; or the like of them did occur; or occurred to others similarly circumstanced, though not to those very persons.[8]

What Newman here says about deeds, we might also say about written works. For example, Athanasius in fact did not write the fourth book against the Arians, or Basil never really called the Spirit "God" and "consubstantial with the Father" as epistle 8 has him do, but they both would have done so "under circumstances." Of course, we cannot uncritically accept such a reading when the tradition suggests it. We must entertain the possibility that not only did Athanasius not write the fourth book but also there were no circumstances under which he would have. And so too for Basil.

What modern critical scholarship, after years of painstaking study, has come to realize, Basil already knew, for he was well aware of the differences between himself and Athanasius, or the similarities between himself and the theological tradition that he following Athanasius was supposed to have rejected. Basil well knew which ascetic practices he drew from his early sojourn in Egypt and Syria, which were from the Anatolian asceticism native to Cappadocia, and which he invented himself. What Basil knew, however, he left for posterity to figure out, and the task has been made exponentially more difficult by the emergence of spurious works, both ascetic and theological, and difficulties in various manuscript traditions.

Tradition and Creativity in Theology

Among the theological sources available to Basil, a few stand out as particularly important. Of course there is Origen who cast a long shadow over everybody. More immediately for Basil were the towering figures of Athanasius and Eusebius of Caesarea. Finally, Basil was very familiar with the thought of the so-called Semi-Arians, or Homoiousians—Basil of Ancyra, George of Laodicea, and (at least at one point in his theological life) Eustathius of Sebaste.

The question of Origen's influence on Basil, as on many other fourth-century Christian thinkers, is vast and complicated. It will suffice for us to focus on the interesting findings of Mark DelCogliano in his study of Basil's sermon on the theophany, *Homily on the Holy Generation of Christ*. After a brief description of the mystery of the Son's eternal birth from the Father and a beautiful discourse of the reason for the incarnation,[9] Basil turns to the substance of his sermon, an explanation of Matthew's account of the birth of the Lord. DelCogliano concludes that Basil borrowed from Origen in seven different ways that range from simple adoption to rejection.[10] We might reduce DelCogliano's seven down to three: Basil uses Origen simply, without editing; he uses him but edits what he borrows (the changes being minor or major, preserving Origen's purpose or putting his arguments to a new one); and he uses him only to reject what he borrows. When Basil explains Matthew 1:18—"When his mother Mary had been betrothed to Joseph, before they came together she was found to be with child of the Holy Spirit"—he simply takes over from Origen one of the reasons why the incarnation took place in the womb of a virgin who was betrothed to a man. "Again I turn the matter over in my mind," writes Origen, "and ask why, when God had decided that the Savior should be born of a virgin, he chose not a girl who was not betrothed, but precisely one who was already betrothed."[11] If it were not so, Origen reasons, then "the state of virginity would be a cause of disgrace," when the Virgin was seen "growing big with a child."[12] While Basil does not take Origen's very words, he does take the point and without any modification.[13]

Origen adds another reason that the Lord's conception took place in the womb of a married virgin, and it is an even clearer instance of Basilian dependence. Origen quotes Ignatius of Antioch who taught that the virginity of Mary escaped the notice of the devil, "the ruler of this age."[14] Basil quotes the same text from Ignatius, and DelCogliano makes a couple of points about his use of Origen here. First, Basil does not mention Ignatius by name, while Origen does. And second, Basil expands Origen's point by explaining why God would conceal the virginal conception from the devil: the virgin's betrothal was a decoy for the devil, who, ever since he heard the prophecy of Isaiah that the Virgin would conceive, lay in wait to ambush virginity.[15] DelCogliano distinguishes this use of Origen from the first, for here Basil expands the point that he had taken over while in the first instance he borrowed without any modification.

Sometimes Basil will take a point from Origen but set it to a new purpose, as he does in his defense of the perpetual virginity of Mary. Basil takes over three different arguments of Origen, though in each case Origen was concerned not with those who denied the perpetual virginity of Mary but some other polemic. The first text that Basil uses is from Origen's *Commentary on Matthew*. Origen was trying to explain Jesus's words that some will not taste death until "they see the Son of man coming in his kingdom" (Matt. 16:28), and he focuses on the scriptural meaning of "until." When the Lord said, "I am with you always, to the close of the age" (Matt. 28:20), no one would "dare to say that after the consummation of the age the Son of God will be no longer with the disciples."[16] Basil applies Origen's point about the meaning of "until" to Matthew 1:25—"but knew her not until she had borne a son."[17]

In his homily on Luke 2:21–24, Origen takes aim at the Gnostic dualism that posited an evil God of the physical world and of the law of the Old Testament, and a good God, the Father of Jesus Christ. Why would the good God have made his Son subject to the law of an evil God? Mary and Joseph, when they brought Jesus to the temple, are said to obey the Scriptures, and Origen makes clear the texts of the Old Testament that they are obeying. The Lord had commanded Moses, "Consecrate to me all the first-born; whatever is the first to open the womb among the people of Israel" (Exod. 13:2); or, as Numbers has it, "For they [the Levites] are wholly given to me from among the people of Israel; . . . I have taken them for myself" (Num. 8:16). Origen goes on to offer a spiritual interpretation of "every male that opens the womb": "in the case of every other woman, it is not the birth of an infant but intercourse with a man that opens the womb."[18]

Basil seems to be taking over Origen's point when he writes that Jesus "is called the firstborn because he was the first one to open the womb of his mother."[19] "Firstborn" here does not mean that Jesus was the first of Mary's children, thus implying that there were others. Rather, it means that Jesus was the first baby to open the womb of his mother because he was the first who had no human father. Mary was the first mother whose womb was not opened by intercourse with a man but by a baby.

There is a third and final point that Basil takes from Origen to defend Mary's perpetual virginity.[20] Origen relates a tradition about Zechariah and in so doing had no intention of defending the perpetual virginity of Mary. Basil turns Origen's point to this purpose. "It is also clear," Basil writes, "from the story about Zechariah that Mary was always a virgin. For there is an account, and it has been handed down to us from the tradition, that Zechariah entrusted

Mary to the place for the virgins after conceiving the Lord."[21] Zechariah was killed by the people, not so much for transgressing the law concerning the place of virgins in the temple, but because "by his actions he established that incredible and famous sign: a virgin gave birth and her virginity was not destroyed."[22] Zechariah was a martyr for the new law, not a transgressor of the old.[23] Thus, Basil redirected what he borrowed from Origen.

Before we take our leave of Origen, let us consider, again with the help of DelCogliano, an example of Basil's rejection of his interpretation of a biblical text. Basil uses Origen to explain the identity of the Magi and the reason for their journey to see the infant Lord. Basil rejects, however, Origen's explanation of the star of Bethlehem: Origen thought that the star was a comet.[24]

Basil, however, disagrees and teaches that the star was a star, though "new and unfamiliar."[25] While, as DelCogliano notes, Basil refused Origen's explanation on scientific grounds—first, comets are on the whole motionless "since their combustion is confined to a circumscribed place" (*Hom. gen. Chr.* 5), while the star of Bethlehem was not, and, second, the star of Bethlehem did not come to be in the same way as a comet—Basil seems "keen to distance himself from any hint of an astrological explanation."[26] Origen had linked the appearance of comets to significant events here below, such as the succession of kings, while Basil calls this "idle curiosity" and offers a completely naturalistic explanation for their appearance: "When the air surrounding the earth overflows and is diffused into the ethereal region, as it rises there it produces something thick and turbid that is like fuel for a fire."[27]

Basil shows the same deference and freedom with Eusebius of Caesarea. He is willing to use Eusebius when he thinks him helpful but does not hesitate to correct or differ when he sees fit. As an example of the former, we may consider Basil's adoption of Eusebius's interpretation of Proverbs 8:22 wherein Wisdom says, "he created me at the beginning of his work"[28] Basil treats the passage once in his corpus and very briefly. Eunomius had used the text to prove that the Son is a creature, and Basil makes three points on the verse: it "is said only once in all Scriptures"; the book of Proverbs is obscure, so that "no one may take anything from it that is either indisputable or crystal-clear"; and "other translators, who have hit upon the meaning of the Hebrew words in a more appropriate way, render it as 'he acquired me' instead of *he created me*" (*Ag. Eun.* 2.20; 160). As DelCogliano points out, Basil took two of these three points from Eusebius.[29] Basil is much less confident than Eusebius, however, that the meaning of the text can be discerned with any certainty. On this point, "Basil goes his own way, rejecting the exegetical optimism of both Eusebius and Athanasius."[30]

We find a far more significant example of Basil's theological independence of Eusebius in his understanding of "unbegotten." We recall that "unbegotten" was central to the theology of the Eunomians who defined God as "unbegottenness." Basil's understanding of this word, then, is crucial not only for his refutation of the Eunomians but also for his own theological understanding of the Father and the Son. For Eusebius, as for so many, "unbegotten" was synonymous with "eternal." Basil, however, parts with this tradition and teaches that the two terms do not communicate the same thing (*Ag. Eun.* 2.17).[31]

This point is of the highest importance, for so long as "unbegotten" remains synonymous with "eternal," and "unbegotten" describes the Father, then the Son can never be eternal in the same sense as the Father but must be thought of as ontologically subordinate to him. We could put the point another way. In the line of theologians who stood in the tradition of Eusebius (and, ultimately, of Origen) there emerged a movement, as DelCogliano puts it, to decentralize "unbegotten," to make this concept less important in the theology of the Trinity and to make the biblical names Father and Son more important. Significant progress in this decentralization was made by Basil of Ancrya and George of Laodicea, who used Athanasius,[32] but the crucial move, the final and clear break between "unbegotten" and "eternal" was made by Basil.[33]

While Basil moves beyond Basil of Ancyra and George of Laodicea, the chief architects of Homoiousian theology, he knew their work well and made use of it. His understanding of "unbegotten," which we just mentioned to differentiate Basil from the Homoiousians, is, in part, derived from them. In *Against Eunomius*, Basil insists that "there is no doctrine in the gospel of our salvation more important than faith in the Father and the Son" (*Ag Eun.* 2.22; 163). Those who deny this, he says, err in the ways of either pagans or Jews. Christians do not put "faith in the Creator and something made . . . [but] have been sealed in the Father and the Son through the grace received in baptism" (*Ag. Eun.* 2.22; 163). Before Basil, his namesake from Ancyra and Athanasius had made similar points, and he echoes their thought and language in using the baptismal formula of Matthew 28:19 to displace "unbegotten" from its position of prominence in the theology of the Eunomians.[34]

St. Basil draws also on George of Laodicea in this polemic against the Eunomians over "unbegotten."[35] Attacking the centrality of "unbegotten" in Eunomius's theology, Basil writes:

> For my part, I would say that we would be justified in passing over . . . "unbegotten" . . . on the grounds that it is nowhere found in Scripture and furthermore is the primary building block of their blasphemy. The term "Father" means the same as "unbegotten," yet it has the additional advantage of implying a relation, thereby introducing the notion of the Son. . . . [And] we should not designate him the "unbegotten" instead of "Father," at least if we are not going to claim a wisdom superior to the teachings of the Savior. (*Ag. Eun.* 1.5; 93–94)

Thus, for Basil, "Father" is superior to "unbegotten" because the latter is unscriptural, it is not a relative term like "Father" is, and it is not a word sanctioned by the Lord, while "Father" is (Matt. 28:19). George of Laodicea makes these same points but in a slightly different way.[36] It is often said that Basil, at the beginning of his theological career, moved in Homoiousian circles, and this is true. We have seen he was dear friends with Eustathius of Sebaste, in the company of whom he wrote *Against Eunomius*, and he attended the 359 Council of Constantinople with Basil of Ancyra. And yet we cannot adequately describe Basil's theology using simple Homoiousian categories.[37] It is Basil's critical use of his sources that explains these two facts. Furthermore, Basil's moments of independence or expansion reveal his deep insight into the truths in defense of which he marshaled and adapted his sources.

Let us turn now to Basil and Athanasius. Even after modern critical scholarship does its work of identifying spurious books and letters, and thus removing the easy evidence that Athanasius passed on the baton to Basil, it remains the case that the two great theologians have much in common and on the most important of theological matters. For example, both make a strict distinction between God and the world, between the uncreated and the created, and both insist on the full transcendence of the Son: for them, it is not the case that the Son is God immanent and the Father, God transcendent. They also shared some common ground in ecclesio-political matters: both agreed, for instance, that the creed of Nicaea together with a confession that the Spirit is not a creature should be the basic terms of doctrinal communion in the church. These similarities and others provoke us to ask the obvious question: is there a relationship of dependence standing behind these common themes and interests? We might treat the matter by investigating three questions. Did Basil adopt Athanasius's view of the relationship between God and the world?[38] Did Basil take over Athanasius's view of the relationship between Father and Son? And was Basil influenced by Athanasius's treatment of the Holy Spirit?

Unlike many of his theological opponents, Athanasius made a strict distinction between God and the world, between uncreated and created. There is no middle ground, no creature unlike the other creatures, as the "Arians" would have it. This means, of course, that the Son does not occupy the place between the almighty Father and his creation; rather, the Son is as transcendent as the Father and in the incarnation the all-transcendent becomes immanent.

Basil is onto the same insight and articulates a strict distinction between God and the world. One of his most eloquent expressions of this truth is his refutation of the position that the Spirit occupies a middle position between God and the world: he is neither servant nor master but free. "O the pitiful boldness," exclaims Basil in a text we have considered once before, "of those who say such things. What do I lament more, their stupidity or their blasphemy? They insult the dogmas of divinity with human analogies, and they thus attempt to apply to the divine and unspeakable nature the custom that differences of rank vary, without considering the fact that no man is a slave by nature" (*On H. Sp.* 20.51; 87). Thus, for Basil, there are no degrees of divinity. God—Father, Son, and Holy Spirit—is master, and creation is slave. If the Spirit "is created," says Basil, "he is clearly a slave along with everything else, for 'everything,' Scripture says, 'is your slave' (Ps. 119 [118]:91); but if he is above creation, he participates in the kingship" (*On H. Sp.* 20.51; 89).[39]

Even though Basil and Athanasius have the same insight, there is no evidence of dependency. On the one hand, Athanasius never uses Basil's image of Master, Slave, and Free. Indeed, Athanasius never cites Psalm 120 [119]:91.[40] On the other hand, Basil never uses some of the typically Athanasian ways to describe God's relationship to the world: he does not say that God exceeds all being but is good;[41] he does not speak of God "remaining" with his creation;[42] he does not stress God's philanthropy;[43] and he does not employ the argument that a transcendently indifferent God is really weak rather than strong.[44]

One of the ways in which Basil and Athanasius overcome the Greek view that God cannot be both transcendent and immanent is to insist on the full transcendence of the Son, whose immanence is made obvious in the incarnation. One of Athanasius's favorite biblical texts on this theme is John 14:10, "I am in the Father and the Father in me. . . . The Father who dwells in me does his works." We can easily see how Athanasius saw in this text an immanent Father and a transcendent Son. Basil, on the other hand, cites John 14:10a only once, in a sermon in praise of a martyr,[45] and he never cites John 14:10b. Athanasius is fond of calling the Son the proper Word of God;[46] Basil never uses the expression "proper Word" or "proper offspring" (*gennēma idion*).

Athanasius had become an ardent defender of the creed of Nicaea's *homoousios* and argued that it was the best word for refuting the Arians and securing a proper understanding of the Son's transcendence. Basil had been far less certain. Like many other theologians of the time, the word gave him serious pause. Yet around 365 Basil confessed that he preferred *homoousios* because the alternatives were more open to perversion. In 359, Athanasius wrote *De synodis* with the expressed purpose of addressing the concerns that people like Basil had with *homoousios*. Did Basil read *De synodis*? Archibald Robertson, who edited John Henry Newman's translations of Athanasius, thought so. He cites two letters, epistles 8 and 9, of Basil that bear the influence of *De synodis*. The trouble here is that epistle 8, which more clearly shows dependency, has been proven inauthentic.[47]

We are left, then, with the possibility that Basil's epistle 9 echoes *De synodis*. Epistle 9 was a watershed for Basil, for here he first indicates that he has changed his mind on *homoousios*. There is no obvious textual dependency, but these documents share some interesting points. First, Basil is now well aware that "like" is open to perversion, and, indeed, Athanasius very clearly exposed the Arian abuse of the word. Second, Basil says that "we are frequently accustomed to entertain the idea of 'likeness' in the case of indistinct resemblances, coming anything but close to the originals" (ep. 9.3; NPNF 2, 8: 123). Finally, Basil accepts *homoousios* insofar as it indicates no variation (*parallagē*) of the Only-begotten's *ousia* in relation to that of the Father (ep. 9.3).

If these similarities point to dependency on *De synodis*, the dependency was not slavish. First, Athanasius never uses the phrase "variation of being" (*parallagē ousias*), the rejection of which is Basil's stated reason for accepting *homoousios*. Second, in *De synodis* Athanasius defends Dionysius of Alexandria (d. 264–65) who rejected *homoousios* to combat Sabellianism but then accepted it in a letter to Dionysius of Rome.[48] Athanasius even wrote a separate work in defense of Dionysius.[49] He refuses to allow the Arians to co-opt his own predecessor's authority. Basil, however, judges Dionysius with a tempered severity. While Dionysius meant well, his teaching nonetheless served as the seed of the doctrine of "unlikeness." "It would have been quite sufficient," writes Basil, for Dionysius "to have pointed out that the Father and Son are not identical in substance [*tauton tō hypokeimenō*]," but he went too far when he posited also a "difference of substance [*ousias diaphoran*], diminution of power [*dynameōs hyphesin*], and variableness of glory [*doxēs parallagēn*]" (ep. 9, 2; NPNF 2, 8: 123).

Finally, we come to our last point of comparison between Basil and Athanasius: the latter's *Letters to Serapion* and the former's third book against Eunomius and *On the Holy Spirit*.[50] Again, on the surface there seems to be a relationship here. Both reject any notion that the Holy Spirit is an angel;[51] both reject the argument that if the Spirit is not a creature, then he must be a son;[52] both appeal to the baptismal formula and call the Holy Spirit "seal";[53] and both refute their opponents' prooftext, Amos 4:13 ("He who has formed thunder and created the Spirit").[54] But again the thematic similarities do not point with any certainty to a textual dependence.[55]

Mark DelCogliano, in fact, has tried to show that Basil used not Athanasius but Didymus the Blind in *Contra Eunomium* 3.[56] So, the argument goes, Basil and Didymus refute the Spirit-fighters' use of Amos 4:13 and John 1:3 (they included the Holy Spirit in the "all things" created through the Word), while Athanasius makes no mention of the latter prooftext.[57] What clinches DelCogliano's argument, however, is that both Didymus and Basil (and not Athanasius) call attention to the tense of the participle in Amos 4:13 (*ho ktizōn pneuma*). Because the present participle is used and indicates repeated action, the "spirit" in question must be the wind and not the Holy Spirit. In addition, Basil and Didymus (and not Athanasius) make the same points in their respective exegesis of John 1:3. The Spirit is not created; he is not among the "all things" that come into being through the Word; and the Spirit's nature surpasses created nature. DelCogliano's arguments are persuasive, and they call for a closer study of the relationship among Basil, Didymus, and Athanasius.

The similarities in theme, in argument, and especially in exegetical details that lead us to posit a relationship between Basil and Didymus are not to be found in *On the Holy Spirit* and Athanasius's *Letters to Serapion*. First, Athanasius and Basil both take up 1 Timothy 5:21. This text is crucial in the argument of the first letter to Serapion because Athanasius's opponents, the Tropici, use the text to defend their position that the Spirit is a creature. Paul had written to Timothy, "In the presence of god and of Christ Jesus and of the elect angels I charge you to keep these rules without favor, doing nothing from partiality" (1 Tim. 5:21). The Tropici, according to Athanasius, say that because Paul "listed the angels only after he mentioned God and Christ . . . , the Spirit must be classified with the angels, and . . . belongs to their order and is an angel that is greater than the others" mentions God and Christ and then the angels, the Spirit must be counted with the angels, and belong himself to their category, and be an angel greater than the others" (*To Serap.* 1.10.4; 69). Athanasius counters this interpretation with an extended refutation. First, he makes the point that Scripture nowhere calls the Holy Spirit an angel. Second, he shows the absurdity of inferring from Paul's omission of the Holy Spirit that the Spirit is not of the Godhead. Paul need not mention the Spirit by name, for when one member of the Trinity is mentioned, the others are implied. "If the Son is named," Athanasius writes, "the Father is in the Son, and the Spirit is not external to the Word" (*To Serap.* 1.14.6; 75). Finally, Athanasius explains the appropriateness of Paul's calling the angels to witness. Quoting Matthew 18:10, Athanasius thinks that Paul may be invoking the angels to witness because they always look upon "'*the face of the Father who is in heaven*,' on behalf of *the little ones* in the Church" (*To Serap.* 1.14.7; 75).

Like Athanasius, Basil too offers an extended interpretation of 1 Timothy 5:21 to oppose the Spirit-fighters' use of the text. We must first notice here that Basil's opponents differed from Athanasius's. Athanasius's opponents use 1 Timothy 5:21 to affirm that the Spirit is an angel; Basil's use it to make that point that just because the Holy Spirit is often numbered with the Father and the Son, he need not also be glorified with them, for in 1 Timothy 5:21 the angels are numbered with God and Christ but they are not worshiped with them. Even still, both Athanasius and Basil offer an explanation of why Paul calls the angels to witness. Athanasius mentions the role of angels in God's providence; Basil dwells on the presence of the angels at the judgment, for whoever denies the Son of Man "before men will be denied before the angels of God" (Luke 12:9; *On H. Sp.* 12.29). If Basil knew Athanasius's interpretation, he did not use it.

John 4 is a second scriptural text that Basil and Athanasius take differently. Here in John's Gospel the Truth himself bears witness that "true worshippers will worship the Father in spirit and in truth" (John 4:23; see vv. 21–24). Athanasius marshals a number of other scriptural texts to argue that here Jesus is saying that true worship is offered in him and in the Holy Spirit (*To Serap.* 1.33.2). He mentions John 14:6, "I am . . . the truth"; Psalm 43 [42]:3, "Send out thy light and thy truth"; and John 15:26 (cf. 14:17), "I shall send to you [the Paraclete] from the Father, even the Spirit of Truth, who proceeds from the Father."

Basil makes the same point but in his own way. With Athanasius he argues that "in spirit and in truth" is a reference to the Holy Spirit and the Son, and like Athanasius, Basil weaves into his interpretation other scriptural texts. Basil, though, makes no mention of Psalm 43 [42]:3 nor of John 15:26; rather, Basil draws on Colossians 1:15 and Hebrews 1:3. The Samaritan woman had wrongly thought that worship is in a particular place, and the Lord, says Basil, corrected her. He says:

> Just as we speak of worship in the Son as worship in the Image of God the Father, so also we speak of worship in the Spirit as worship in him who manifests the divinity of the Lord. Therefore, in worship the Holy Spirit is inseparable from the Father and the Son, for if you are outside of him, you will not worship at all while if you are in him, you will in no way separate him from God. . . . For it is impossible to see the Image of the invisible God, except in the illumination of the Spirit, and it is impossible for him who fixes his eyes on the image to separate the light from the image. . . . We behold the radiance of the glory of God through the illumination of the Spirit, and, then, we are led up through the character to him of whom he is the character and identical seal. (*On H. Sp.* 26.64; 103)

Again, we see that Basil's interpretation is different from Athanasius's.

I wish to mention one final example of a superficial similarity between Basil's and Athanasius's argument for the divinity of the Holy Spirit. Both use the rite of baptism as a weapon against their opponents. But here again the similarity is not profound and certainly not impressive enough to make us think that Basil is developing the thought of Athanasius. Athanasius warns his opponents, the Tropici, that if they count the Spirit with creatures, then the rite of initiation that they think they "perform does not initiate completely into the divinity, for a creature is mixed with it" (*To Serap.* 1.29.2; 98). "Who will join you to God," Athanasius asks them, "if you do not have the Spirit of God himself but the spirit of the created order?" (*To Serap.* 1.29.2; 98). The baptism of the Tropici is "rendered insecure" because it mixes the divine and the created; it "is divided here and there" (*To Serap.* 1.29.3; 98).

Basil's use of baptism in *On the Holy Spirit* is far more extensive than Athanasius's. Even still, Basil does not seem to be picking up Athanasius's argument. Athanasius implied that heretical baptism profits one nothing, while Basil says so directly. If one renounces the trinitarian faith into which he was baptized, he is turning back to idols and making himself a stranger to the promises of God (*On H. Sp.* 10.26). In another place, Basil explains baptism as the means whereby we imitate the death and resurrection of Christ (*On H. Sp.* 15.35), and in still another he correlates baptism with faith and doxology. "Let them teach us not to baptize as we have received, or not to believe as we have been baptized, or not to give glory as we have believed" (*On H. Sp.* 27.68; 80). In all of these texts, there are no echoes of Athanasius.

So far I have been stressing the differences between Basil's *On the Holy Spirit* and Athanasius's *Letters to Serapion*, but now I would like to turn to a piece of evidence that may tell for rather than against Athanasian influence on Basil. At a council in 362 in Alexandria, Athanasius set out the terms whereby the church might achieve communion in faith. At the heart of these terms is a confession of the creed of Nicaea, but Athanasius wished to be sure that those who confessed three *hypostaseis* in God were not "Arian," and so he asked them what they meant. Athanasius reported their response, which included a confession of the consubstantiality of the Son and a confession that the Holy Spirit is "not a creature, nor external, but proper to and inseparable from the Essence of the Father and the Son."[58] It was precisely this that Basil set out as the terms of communion for Eustathius of Sebaste: he had to confess the creed of Nicaea and anathematize, Basil writes, "all who call the Holy Spirit a creature, and all who so think; all who do not confess that he is holy by nature, as the Father is holy by nature, and the Son is holy by nature, and refuse Him His place in the blessed divine nature" (ep. 125.3; NPNF 2, 8: 195). Basil goes on to give arguments for the divinity of the Spirit that appear also in *On the Holy Spirit*.

This passage typifies the basic relationship between Basil and Athanasius. Here there is a clear reminiscence of Athanasius and a similarity in context, but there is not enough evidence to draw the conclusion that Basil has Athanasius's work on his lap as he wrote his own. If Basil was influenced by Athanasius here, he felt the freedom to put Athanasius's point in his own words and in the context of his own distinctive theological emphases. Similarities of theme and argument give rise to the hope of establishing a significant relationship, but this hope quickly dissipates into an inconclusive wonder. If Basil took anything from Athanasius, he left behind the hallmarks of Athanasius's thought and language.

Tradition and Creativity in Asceticism

It was not only in his theological thought but also in his ascetic that Basil proved himself to be a traditional but innovative thinker, strictly bound to the Scriptures though more or less informed by the Christian ascetic tradition. If in some ways the tradition has underestimated the theological creativity and independence of St. Basil, the originality of his ascetic thought has for long centuries been appreciated, at least insofar as he is regarded as a founder of Eastern (and, indirectly, Western) asceticism. Modern scholars have in various ways confirmed and corrected this basic insight of the tradition.

We can begin with a few simple questions, at least simple to ask if not to answer. Where did Basil get his ascetic theology? What were the influences upon him? What in his ascetic thought is a re-presentation of the traditions available to him, and what is genuinely new? W. K. L. Clarke located three basic sources for Basil's ascetic thought: "the unorganized ascetic life which was found in Cappadocia and Pontus during Basil's childhood and youth, of which such striking examples had existed in his own family circle"; Pachomian monastic life; and Basil's own contribution, "the innovations which commended themselves to his mature judgment as desirable in view of the needs of the Church and character of his fellow countrymen."[59] Thus, for Clarke, "Basilian monachism was composed of three strands": the first is of "slight importance," and Basil's own ideas were far more important than his debt to Pachomius.[60]

Only part of Clarke's assessment has stood the test of time. Essentially, his first strand, asceticism native to Cappadocia, has assumed far greater significance than he realized, and his second strand, Pachomian influence, far less.[61] Andrea Sterk is right, I think, when she writes that "Basil had very little exposure to Pachomian patterns of monastic life."[62] Basil's sojourn in the late 350s to Syria and Egypt had more to do with finding Eustathius of Sebaste than with "collecting data for his own monastic establishment."[63] Moreover, "it is certain," Emmanuel Amand de Mendieta notes, "that Basil himself never went to the Thebaid (Upper Egypt) and that he did not visit Pachomian monasteries."[64] The Pachomian and the Basilian ways of life, in fact, differ greatly: Basil's was more theological and biblical; Basil's was more communitarian; Basil saw a need for a novitiate whereas Pachomius did not; Basil established a harmonious equilibrium between work and prayer; Basil forbids severity in ascetic practice; and Basil put monastic communities in the service of the church.[65]

So Clarke overestimated the influence of Pachomius on Basil (even as he asserted Basil's independence of Pachomius) and underestimated the influence of Eustathius of Sebaste. Anna Silvas stands at the end of a long line of scholars who have underscored the importance of Eustathius and the ascetic movement around him. So what in Basil's thought may be traced to Eustathius? The question is difficult to answer because, as we saw early on in this study, Eustathius was a moving target. Basil certainly disavowed the ascetic practices of the Eustathian ascetic extremists who were condemned at the Synod of Gangra, but so did Eustathius himself. It seems safe to say that Eustathius's influence was strongest in Basil's early ascetic practice and theology—indeed, Silvas says that in the 360s Basilian and Eustathian communities would be indistinguishable (Silvas, 86)—but that Eustathius's influence grew weaker over time as Basil came into his own as a leader of ascetic communities and a mature theologian of the ascetic life.[66]

Basil was inspired by Eustathius's holiness, but the latter's monastic practice was clearly a starting point rather than an end. Concretely speaking, Basil saw in the bishop Eustathius an urban asceticism put to the service of the church, and before Basil established a hospice, Eustathius had done so.[67] There is good reason to think, however, that Basil's ascetic thought is much more than the working out of principles he took over from Eustathius, for this view underestimates both the role of Basil's own family in his monastic development and the power of his mind. Amand de Mendieta overstates the case when he says that Basil's *Rules* "could be considered, in large part, as the spiritual property" of Eustathius.[68] By 363, Basil's family had become an organized ascetic community with separate houses for male and female members.[69] We might see this as the natural and logical consequence of his sister Macrina's ascetic aspirations. Silvas suggests that the ascetic transformation that took place in Basil's family, culminating with the profession of his brother Peter, was very important in Basil's life. Perhaps Basil's thought on the ascetic life moved his family in the direction of a more formal arrangement, or "perhaps Basil met the final synthesis of community arrangements at Annisa when he returned to Pontos in early 363, and it then crystallized for him the tenor of his own groping toward the cenobitic life" (Silvas, 93). In whichever direction the influence ran—and it could well have been mutual—Macrina and Peter, and not just Eustathius, had something to do with Basil's emerging ascetic theology that eventually found its most mature form in the *Longer* and *Shorter Rules*.

Besides Eustathius and his own family, there is yet another driving force behind Basil's ascetic thinking, and this may be *the* driving force. We must mention (again) in this context Basil's devotion to Scripture. He exercised the great powers of his mind upon the Word of God and ever strove to discern the way of life commanded therein. *On Judgment* had diagnosed the problems in the church as a failure to follow Scripture. The *Moralia* is little more than a collection of New Testament passages given subheadings and arranged thematically. From about the mid-360s, Basil had begun to "interiorize" Scripture and the process was near complete by the time the Great Asceticon reaches its final form (Silvas, 88). Basil's ascetic theology developed as much from his own study of Scripture as it did from the influence of his friends and family.

Let us consider now two very concrete examples of the originality of Basil's ascetic thought: double monasteries and dispositions.[70] Just as Basil reworked the trinitarian theologies of his predecessors and contemporaries and reformulated them according to his own lights, so he did not invent his understanding of the double monastery whole cloth; rather, it was in the lived experience of his own community and that of Annesi "that his ideas took shape and later became 'codified.'"[71] The double monastery is an icon of Basilian anthropology, of redeemed man, male and female, and Basil's answer both to mixed monasteries, wherein men and women cohabitated, and to the anthropological and eschatological theory that lay behind it.

Augustine Holmes is right, I think, to emphasize the eschatological motivation behind the practice of male and female celibates cohabitating and other controverted practices (such as women ascetics wearing men's clothing). Texts like Galatians 3:28—"There is neither Jew nor Greek, there is neither slave nor free, there is neither male nor female; for you are all one in Christ"—and Luke 20:34–36—"The sons of this age marry and are given in marriage; but those who are accounted worthy to attain to that age and to the resurrection from the dead neither marry nor are given in marriage, for they cannot die any more, because they are equal to angels"—were taken to mean that "through celibacy and ascetic struggle the lost likeness to God is restored, sexual differences are transcended and the life of the resurrection is lived on earth."[72] It is a distorted and "over-realized" eschatology that stands behind the ascetic extremism condemned by the Synod of Gangra. In the ascetic eschaton made real now, there is no marriage, no slavery, no institutional church, no feasting on Sundays, no male and female (and, therefore, no gender-specific dress or hairstyle). Thus the extremists advocated one spouse leaving another to become an ascetic, slaves abandoning masters, separation from the local bishop and his liturgies, fasting on Sundays, and the same dress and hairstyles for men and women. For these ascetics, the secular order between the first and second coming of the Lord has no legitimacy; it is the age that has passed.

While Basil clearly sees the ascetic life as the living out of the resurrected life, he does not make the mistake of devaluing sexual differentiation or of underestimating sexual passion and temptation in the ascetic, resurrected life this side of heaven. Holmes makes the interesting observation that Basil never cites Galatians 3:28 in the *Rules*, and he challenges Stramara's view that the Galatians text served as the theological ground for the equality of men and women as they lived ascetic lives in double monasteries. Holmes thinks that the Galatians text is the theological charter for the mixed monasteries of the ascetic extremists rather than the double monasteries of the sort that Basil advocated.[73] Indeed, the double monastery is Basil's reforming answer to what he viewed as a dangerous mixing of the sexes in contradiction of the demands of the gospel. In Basil's *Rules*, the double monastery preserves male and female communion in governance of the community, in prayer, and in work, all without jeopardizing chastity.[74]

Daniel Stramara eloquently sums up Basil's achievement in molding the existing ascetic practices of his time into the way of life of the double monastery: "Basil of Caesarea was a theologian of vision who not only provided for the experiential needs of monks and nuns, but supplied the theological and spiritual inspiration for their lives shared chastely together in one community mirroring the apostolic body of believers."[75] Basil would refuse, of course, to see himself as an innovator. Double monasticism was nothing new; rather, "it embodied the charism of the apostolic community of men and women and carried on the living tradition of the church [and] was the prophetic witness to the equality of men and women in Christ, forming one *adelphotēs*," one brotherhood.[76] Stramara credits Basil for the enduring tradition of double monasticism, from the fourth century on.

The other example that I wish to offer of Basil's creativity in ascetic theology or spirituality is his profound understanding of disposition, *diathesis*. Basil's spirituality rests, Augustine Holmes points out, on four pillars: withdrawal or separation, the goal (*skopos*) of a life pleasing to God, disposition (*diathesis*), and the memory of God.[77] *Shorter Rules* 196, on food and drink, recapitulates all of the pillars and implies the relations they have one to another. One eats and drinks to the glory of God

> through mindfulness of God our benefactor, and by a disposition of soul that is witnessed in the comportment of the body, so that one does not eat carelessly, but as one who always has God as overseer, and by keeping as one's goal at mealtime not to eat as a *slave of the stomach* (cf. Rom. 16:18) for pleasure, but as God's worker for strength to fulfill one's tasks according to the commandment of Christ. (*Sh. Rul.* 196; 379–80)[78]

The end comes first. That is to say the goal (*skopos*) of pleasing God, the aspiration to be a Christian ascetic, comes before all else. One will not remember God or develop a good disposition or bother to withdraw from the world unless one first presses "on toward the goal for the prize of the upward call of God in Christ Jesus" (Phil. 3:14).[79] Holmes indicates that, for Basil, the difference between *skopos* and *telos* (both meaning "goal" or "end") is that *telos* describes the reality in itself while *skopos* "describes it from the perspective of the person aiming at it."[80]

Memory, disposition, and withdrawal are the means whereby the goal is realized. Withdrawal or separation, we have seen, is an aid, an indispensable aid, to memory of God. It remains for us to consider the role of memory and *diathesis* (disposition), and here the chief study is that of John Eudes Bamberger.[81] While memory of God has clear pagan and Christian roots, of which Basil was well aware, Bamberger suggests that Basil's use of the word is different, for in his thought "it is decidedly oriented towards the experiential and practical and relatively unconcerned with theories of knowledge and of man's nature for their own sake."[82] Memory is so powerful that it can change one's character to the point that virtuous activities that used to be repulsive are now attractive, and vicious activities that used to be appealing are now repulsive.[83]

While memory is no doubt central in Basil's thought, Bamberger more persuasively argues that a profound notion of disposition (*diathesis*) should be credited to Basil.[84] He notes that the word was never prominent in the earlier tradition and that the elements of Basil's psychology "as an articulated whole" are "based upon his personal observations, intuitions, and reflections."[85] It should be mentioned that *diathesis* was important not only for Basil but also for the monks whom he advised, for the word shows up in a number of questions. Perhaps it was Basil's guidance in the first place that led the monks to ask about dispositions; perhaps their questions about disposition set Basil to thinking about it. In any case, the answers to the questions are his, together with, if I may so put it, the theology of *diathesis* that they contain.[86] *Diathesis*, in a few words, is a second nature produced by the memory of God.[87] It is a

stable attitude of love, the habit of loving God that results in spiritual joy.[88]
This disposition is so deep that it manifests itself in the unconscious as is
evident in Basil's explanation of dreams: they are "a reflection of the psychic
life as it is active during its conscious state."[89] Or, as Basil puts it, if the soul
occupies "itself with the judgments of God, continually practicing what is good
and pleasing to God, then it shall have dreams of a similar kind (*Sh. Rul.* 22;
287).[90] In his homily on the martyrdom of Julitta, he exhorts his congregation:

> Let your slumbers be themselves experiences in piety; for it is only natural that
> our sleeping dreams should be for the most part echoes of the anxieties of the
> day. As have been our conduct and pursuits, so will inevitably be our dreams.
> Thus will you pray without ceasing; if you pray not only in words, but unite
> yourself to God throughout the course of your life, which will then become one
> ceaseless and uninterrupted prayer.[91]

Thus, in a way, we can be mindful of God in our sleep and so pray unceasingly.

While Bamberger's work is very illuminating, I am uncertain about his comparisons between Freud and Jung on the one hand and Basil on the other. It is
not clear—at least to me—that Basil, with his views on memory and disposition, is articulating even implicitly a theory of the "dynamic unconscious." It
is very clear, however, that the memory of God, made possible by withdrawal
from distraction, creates in the soul the stable disposition of loving God, and
that thus the Christian accomplishes his *skopos*.

Conclusion

In both theology and asceticism, we see a consistent picture emerging of how
Basil handles the great tradition that he inherited. Elm, too, notes this parallel
between Basil's doctrinal and ascetic theology:

> Basil of Caesarea—in his doctrine as well as his ascetic concepts—was an out-
> standing reformer, and in that sense he was an innovator. Like most reformers,
> he derived his new concepts—such as his reinterpretation of the Trinity—from
> existing structures and models, but he invested these with new meaning and
> thereby subjected them to change.[92]

He used what he received to help him understand the Scriptures to which he
gave his every intellectual effort and his unconditional assent. In the course
of this exercise, he often came upon fresh insights that inevitably entailed the
modification, correction, and deepening of the tradition that Basil, in turn,
passed on to his successors.

Conclusion

Theology and Spirituality in the Thought of St. Basil

It is easy for us to divide and separate what Basil did not. His trinitarian thought, for example, is one thing, his ascetic and spiritual thought, another. But it was not so for him. This fact is evident both on the level of history and on that of theology. It is a matter of fact that Basil's two great trinitarian works, *Against Eunomius* and *On the Holy Spirit*, originated in an ascetic context.[1] We have seen that Basil would often participate in what we may call ascetic conferences. He and other ascetic leaders met to talk about various issues that arose in the lives of the monks. They spoke not just of spiritual matters but of properly theological ones. They discussed the meaning of particular scriptural texts and words. It is not the case, moreover, that this study of the Scripture happens to take place in an ascetic context, as if there could be another. "For Basil," writes Peter Martens, "the attentive reading of the Bible is closely related to asceticism: not only does this way of reading Scripture guide the life of virtue, but this very life of virtue, in turn, is a presupposition for, and even constitutive of, attentive biblical exegesis."[2] God has written the Bible, so to say, for the ascetically minded, and only they can understand the meaning of what God has written.

Thus, the study of Scripture with a view toward the doctrine of the Trinity must nonetheless be an ascetic study. And so it was for Basil. He is shocked that Eustathius could accuse him of mistakes in trinitarian doctrine, for Eustathius was present with Basil at the monastic discussions of such things.

> Ask yourself: How often did you visit us in the monastery on the river Iris, when, moreover, our most divinely-favoured brother Gregory was present with me, achieving the same purpose in life as myself? Did you ever hear any such [mistake in doctrine]? Did you receive any suggestion of it, small or great? And how many

days did we spend in the village opposite, at my mother's, living there as a friend
with a friend, with conversation astir among us both night and day? Were we
found to hold any kindred thought in our minds? And when we set out at the
same time to visit the blessed Silvanus, did not our journey include discussions
on these matters? And at Eusinoe, when you, about to set out for Lampsacus
with several bishops, summoned me, was not our conversation about faith? And
all the time were not your short-hand writers present as I dictated objections to
the heresy? Were not the most faithful of your disciples in my presence the whole
time? While visiting the brotherhoods, and spending whole nights with them in
prayer, always speaking and hearing opinions about God without contention,
did I not furnish precise proofs of my own mind? (ep. 223.5; 303–5)

Basil here seamlessly weaves together the dogmatic and the ascetic. Gregory
and he were trying to radically live the gospel, and Eustathius's "disciples" are
certainly his fellow ascetics. Basil mentions in the same breath the spending
of whole nights in prayer and theological discourse about God. There was
nothing more natural than that these spiritual athletes would talk about God.

We should see *On the Holy Spirit* in a similar light. Basil wrote the work to
answer the questions of Amphilochius of Iconium. Amphilochius put questions to Basil, however, not as one theologian to another, or one bishop to
another, but above all as one ascetic to another. Amphilochius was much like
the young Basil: he had given up a secular career in rhetoric to pursue the philosophic life.[3] Old Basil, however, convinced Amphilochius to live the ascetic life
more on his own coenobitic model, and this began a dear friendship in which
Amphilochius asked for counsel (a "word," we might say) and Basil gave it.
One of the matters on which Amphilochius asked for advice was the Spirit,
and Basil's answer was the treatise *On the Holy Spirit*. Their correspondence,
in other words, might well be thought of as a monastic conference—the same
kind that gave us *Against Eunomius*—but at a distance.

The historical contexts of Basil's two great dogmatic works point toward
a theological coherence. The single theological vantage point from which
we can view the whole of Basil's thought, I think, is his anthropology. The
fundamental truth here is that God made man both incomplete and bodily,
so that man comes to perfection and completion by his life in the body. Basil
views the whole economy of salvation as the set of those divine measures
whereby God aims to bring us out of our liminal position and toward himself.
Two such measures, we saw, are the world itself (including the human body)
and the Scriptures. Man reads these two books to find out what God wishes
to say to him. The chief point related in the books is that God has acted for
the salvation of man. The books, that is, describe God's great benefactions,
his great acts of love toward man—above all, the incarnation, passion, and
death of the Lord.

How does God telling us what he has done for us help us? It helps us because
once we call to mind God's mercy and keep it ever in our memory, we will

naturally turn to him in love, for we cannot refuse to love such a benefactor. Our mindfulness of God, a mindfulness that he provoked through creation itself and through scriptural revelation, leads not to a transient and ephemeral love but to an abiding disposition of love. Thus disposed, we can now render to God the bodily service in continent fasting, in work, and in prayer—briefly put, in keeping all the commands—that will realize ever more profoundly in us the eschatological life of the resurrection. In this way God brings us from our state of imperfection to a state of perfection. His love of us, encoded in creation and proclaimed in Scripture, makes us to love him. His self-abasement for our good makes us to praise him and to deny our own will—by not eating what we please, or doing the kind of work that we please, or wearing what we please, or speaking how we please and with whom we please, or giving spiritual counsel as we please—so that we might do his will.

The subjects of Basil's chief dogmatic works, the nature and identity of the Son and the Spirit, have an essential place in the spiritual process just outlined. Basil realized that if Eunomius and Eustathius were right on the Son and the Spirit, then the whole Christian (ascetic) life as he understood would be ruined. As he so often said, Eunomius and Eustathius cut off our access to God. If the Son is not equal to the Father, then his humiliations are not the humiliations of God and our imitation of them cannot make us like God. That is to say, if the Son is not consubstantial with the Father, then a life lived according to his commands cannot bring us to the Father. Something similar holds with the Spirit. When we are baptized into the Spirit, Basil says that we become that into which we were baptized; we become Spirit (*Mor.* 80.22). But, again, if the Spirit is a creature, then he cannot make us to be like God. He recognized that if the Spirit-fighters were right, then he was living a fantasy and a fraud. Understood in this way, it was impossible for ascetics to stand above dogmatic controversy. For ascetics to be unconcerned with theology and with theological mistakes is for them to be unconcerned for the purported object of their lives. In the end, Basil's theology and spirituality converge into a single movement of the person—or rather, the human community—toward God.

Notes

Acknowledgments

1. *The Ascetic Works of Saint Basil*, trans. W. K. L. Clarke (New York: MacMillan, 1925), 6.

Preface

1. John Behr, *The Nicene Faith*, Formation of Christian Theology 2 (Crestwood, NY: St. Vladimir's Seminary Press, 2004), 8–9.
2. Ibid., 9.
3. Often I use words like *man* and *he* inclusively rather than exclusively. I do not hereby wish to make a theological and certainly not a political statement. Really it is a matter of stylistic preference: I find the inclusive alternatives less eloquent than the exclusive term used inclusively. I ask the reader's indulgence if we disagree.

Abbreviations

1. I cite the *Morals* according to the numbering of Clarke, which differs from that of Wagner, who follows Garnier's edition in PG 31. Garnier gave chapter numbers to the selection of New Testament texts that follow each rule, while in Clarke these numbers apply to the rules themselves, and this makes better sense.

Chapter 1: Awakenings

1. John Henry Newman, *An Essay on the Development of Doctrine*, 6th ed. (1878; repr., Notre Dame, IN: University of Notre Dame Press, 1989), 127.
2. Ibid., 128.
3. W. K. L. Clarke writes that "in spite of his strict life at Athens, [Basil's] religion had been conventional, and the term 'conversion' is as applicable to him as to St. Augustine" (*The Ascetic Works of St. Basil*, trans. W. K. L. Clarke [New York: MacMillan, 1925], 49).
4. The relation between organized asceticism and its less organized forms is complex. Sometimes the connection seems to be rather strong, as, e.g., in St. Basil's family, but we should not suppose that there is always such a domestic background to an organized form of asceticism. As one example of the institutionalization (and I do not intend here any pejorative connotations) of asceticism, consider the emergence in the West of a public ritual for the consecration of virgins. See Nathalie Henry, "A New Insight into the Growth of Ascetic Society in the Fourth Century AD: The Public Consecration of Virgins as a Means of Integration and Promotion of the Female Ascetic Movement," in *Studia Patristica 35, Papers Presented at the Thirteenth*

International Conference on Patristic Studies Held in Oxford, 1999, pt. 4, *Ascetica, Gnostica, Liturgica, Orientalia,* ed. M. F. Wiles and E. J. Yarnold, 102–9 (Louvain: Peeters, 2001).

5. I do not know whether the experience of Basil's family was typical in any way, but there seems no reason to suppose it idiosyncratic. Presumably, there were other families similarly affected.

6. The council of Nicaea (325) testifies to these problems in the canonical remedies that it legislated. Canon 2 of Nicaea states that "since . . . there have been many breaches of the church's canon, with the result that men who have recently come from a pagan life to the faith after a short catechumenate have been admitted at once to the spiritual washing, and at the same time as their baptism have been promoted to the episcopate or the presbyterate, it is agreed that it would be well for nothing of the kind to occur in the future" (can. 2; trans. Edward Yarnold, in *Decrees of the Ecumenical Councils,* ed. Norman Tanner, Giuseppe Alberigo et al., vol. 1, *Nicaea I to Lateran V* [Washington, DC: Georgetown University Press, 1990], 6).

7. Socrates, apparently erroneously, places Eulalius in Caesarea; as Silvas mentions (53) scholars since the time of F. Loofs place him in Sebaste. See Loofs, *Eustathius von Sebaste und die Chronologie der Basilius-Briefe* (Halle: Niemeyer, 1898).

8. On the dating of the council, see Silvas, 486n1.

9. Sozomen's report on Eustathius's dress may conflict with the testimony of Basil himself, who provides us with a possible allusion to Eustathius's adoption of the philosopher's mantle: "I thought," he writes, "that lowliness of dress was sufficient evidence of lowliness of mind; and sufficient for my full assurance was the thick cloak, and the girdle and the sandals of untanned hide" (ep. 223.3; 3:297).

10. Basil's brother Gregory of Nyssa also wrote an oration in honor of Basil, but it is far less informative than Gregory of Nazianzus's and than Nyssa's *Life of Macrina.* See Anthony Meredith, "Gregory of Nazianzus and Gregory of Nyssa on Basil," in *Studia Patristica 32, Papers Presented at the Twelfth International Conference on Patristic Studies Held in Oxford 1995: Athanasius and His Opponents, Cappadocian Fathers, Other Greek Writers after Nicaea,* ed. Elizabeth A. Livingstone, 163–69 (Louvain: Peeters, 1997).

11. In ep. 1, Basil tells Eustathius of Sebaste that he left Athens "owing to the repute of your philosophy" (ep. 1; 1:3). This need not contradict Silvas's view that Basil left Athens because of the death of Naucratius, especially when we take it together with the evidence in the *Life of Macrina.* Basil may here be singling out one in a confluence of factors that brought him to leave Athens: his agreement with Gregory of Nazianzus to pursue philosophy (see Gregory, ep. 1); the death of Naucratius; the example and counsel of Macrina; and his knowledge of Eustathius of Sebaste, with whom and with whose way of life, it seems obvious, Basil was familiar as he studied in Athens.

12. In ep. 1, addressed to "Eustathius the Philosopher" (certainly Eustathius of Sebaste), Basil indicates that he set out on this ascetic tour trying to catch up with Eustathius.

13. Silvas follows Fedwick's chronology; see Paul Fedwick, "A Chronology of the Life and Works of Basil of Caesarea," in *Basil of Caesarea, Christian, Humanist, Ascetic: A Sixteen-Hundredth Anniversary Symposium,* ed. Paul Fedwick (Toronto: Pontifical Institute of Mediaeval Studies, 1981), 1:6–8.

Anthony Meredith suggests that some of the philosophical character of ep. 2 may be a rhetorical device to appeal to Gregory of Nazianzus rather than an indication of his own disposition toward philosophy, for Basil "sometimes starts from the position of his addressee in order to convert him to his point of view" ("Asceticism—Christian and Greek," *Journal of Theological Studies,* n.s., 27 [1976]: 326).

14. See Silvas, 87. The reference to the philosopher's cloak in ep. 4 is indirect. Basil writes to Olympius, whose generosity threatened Basil's embrace of poverty. Basil writes in the person of his friend Poverty, who herself quotes Zeno, "who, on losing all in a shipwreck, uttered no ignoble word, but only 'Bravo, Fortune! You lend a hand in driving me into the philosopher's cloak [*tribōnion*]'" (ep. 4; 1:31).

15. See, e.g., ep. 2.2.

16. "Tranquility" is also important in ep. 14, to Gregory of Nazianzus, wherein Basil describes his retreat at Pontus and praises it for nourishing tranquility (see 14.2).

17. Fedwick, in a note rejecting Gribomont's late dating of ep. 22, remarks that "the older Basil grew the more he turned to Scripture." While Basil had been acquainted with Scripture

from youth, "such a comprehensive understanding of the theoretical and practical implications of the Scriptural message as exhibited in the *Reg. mor.* but not yet in [ep. 22] could only have been achieved later in life" ("Chronology," 8n29).

18. On the date of the *Morals*, see Léon Lèbe, "S. Basile et ses *Règles Morales*," *Revue bénédictine* 75 (1965): 193–200. Rousseau discusses the matter and favors an early date (228n211) (*Basil of Caesarea* [Berkeley: University of California Press, 1994], 228n211). At the very least the *Morals* may have been at least drafted early, though edited over the years. Gregory Nazianzus seems to indicate as much when he describes his aforementioned experience with Basil in Pontus. "O for the contest and incitement of virtue which we secured by written Rules and Canons; O for the loving labour in the Divine Oracles, and the light we found in them by the guidance of the Holy Ghost" (ep. 6; 448). Fedwick dates the *Morals* 1–68 to 372–75; and *Morals* 69–80 to 376–77 (see "Chronology," 14n80). Fedwick does not indicate why 1–68 (69) receives so late a date; 70–80, for reasons indicated below, need only date to after his ordination to the episcopate in 370.

19. This passage bears similarities to the opening of ep. 22.

20. Basil does not explicitly say that the "preacher of the Word" is a bishop, but he implies it. First, he writes that "these who are entrusted with the preaching of the Gospel should with supplication and prayer, appoint as deacons or priests men that are blameless and respectable as to their former life" (*Mor.* 70.1; 120). Second, Basil writes "that he who is set over the word must go the round of all the villages and cities entrusted to him," and this activity seems appropriate to a bishop (*Mor.* 70.12; 169). It is possible to translate several texts so as to include himself among the preachers of the Word, even though, strictly speaking, the Greek text does not. Thus, the Latin translation uses the first person several times (*Mor.* 70.21, 23, 27, 34; 72.5), and Clarke's English translation even more often (*Mor.* 70.6, 8, 13–14, 16–18, 21, 23, 27, 34–36; 72.3, 5–6). Consider the following example, wherein Clarke, understandably, renders the Greek impersonal verb with a first-person one: "That *we* should strengthen those who receive the word of truth by a visitation" (*Mor.* 70.18; 122, my emphasis). Finally, and most persuasively, Rule 71 is titled, "what the Scripture says about bishops and presbyters jointly," implying that the foregoing applies to bishops alone (*Mor.* 71.1; 124).

Chapter 2: Man

1. Philip Rousseau, "Human Nature and Its Material Setting in Basil of Caesarea's Sermons on the Creation," *Heythrop Journal* 49 (2008): 225.

2. Quoted by Stephen Lewis, "*Quid animo satis?* A Question that Generates an Education," lecture, Franciscan University of Steubenville, Steubenville, OH, November 18, 2011. Lewis remarks that

> Claudel learned this approach to things from one of his masters, the great *symboliste* poet Stéphane Mallarmé (an atheist): "Mallarmé est le premier qui se soit placé devant l'extérieur, non pas comme devant un spectacle, ou comme un thème à devoirs français, mais comme devant un texte, avec cette question: *Qu'est-ce que ça veut dire?*" Claudel goes on to describe how this question became for him one with the explicitly Christian approach to reality as composed of signs, given by a Creator: "Nous savons que le monde est en effet un texte et qu'il nous parle, humblement et joyeusement, de sa propre absence, mais aussi de la présence éternelle de quelqu'un d'autre, à savoir son Créateur." (Paul Claudel, *Œuvres en prose*, ed. Jacques Petit and Charles Galpérine [Paris: Gallimard, Bibliothèque de la Pléiade, 1965], 511–12).

3. The authenticity of *Hexaëmeron* 10 and 11 is uncertain, though I share the judgment of Philip Rousseau that whatever the particulars of transmission and editing, "Basil was . . . the source of all that these subsequent sermons contain" ("Human Nature and Its Material Setting," 222).

4. Trans. in Rousseau, "Human Nature and Its Material Setting," 225. Cf. Harrison, 33. Rousseau's translation is less literal but captures well the spirit of Basil's point.

5. All references to the Psalms are to the Septuagint.

6. If we cannot say that angels are bodiless while men have bodies, at least we can say that angels and men have different kinds of bodies. The question of whether or not the Cappadocians attributed bodies to angels, Morwenna Ludlow rightly thinks, calls for further research. "Some statements," she writes, "from the Cappadocians seem to suggest that demons have light, airy

bodies, such as Gregory of Nazianzus, *Carm.* 1.1.7.60 . . . but some modern authorities think that at least Basil and Gregory of Nyssa denied that demons had bodies" ("Demons, Evil, and Liminity in Cappadocian Theology," *Journal of Early Christian Studies* 20 [2012]: 183n15). Of angels, Basil writes that "their substance [*ousia*] is ethereal spirit, perhaps, or immaterial fire. . . . On account of this they have place and become visible, appearing to those who are worthy in the form of bodies proper to them" (*On H. Sp.* 16.38; 72).

7. Rousseau, "Human Nature and Its Material Setting," 229.

8. This paragraph seems out of place, for it is really an explanation of a text ("And God made the human being according to his image") that Basil has already treated. Moreover the next paragraph (19) treats man's rule over the fish and the animals. Perhaps this oddity is related to the difficulties that surround its authorship.

9. Cited in Augustine Holmes, *A Life Pleasing to God: The Spirituality of the Rules of St. Basil* (London: Darton, Longman, & Todd, 2000), 213.

10. Ludlow, "Demons, Evil, and Liminity in Cappadocian Theology," 189.

11. Ibid., 211.

12. Ibid.

13. In the preface, Basil does not emphasize the agency of God but only human striving and human help, although, contrasting this earthly life with the judgment, he writes, "Now, God is the helper of those who turn from the evil way: then he will be the dread and inexorable examiner of all human deeds, words, and motives" (*Lg. Rul.* prol. 1; 154).

14. Plato's thought on the body and soul can appear more or less dualistic—more dualistic, for example, in the *Phaedo* and less in the *Republic*. For a discussion of this issue and the place of the *Timaeus* in it, see John M. Rist, "Plato Says that We Have Tripartite Souls. If He Is Right, What Can We Do About It?" in *SOPHIÊS MAIÊTORES. "Chercheurs de Sagesse." Hommage à Jean Pépin*, ed. M.-O. Goulet-Cazé, G. Madec, and D. O'Brien, 103–24 (Paris: Institut d'Études Augustiniennes, 1992). Rist explains that Plato's concern in the *Timaeus* is to explain how the "original nature of soul" is involved in all manner of ungodly activities because of its insertion into the body (119).

15. Plato, *Timaeus* 41C; trans. Desmond Lee, *Timaeus and Critias* (New York: Penguin, 1977), 57.

16. Ibid., 44D; 61.

17. See ibid., 69D.

18. Ibid., 69E; 97.

19. See ibid., 41E–42.

20. One important and controverted question is whether or not matter emanates from or is produced by soul and, therefore, ultimately emanates from or is generated by the One itself. Denis O'Brien, one of the key players in the controversy, offers a synopsis of the debate in his dryly humorous and sometimes sarcastic response to H.-R. Schwyzer's and K. Corrigan's independent (and different) criticisms of his own interpretation of Plotinus, which holds that for Plotinus, soul does in fact produce matter (and body) even though matter is considered evil. See Denis O'Brien, *Plotinus on the Origin of Matter: An Exercise in the Interpretation of the "Enneads,"* Elenchos: Collana di testi e studi sul pensiero antico 22 (Napoli: Centro di studio del pensiero antico, 1991); and K. Corrigan, *Plotinus' Theory of Matter-Evil and the Question of Substance: Plato, Aristotle, and Alexander of Aphrodisias*, Recherches de Théologie Ancienne et Médiévale (Louvain: Peeters, 1996).

21. Denis O'Brien assembles the relevant texts and succinctly states the problem. See "Plotinus on Matter and Evil," in *The Cambridge Companion to Plotinus*, ed. Lloyd P. Gerson (New York: Cambridge University Press, 1996), 171.

22. Ibid., citing Plotinus, *Ennead* 3.4.1.

23. Plotinus, *Ennead* 2.4.5; trans. Stephen MacKenna, *The Enneads: A New, Definitive Edition with Comparisons to Other Translations on Hundreds of Key Passages* (Burdett, NY: Larson, 1992), 122. O'Brien cites this passage, but his translation is more vivid: matter cannot but be "a corpse adorned" ("Plotinus on Matter and Evil," 180).

24. See O'Brien, "Plotinus on Matter and Evil," 181, 189–90.

25. See Stephen Clark, "Plotinus: Body and Soul," in *Cambridge Companion to Plotinus*, 279. Dominic O'Meara also draws the comparison to Descartes but more positively; see *Plotinus: An Introduction to the Enneads* (Oxford: Clarendon, 1995), 19–21.

26. Clark, "Plotinus: Body and Soul," 276, 279.

27. Ibid., 289.

28. See *Ennead* 1.8.14; 1.4.14; 1.4.8.

29. *Ep. to Diognetus* 6; trans. Cyril Richardson, *Early Christian Fathers* (New York: Touchstone, 1996), 218.

30. Plotinus, *Ennead* 2.9.18; trans. MacKenna, 170.

31. Ibid. 1.9; 90.

32. Clark, "Plotinus: Body and Soul," 289.

33. Ibid. See *Ennead* 1.4.8.

34. See Clark, "Plotinus: Body and Soul," 289; and Porphyry, *Life of Plotinus* 9.13–16.

35. I draw this statement of the paradox from Denis O'Brien, "Plotinus on Matter and Evil," in *Cambridge Companion to Plotinus*, 171. O'Brien sees his own work as maintaining the paradox while other scholars, such as Schwyzer, Rist, and Pistorius, resolve it in one direction or another. See H.-R. Schwyzer, "Zu Plotins Deutung der sogenannten platonischen Materie," in *Zetesis: Festschrift E. de Strycker*, ed. Th. Lefevre, 266–80 (Antwerp: De Nederlandsche Boeklandel, 1973); John M. Rist, *Plotinus: The Road to Reality* (New York: Cambridge University Press, 1967); and P. V. Pistorius, *Plotinus and Neoplatonism: An Introductory Study* (Cambridge: Bowes & Bowes, 1952).

36. *Ennead* 1.8.8; 1.8.13.

37. O'Brien, "Plotinus on Matter and Evil," 171; see *Ennead* 1.8.14.

38. O'Brien, "Plotinus on Matter and Evil," 171; see *Ennead* 3.9.3; 3.4.1. In the same place, O'Brien comments that the "paradox is only heightened by Plotinus's repeated claim that matter, 'primary evil' and 'evil' *per se* (I.8.3.35–40), is also 'non-being'" (II.4.16.3; II.5.4–5; III.6.7.1–19).

39. As with many other matters in *On First Principles*, there is the question of the fidelity of Rufinus's translation to what Origen really said and thought, and the question of fidelity is complicated further by the controversy over Origen's views on the resurrection. Rufinus was his defender against Methodius and Jerome. Koetschau's critical text of *On First Principles* includes some of the anathemas from the second Council of Constantinople (553) at which certain alleged doctrines of Origen were condemned and includes also excerpts from Justinian's *Epistula ad Mennam*. We should be wary of attributing these positions to Origen without qualification. Without descending into the particulars of the controversy, I will regard Rufinus as faithful to Origen where his translation is consistent with the views articulated in *Against Celsus*, though *Against Celsus* was written later than *On First Principles*, and Origen's views may have developed in the interim.

40. See Enrica Ruaro, "'Lovers of the Body:' The Platonic Primacy of Soul vs. the Christian Affirmation of the Body," in *Conversations Platonic and Neoplatonic: Intellect, Soul, and Nature. Papers from the 6th Annual Conference of the International Society for Neoplatonic Studies*, ed. John F. Finamore and Robert M. Berchman (Sankt Augustin: Academia Verlag, 2010), 155–60.

41. Origen, *Commentary on Matthew* 12:43; trans. John Patrick, in *The Gospel of Peter, The Diatesseron of Tatian, The Apocalypse of Peter, The Vision of Paul, The Apocalypses of the Virgin and Sedrach, The Testament of Abraham, The Acts of Xanthippe and Polyxena, The Narrative of Zosimus, The Apology of Aristides, The Epistles of Clement (complete text), Origen's Commentary on John, Books 1–10, and Commentary on Matthew, Books 1, 2, and 10–14*, ANF (1896; repr., Peabody, MA: Hendrickson, 1994), 473.

42. Ibid. 37; trans. Patrick, 470.

43. This text is from Justinian's *Epistula ad Mennam*.

44. Ruaro, "Lovers of the Body," 161.

45. Enrica Ruaro, "'Resurrection: The Hope of Worms.' The Dispute between Celsus and Origen on the Resurrection of the Body," in *Perspectives sur le néoplatonisme: International Society of Neoplatonic Studies. Acts du colloque de 2006*, ed. Martin Achard, Wayne Hankey, and Jean-Marc Narbonne (Québec: Les Presses de l'Université Laval, 2009), 168.

46. Ibid.

47. See Ruaro, "Lovers of the Body," 161–62.

48. Tertullian, *On the Resurrection of the Flesh* 9; trans. P. Holmes, in *Latin Christianity: Its Founder, Tertullian. Three Parts: I. Apologetic; II. Anti-Marcion; III. Ethical*, ANF 3 (1885; repr., Peabody, MA: Hendrickson, 1994), 552. See Ruaro, "Lovers of the Body," 162.

49. Ruaro, "Lovers of the Body," 163.

50. Tertullian, *On the Resurrection of the Flesh* 53 (my trans.): "resurget igitur caro, et quidem omnis, et quidem ipsa, et quidem integra." See Ruaro, "Lovers of the Body," 165.

51. Eusebius, Letter to Constantia, cited in Christoph Schönborn, *God's Human Face: The Christ-Icon*, trans. Lothar Krauth (San Francisco: Ignatius, 1994), 58–59. The authenticity of this text is debated, and it is preserved only in the work of a much later author, Nicephorus of Constantinople (d. 829), who wrote a treatise against Eusebius in the course of the Iconoclast controversy. The critical text is in H. Hennephof, *Textus byzantinos ad Iconomachiam pertinentes* (Leiden: Brill, 1969), 42–44; and in PG 20, 1545–49.

52. Eusebius of Caesarea, *Theophania* (Syriac), 1, 68–69 (70, 18–71, 14 in the Syriac); cited in Schönborn, *God's Human Face*, 74.

53. Ibid.

54. See Elizabeth A. Clark, *The Origenist Controversy: The Cultural Construction of an Early Christian Debate* (Princeton: Princeton University Press, 1992), 85–158.

55. Silvas comments that "Basil . . . like all the Cappadocians, refuses the pre-existence of the soul and affirms a strict scriptural doctrine of creation" (164n53).

56. Basil makes the same point in another sermon. "We ourselves are one thing, and what is ours is another, and the things around us are another. Thus we are the soul and the mind, through which we have come into being according to the image of the Creator, but the body is ours and the sense perceptions through it, while around us are possessions, skills, and the other equipment of life" (*Hom. Attend* 3; 96).

57. Rousseau, "Human Nature and Its Material Setting," 232.

58. Ibid.

59. Ibid.

60. Ibid.

61. Verna Harrison, "Male and Female in Cappadocian Theology," *Journal of Theological Studies*, n.s., 41 (1990): 453.

62. This sermon, *Hom. Attend*, according to Fedwick—and he seems right—cannot be determined more precisely than the period of Basil's presbyteral and episcopal ministry, so 362–78. Fedwick notes that a couple of manuscripts assign this homily for Lenten reading and that it is a "fitting complement to the unfinished" *Hexaëmeron*, though it was probably written before it. See Paul Fedwick, "A Chronology of the Life and Works of Basil of Caesarea," in *Basil of Caesarea, Christian, Humanist, Ascetic: A Sixteen-Hundredth Anniversary Symposium*, ed. Paul Fedwick (Toronto: Pontifical Institute of Mediaeval Studies, 1981), 1:9nn31–32.

63. Rousseau, "Human Nature and Its Material Setting," 231.

64. Ibid. It is this paradox of human smallness and human dignity that Rousseau identifies as Basil's central theme: man is at once small and great (see ibid., 228).

65. Consider, for example, his early sermon that God is not the author of evil, wherein the suffering of the body is ordered to the cessation of sin (see *Hom. Evil* 4–5).

66. There is a strange and, as far as I can tell, unique passage in the *Morals* that speaks to the physicality of Jesus's second coming. "We must not expect," Basil writes, "the coming of the Lord to be local [*topikēn*] or bodily [*sarkikēn*], but must look for a coming in the glory of the Father through all the world at once" (*Mor.* 68.2; 119, altered).

Chapter 3: The Two Books

1. I have written on this theme previously and here have edited and revised an earlier treatment. See *The Trinitarian Theology of Basil of Caesarea* (Washington, DC: Catholic University of America Press, 2007), 102–49.

2. See Plato, *Laws* 7 (811A); and Henry Chadwick, "Florilegium," in *Reallexikon für Antike und Christentum*, ed. T. Klauser (Stuttgart: Hiersemann, 1969), 7:1131–60.

3. John M. Rist, "Basil's 'Neoplatonism': Its Background and Nature," in *Basil of Caesarea: Christian, Humanist, Ascetic*, 205.

4. Aristotle, *De generatione et corruptione* 2.4; and *Hex.* 4.5.

5. Frank Robbins, "The Hexaemeral Literature" (PhD diss., University of Chicago, 1912), 17. See Diogenes Laertius 7.156; *Hex.* 5.1; and *Hex.* 9.2.

6. Diogenes Laertius 7.141; and *Hex.* 1.3.

7. Y. Courtonne, *Saint Basile et l'Hellénisme: Étude sur la recontre de la pensée chrétienne avec la sagesse antique dans l'Hexaméron de Basile le Grand* (Paris: Firmin Didot, 1934).

8. J. Levie, "Les sources de la 7ᵉ et la 8ᵉ homélies de saint Basile sur l'Hexaméron," *Musée belge* (1920): 113–49.

9. M. Berger, *Die Schöpfungslehre des hl. Basilius des Grossen*, 2 vols. (Rosenheim: Druck von M. Niedermayr, 1897–98).

10. E. Fialon, *Étude historique et littéraire sur saint Basile suive de l'Hexaméron* (Paris: Ernest Thorin, 1869).

11. Theodore Leslie Shear, *The Influence of Plato on St. Basil* (Baltimore: J. H. Furst, 1906).

12. Robbins, "Hexaemeral Literature."

13. See "*theopneustos,*" in *Patristic Greek Lexicon*, ed. G. W. H. Lampe (Oxford: Clarendon, 1976).

14. See his *Commentary on John* 1.5.

15. David is constantly called a prophet in his homilies on the Psalms; Basil calls Moses a prophet in *Hex.* 2.4.

16. William Tieck cites this text ("Basil of Caesarea and the Bible," [PhD diss., Columbia University, 1953], 101).

17. See ibid., 93.

18. See also *Hex.* 8.8; 132: "The words of Scripture, if simply read, are a few short syllables . . . ; but when the meaning in the words is explained, then the great marvel of the wisdom of the Creator appears."

19. For similar interpretations, see also *Hom. on Ps.* 44.2; 44.4; 48.1.

20. See *Hex.* 4.5; 62: "'And so it was' [Gen. 1:10]. This introduction is sufficient to show that the voice of the Creator passed into action. But in many copies there is added, 'And the waters below the heavens were gathered into their places, and the dry land appeared,' words which, indeed, some of the rest of the interpreters have not given, and which the usage of the Hebrews does not appear to retain." The added words, Basil tells us, are superfluous and marked with an obelus.

21. The categories themselves have come under some scrutiny, especially by Frances Young. See *Biblical Exegesis and the Formation of Christian Culture* (New York: Cambridge University Press, 1997), 162–69; "The Rhetorical Schools and Their Influence on Patristic Exegesis," in *The Making of Orthodoxy: Essays in Honour of Henry Chadwick*, ed. Rowan Williams, 182–99 (New York: Cambridge University Press, 1989); and "Exegetical Method and Scriptural Proof: The Bible in Doctrinal Debate," in *Studia Patristica 29: Papers Presented to the Tenth International Conference on Patristic Studies Held in Oxford 1987*, ed. Elizabeth A. Livingstone, 291–304 (Louvain: Peeters, 1989).

22. John J. O'Keefe, "'A Letter that Killeth': Toward a Reassessment of Antiochene Exegesis, or Diodore, Theodore, and Theodoret on the Psalms," *Journal of Early Christian Studies* 8 (2000): 86.

23. Ibid., 92. Here O'Keefe reports the judgments, respectively, of Christoph Schäublin (*Untersuchungen zu Methode und Herkunft der Antiochenischen Exegese* [Köln-Bonn: Peter Hanstein, 1974]) and Frances Young, *Biblical Exegesis*. O'Keefe describes Young's book as "an attempt . . . to give the Antiochene tradition a chance it did not have in antiquity" ("Toward a Reassessment of Antiochene Exegesis," 92n22).

24. Origen, *Homilies on Luke*, hom. 5.1; trans. Joseph T. Lienhard, Fathers of the Church 94 (Washington, DC: Catholic University of America Press, 1996), 20.

25. Ibid., hom. 2; trans. Lienhard, 21.

26. Ibid., hom. 12.2; trans. Lienhard, 48.

27. Ibid., hom. 4; trans. Lienhard, 49.

28. Cited in J. Philip de Barjeau, *L'école exégétique d'Antioche* (Toulouse: Imprimerie A. Chauvin et Fils, 1898), 35n3.

29. Theodore, *Commentary on Galatians* 4:24, trans. Maurice Wiles and Mark Santer, *Documents in Early Christian Thought*, ed. Maurice Wiles and Mark Santer (New York: Cambridge University Press, 1975), 151–52.

30. See O'Keefe, "Toward a Reassessment of Antiochene Exegesis." Young called her own explanation of the exegesis of Eusebius (in *From Nicaea to Chalcedon*) "a description that could

be regarded as typical of standard accounts but is surely, though I now say it myself, somewhat misleading" (*Biblical Exegesis*, 121).

31. Young, *Biblical Exegesis*, 167.

32. Ibid., 169. Young makes a couple of other points against the traditional understanding of the categories: "All patristic commentary on scripture draws on a common approach to literary texts; and where they differ, they have appropriated different parts of ancient paideia" (in addition to *Biblical Exegesis*, see Frances M. Young, "The Rhetorical Schools and Their Influence on Patristic Exegesis," in Williams, *Making of Orthodoxy*).

33. O'Keefe, "Toward a Reassessment of Antiochene Exegesis," 97.

34. Ibid., 95. See Erich Auerbach, *Mimesis: The Representation of Reality in Western Literature*, trans. Willard R. Trask (Princeton: Princeton University Press, 1953); and *Scenes from the Drama of European Literature* (Minneapolis: University of Minnesota Press, 1984).

35. O'Keefe, "Toward a Reassessment of Antiochene Exegesis," 104.

36. See ibid., 95.

37. Ibid., 85.

38. Ibid., 94.

39. Ibid., 104.

40. Richard Lim, "The Politics of Interpretation in Basil of Caesarea's *Hexaëmeron*," *Vigiliae Christianae* 44 (1990): 351–70.

41. For further examples of historical questions and psalmic inscriptions, see *Hom. on Ps.* 59.2 and 61.1.

42. Basil also applies Psalm 7:15 to David and Absalom; see *Hom. on Ps.* 7.18.

43. See *Hom. on Ps.* 46 [45].3 and 28.1–3, wherein the tabernacle stands for the flesh, the ram for the bishop, and the holy court for the church; and *Hom. on Ps.* 32.2, wherein the harp is the body and the ten-stringed psaltery is the Ten Commandments.

44. Basil goes on to explain that the cedars of Psalm 29 [28]:5 are the puffed up wicked (*Hom. on Ps.* 29 [28].5).

45. "Hear these things, all ye nations; give ear, all ye inhabitants of the world. All you that are earthborn, and you sons of men: both rich and poor together."

46. See Tieck, "Basil of Caesarea and the Bible," 159.

47. Ibid.

48. On the date of the homilies on the Psalms, see Jean Bernardi, *La Prédication des pères cappadociens: Le Prédicateur et son auditoire* (Marseille: Presses universitaires de France, 1968), 23–29. He dates the homilies to 368–75. On the date of the *Hexaëmeron*, see Philip Rousseau, *Basil of Caesarea* (Berkeley: University of California Press, 1994), 360–63.

49. Lim, "Politics of Interpretation," 355.

50. See ibid., 355–60.

51. Ibid., 361.

52. Ibid. See *Hex.* 7.5–6; 8.8.

53. Bernardi, *La Prédication des pères cappadociens*, 33–34. Indeed, Bernardi thinks that in Basil's congregation the baptized are a minority.

54. Cited in Margaret Murphy, *St. Basil and Monasticism* (Washington, DC: Catholic University of America Press, 1930), 89.

Chapter 4: The Trinity, Simply

1. The chronological ordering of the *Morals* and its prefaces, we have seen, is not straightforward, and the prefaces may be later than at least parts of the *Morals*. In any case, with the prefaces we may say that Basil is, as it were, reissuing the *Morals* and setting them in a different context from their original conception.

2. That it is his polemical work against Eunomius that has been misunderstood seems probable both because of the dates of the works in question and because of the themes stressed in *On Faith*, which are very similar to the themes stressed in *Against Eunomius*—namely, the incomprehensibility of God and the consubstantiality of the Father, Son, and Holy Spirit, who, nonetheless, have different characterizing properties.

3. This is one text wherein Clarke's translation is better than Wagner's, for she misses, I believe, Basil's point when she translates Basil's words thus: "I thought it appropriate to the

specific nature of the impiety sown by the Devil that I should check [it] . . . by arguments gleaned from various sources as the need of those weak in faith required; and in many cases these *were not written down* [*agraphois*], yet were not out of harmony with sound scriptural teaching" (Wagner, 58). Given the context, Basil is not contrasting written and oral teachings but scriptural and nonscriptural. I, he goes on, will "declare what I have learned from the Holy Scripture, making a sparing use of titles and words which are not found literally in Holy Writ, even though they preserve the sense of the Scripture" (Wagner, 58–59).

4. Basil seems to indicate that the man to whom he is writing had something to do with his own becoming a minister of the new covenant.

5. As he does so often, for example in his letters to bishops, Basil uses the plural pronoun. He very often, as here in *On Faith*, will use the first-person plural pronoun of himself.

6. Eusebius of Caesarea, *Letter to His Church concerning the Synod of Nicaea* 4; trans. William Rusch, in *The Trinitarian Controversy*, Sources of Early Christian Thought (Philadelphia: Fortress, 1980), 57.

7. One might think of the Roman Creed or Apostles' Creed.

8. Gregory of Nazianzus openly confesses the divinity and consubstantiality of the Spirit: "*What, then? Is the Spirit God? Certainly. Is he consubstantial?* Yes, if he is God" (*Or.* 31.10; trans. Wickham, 123).

9. The faith that Eusthathius signed was the Nicene Creed, with the addition of anathemas protecting the divinity of the Holy Spirit.

10. Andrew Radde-Gallwitz made this point in a public address ("Creed as Apology: The Pneumatological Letters of Basil of Caesarea and Gregory of Nyssa") given at the Boston Colloquy for Historical Theology, Boston College, July 30, 2011.

11. This suspicion of asceticism may have been very painful for Basil, for, as we will see in later chapters, he identifies the ascetic life with the only true Christian life.

12. See ep. 99 and 214. Ep. 99 is an account of Basil's failed mission to Armenia and the problems encountered with Theodotus and Eustathius, while in ep. 214 Basil vents his frustration with the Paulinians in Antioch and with Pope Damasus, who established communion with Paulinus rather than Basil's man, Meletius.

13. Radde-Gallwitz notes the slightly defensive or admonitory character of this letter and wonders whether Basil is also writing to clear his name, for at the same time as this correspondence with the daughters of Terentius, Basil was corresponding with Eusebius of Samosata regarding his dealings with Theodotus and Eustathius (Radde-Gallwitz, "Creed as Apology").

14. Ibid.

15. It must be admitted, nevertheless, that certain aspects of Basil's confession, and not just those aspects added by him, derive ultimately from a polemical context. Of course, this is true of *homoousios* itself, just as it is of Basil's own statements regarding the divinity of the Holy Spirit.

16. I have considered in more detail elsewhere the structure of *On the Holy Spirit*. See *The Trinitarian Theology of Basil of Caesarea* (Washington, DC: Catholic University of America Press, 2007), 179–80. Gregory of Nazianzus employs the same strategy in his third theological oration (*Or.* 29). "Every speech," he writes, "has two parts to it. One part aims at establishing one's own position; the other refutes the opposing case" (*Or.* 29.1; trans. Frederick Williams and Lionel Wickham, *On God and Christ: The Five Theological Orations and Two Letters to Cledonius*, Popular Patristics 23 [Crestwood, NY: St. Vladimir's Seminary Press, 2002], 69). Gregory states his own position on the Godhead in the next paragraph and then spends the rest of the oration replying to the objections.

17. The three sections are *On H. Sp.* 9.22–23, 16.37–40, and 21.52–24.57.

18. Basil quotes the Lord, "O Righteous Father, the world has not known thee" (John 17:25; *On H. Sp.* 22.53).

19. Basil cites John 14:19, "Yet a little while, and the world will see me no more, but you will see me" (*On H. Sp.* 22.53).

20. Compare with 24.56: "He is good in nature, as the Father is good and the Son is good, but creation participates in goodness by choosing the good. Know the depths of God: creation perceives the revelation of mysteries through the Spirit. He gives life along with God who enlivens all things, and with the Son, the life-giver" (94–95).

21. See Paul Fedwick, "A Chronology of the Life and Works of Basil of Caesarea," in *Basil of Caesarea, Christian, Humanist, Ascetic: A Sixteen-Hundredth Anniversary Symposium*, ed.

Paul Fedwick (Toronto: Pontifical Institute of Mediaeval Studies, 1981), 15. Fedwick notes that references to *On Judgment* (*On Bap.* 2.5) and *Longer Rules* place it after those works but that it antedates the *Hypotyposis vitae asceticae* (15n83).

Chapter 5: The Trinity in Controversy

1. See J. T. Lienhard, "The 'Arian' Controversy: Some Categories Reconsidered," *Theological Studies* 48 (1987): 415–37; reprinted as chap. 2 in J. T. Lienhard, *Contra Marcellum: Marcellus of Ancyra and Fourth-Century Theology* (Washington, DC: Catholic University of America Press, 1999), 28–46.

2. See Richard Paul Vaggione, *Eunomius of Cyzicus and the Nicene Revolution*, Oxford Early Christian Studies (New York: Oxford University Press, 2000).

3. Jon M. Robertson, *Christ as Mediator: A Study of the Theologies of Eusebius of Caesarea, Marcellus of Ancyra and Athanasius of Alexandria*, Oxford Theological Monographs (New York: Oxford University Press, 2007), 220–21.

4. See ibid., 221.

5. Vaggione, *Eunomius of Cyzicus*, 110–11.

6. Ibid., 141.

7. Ibid.

8. John Behr, *The Nicene Faith*, Formation of Christian Theology 2 (Crestwood, NY: St. Vladimir's Seminary Press, 2004), 14. This last phrase—"created but not as one of the creatures"—is, of course, a classic expression of non-Nicene theologies. Arius uses it, for example, in his letter to Alexander of Alexandria: the Father "begot him . . . an immutable and unchangeable perfect creature of God, but not as one of the creatures—an offspring, but not as one of those born" (*Letter to Alexander* 2–3; trans. William Rusch, 31), in *The Trinitarian Controversy*, Sources of Early Christian Thought [Philadelphia: Fortress, 1980], 31). Eusebius of Caesarea also uses it in his interpretation of Nicaea(!), as we will see below.

9. Behr, *The Nicene Faith*, 14.

10. Vaggione, *Eunomius of Cyzicus*, 104.

11. Ibid.

12. Ibid., 123.

13. See Vaggione's introduction to Eunomius's *Exposition of Faith* in *Eunomius: The Extant Works*, Oxford Early Christian Texts (New York: Oxford University Press, 1987), 131.

14. Vaggione omitted the phrase "as son to father."

15. Gregory of Nazianzus deals with this aspect of Eunomius's thought in his second theological oration on the Son (*Or.* 29). Gregory reports the Eunomian line of thought: "'*Father,*' they say, *is a designation either of the substance or the activity; is it not?*" Gregory escapes the dilemma by asserting that "'Father' designates neither the substance nor the activity, but the relationship, the manner of being, which holds good between the Father and the Son" (*Or.* 29.16; trans. Wickham, 83–84).

16. Lienhard, *Contra Marcellum*, 45.

17. Maurice Wiles, "Eunomius: Hair-splitting Dialectician or Defender of the Accessibility of Salvation?" in *The Making of Orthodoxy: Essays in Honour of Henry Chadwick*, ed. Rowan Williams, 157–72 (New York: Cambridge University Press, 1989), 169.

18. See Vaggione, *Eunomius of Cyzicus*, 257.

19. Ibid., 254.

20. See Mark DelCogliano, *Basil of Caesarea's Anti-Eunomian Theory of Names: Christian Theology and Late-Antique Philosophy in the Fourth Century Trinitarian Controversy*, Supplements to Vigiliae Christianae 103 (Boston: Brill, 2010), 49–134.

21. See ibid., 25–37.

22. The Pneumatomachian argument here is similar to that of the homoians.

23. See Vaggione, *Eunomius of Cyzicus*, 98–147.

24. *Synodal Letter of Antioch* 14; trans. Rusch, 48.

25. See Eusebius, *Letter to His Church concerning the Synod of Nicaea* 7, 10, and 12.

26. Ibid., 11; trans. Rusch, 59.

27. See ibid., 15.

28. Ibid., 16; trans. Rusch, 60.

29. Though not by the Cappadocians, Macedonius's name became associated with the Pneumatomachians by the late fourth century. It seems that the association is unfounded: Macedonius was not a Macedonian (see R. P. C. Hanson, *The Search for the Christian Doctrine of God: The Arian Controversy, 318–381* [Edinburgh: T&T Clark, 1988; repr., Grand Rapids: Baker Academic, 2006], 760–62).

30. Ibid., 766.

31. On the distinction between "theology" and "economy" in Basil, see the introduction to DelCogliano and Radde-Gallwitz's translation of *Against Eunomius*, 51–53; and Behr, *Nicene Faith*, 290–93.

32. See Behr, *Nicene Faith*, 292.

33. Deferrari's facing Greek text contains a phrase that, Behr points out, Courtonne rejected as spurious in his critical edition. The phrase is a participial clause parallel to "who advanced in wisdom and grace." Thus Deferrari's translation, again altered, reads, "who applies the ignorance to him *who had received all things economically and* advanced in wisdom" (my emphasis). If Courtonne is right about the text, then the interpolation makes explicit what is already in the text and simply names with a technical term the interpretive move that Basil makes in any case.

34. Eunomius, *Apology for the Apology*, preserved in Gregory of Nyssa, *Ag. Eun.* 5.2; trans. H. A. Wilson, in *Select Writings and Letters of Gregory, Bishop of Nyssa*, NPNF 2, 5 (1893; repr., Peabody, MA: Hendrickson, 1995), 175.

35. Vaggione, *Eunomius of Cyzicus*, 109, his emphasis.

36. I use "Nestorian" to name a theological position and prescind from the debated question as to whether Nestorius was a Nestorian.

37. Behr opines that Vaggione's book is better at sympathetically presenting the non-Nicene position than it is at explaining the Nicene (see *Nicene Faith*, 11, and 13n41).

38. I take it as obvious that partitive exegesis could be deployed in a nestorianizing way; the question, however, is whether it need be so.

39. By a later standard, Basil's language here is odd not only because it is open to a Nestorian interpretation but also because he uses the phrase "*ousia* of the Word" instead of "*hypostasis* of the Word."

40. Behr considers this text from a different angle in his treatment of the economy in Basil; see *Nicene Faith*, 318–19.

41. Behr treats Basil's anti-Apollinarian polemic; see *Nicene Faith*, 318–24.

42. Writing on the univocity of Eunomius's Jesus, Vaggione states that "Eunomius's argument rests on the assumption that only one voice was heard in Jesus, that of the Only-begotten God, for the Only-begotten God's knowledge was simple, the reflection of his nature, not the outcome of a process of mental analysis" (Vaggione, *Eunomius of Cyzicus*, 110n200).

43. Ibid., 123.

44. See ibid.

45. Ibid., 124.

46. Basil had said something similar of the Son:

> Now there are two realities, creation and divinity: while creation is assigned to the rank of service and submission, divinity rules and is sovereign. Isn't it clear that the one who deprives the Only-Begotten of the dignity of sovereignty and casts him down into the lowly rank of servitude also by the same token shows that he is co-ordinate with all creation? Indeed, there is nothing noble about him being set at the head of fellow-servants. Rather, unless one confesses that he is king and sovereign, and that he accepts submission not because of the inferiority of his nature but because of the goodness of his free choice, this is objectionable and horrible, and it brings destruction upon those who deny this. (*Ag. Eun.* 2.31; 178)

This phrase, "because of the goodness of his free choice," seems to refer to the economy.

47. I am heavily indebted in what follows to the excellent monograph of Mark DelCogliano on Eunomian and Basilian theories of names and their roles in their respective theologies. See *Basil of Caesarea's Anti-Eunomian Theory of Names*, 25–48.

48. Ibid., 38.

49. DelCogliano uses these expressions; see ibid., 185.

50. Ibid., 162.

51. See ibid., 190–211 on proper names, 212–22 on absolute names, and 222–53 on relative names. DelCogliano also treats what he calls "derived names," names that refer to conceptualizations or derived notions; see 254–59. On proper names, see also Paul Kalligas, "Basil of Caesarea on the Semantics of Proper Names," in *Byzantine Philosophy and Its Ancient Sources*, ed. Katerina Ierodiakonou, 31–48 (Oxford: Clarendon, 2002); and on relatives, see also David G. Robertson, "Relatives in Basil of Caesarea," in *Studia Patristica 37, Papers Presented at the Thirteenth International Conference on Patristic Studies Held in Oxford, 1999: Cappadocian Writers, Other Greek Writers*, ed. Maurice F. Wiles and Edward J. Yarnold, 277–87 (Louvain: Peeters, 2001).

52. See DelCogliano, *Basil of Caesarea's Anti-Eunomian Theory of Names*, 165–71; DelCogliano draws the four stages from Andrew Radde-Gallwitz, *Basil of Caesarea, Gregory of Nyssa, and the Transformation of Divine Simplicity*, Oxford Early Christian Studies (New York: Oxford, 2009), 145–54.

53. On Basil's pagan and Christian sources, see DelCogliano, *Basil of Caesarea's Anti-Eunomian Theory of Names*, 171–87. He concludes his investigation of Basil's sources suggesting that Basil's theory "represents an appropriation of an interpretation of Aristotle that emerged among second-century Aristotelians (and is witnessed to by Clement) and was adopted by third- and fourth-century Neoplatonists such as Porphyry and Dexippus." The evidence is not strong enough, however, to infer direct influence, and so DelCogliano points to the Homoiousians as proximate sources for Basil. "Like him, they made the notions connected with names central in their theology, [and] Basil may have recognized the seeds that they planted and nurtured them into maturity" (187).

54. Ibid., 186.

55. Ibid., 185.

56. I draw here on my earlier treatments of this theme. See *The Trinitarian Theology of Basil of Caesarea* (Washington, DC: Catholic University of America Press, 2007), 141–49; and "Scripture, Worship, and Liturgy in the Thought of St. Basil the Great," *Letter and Spirit* 7 (2011): 85–97.

57. Emmanuel Amand de Mendietta, *The "Unwritten" and "Secret" Apostolic Traditions in the Theological Thought of St. Basil of Caesarea*, Scottish Journal of Theology Occasional Papers 13 (London: Oliver and Boyd: 1965), 23.

58. Basil writes: "Doctrine is one thing, and proclamation is another. One is kept in silence, but proclamations are made public. Now obscurity is a form of silence used in Scripture, which makes the meaning of dogmas difficult to see for the benefit of the readers" (*On H. Sp.* 27.66; 105–6).

59. Emmanuel Amand de Mendieta, trans., *The "Unwritten" and "Secret" Apostolic Traditions in the Theological Thought of St. Basil of Caesarea*. Scottish Journal of Theology Occasional Papers 13 (London: Oliver & Boyd: 1965), 6–8, with his notations as to what is *dogma* and what, *kērygma*.

60. See Jean Gribomont, "Esotérisme et Tradition dans le Traité du Saint-Esprit de Saint Basile," in *Oecumenica, an Annual Symposium of Ecumenical Research* (Minneapolis: Augsburg, 1967), 44.

61. See R. P. C. Hanson, "Basil's Doctrine of Tradition," *Vigiliae Christianae* 22 (1968): 249–52.

62. R. P. C. Hanson, *Tradition in the Early Church* (London: SCM, 1962), 184; cited in Gribomont, "Esotérisme et Tradition," 24n15.

63. Florovsky thinks to render *en mystēriō* (*On H. Sp.* 27.66) as "in secret" is a "flagrant mistranslation." Georges Florovsky, "The Function of Tradition in the Ancient Church," *Greek Orthodox Theological Review* 9 (1963): 194. De Mendieta disagrees because *mystēriō* is singular and no article is used (*"Unwritten" and "Secret" Apostolic Traditions*, 31 and n1). Gribomont sympathizes with Florovsky and judges that de Mendieta has not reckoned with "une certaine contrainte faite aux habitudes de la langue" that the biblical allusion justifies (*en mystēriō* here harkens back to 1 Cor. 2:7) ("Esotérisme et Tradition," 52–53).

64. Florovsky, "The Function of Tradition in the Ancient Church," 195.

65. Ibid., 193.

66. See de Mendieta, "The Pair *KĒRYGMA* and *DOGMA* in the Theological Thought of St. Basil of Caesarea," *Journal of Theological Studies*, n.s., 16 (1965): 136.

67. Ibid., 136–39. See also Michael Kane, "St. Basil's *On the Holy Spirit*: A Secret Tradition or the Rule of Faith?" *Diakonia* 35 (2002): 30–33.

68. Gribomont, "Esotérisme et Tradition," 51.

69. In fact he saw the progression in his own; see ep. 223.3.

70. Hanson, "Basil's Doctrine of Tradition," 244–45.

71. Ibid., 246–48.

72. Ibid., 252. Kane, following de Mendieta, holds that Basil so stressed the secrecy of the tradition for rhetorical effect (Kane, "Secret Tradition or the Rule of Faith?" 36; de Mendieta, *"Unwritten" and "Secret" Apostolic Traditions*, 40).

73. See Hanson, "Basil's Doctrine of Tradition," 252.

74. Hanson, *Tradition in the Early Church*, 184; cited in de Mendieta, *"Unwritten" and "Secret" Apostolic Traditions*, x.

75. See Gribomont, "Esotérisme et Tradition," 54–55.

76. Ibid., 54.

77. Ibid., 55.

78. William Tieck, "Basil of Caesarea and the Bible," (PhD diss., Columbia University, 1953), 145.

Chapter 6: Heavenly *Politeia*

1. *The Ascetic Works of St. Basil*, trans. W. K. L. Clarke (New York: SPCK, 1925), 86n2.

2. Peter Brown, *Augustine of Hippo: A Biography*, rev. ed. (Berkeley: University of California Press, 2000), 342, citing E. Portalié, *A Guide to the Thought of St. Augustine* (London: Burns and Oates, 1960), 188.

3. See Dale C. Allison Jr., *Resurrecting Jesus: The Earliest Christian Tradition and Its Interpreters* (New York: T&T Clark, 2005), 27–41.

4. See ibid., 29.

5. One of the nice features of Silvas's book is that it is printed in such a way as to allow comparison among the various editions of the rules.

6. Silvas, 29n20.

7. Ibid.

8. See Paul J. Fedwick, *The Church and the Charisma of Leadership in Basil of Caesarea*, Studies and Texts 45 (Toronto: Pontifical Institute of Mediaeval Studies, 1979), 18.

9. Ibid., 164. See also Jean Gribomont, "Obéssance et Évangile selon s. Basile le Grand," in *Supplément de la Vie spirituelle* 21 (1952): 192–215; and "Le Renoncement au monde dans l'idéal ascétique de s. Basile," *Irénikon* 31 (1958): 282–307; 460–75.

10. See *Reg. Bas.* 6.9; 15.Q; 192.Q; 196.Q; and Silvas, 23n11.

11. Silvas, 28–29.

12. Ibid., 23.

13. *The Excellence of Marriage* 23.30; trans. Ray Kearney, in *Marriage and Virginity: The Excellence of Marriage, Holy Virginity, The Excellence of Widowhood, Adulterous Marriages, Continence*, The Works of St. Augustine: A Translation for the 21st Century, vol. 9, pt. 1 (New York: New City Press, 1999), 55. Augustine says the same thing in *Holy Virginity* 14.14.

14. See *Holy Virginity* 14.14.

15. Ibid. 30.30; trans. Kearney, 86.

16. Augustine, *On Faith and Works* 20; trans. Kearney, in *On Christian Belief*, The Works of St. Augustine, vol. 8, pt. 1 (Hyde Park, NY: New City Press, 2005), 240.

17. Ibid.

18. Silvas, 28.

19. See ibid., 25–28.

20. Ibid., 29.

21. Basil makes this comment in reference to second marriage.

22. Basil cites this text in the next sentence.

23. Philip Rousseau, *Basil of Caesarea* (Berkeley: University of California Press, 1994), 197.

24. Ibid., 205–6.

25. Eusebius, *Demonstratio Evangelica* 1.8, cited in Allison, *Resurrecting Jesus*, 29.

26. Ibid.

27. See ibid.

28. Walter Bauer, *A Greek-English Lexicon of the New Testament and Other Early Christian Literature*, trans. and ed. William Arndt, F. W. Gingrich, and F. W. Danker (Chicago: University of Chicago Press, 1979), 686.

29. I have treated this theme similarly in *The Trinitarian Theology of Basil of Caesarea* (Washington, DC: Catholic University of America Press, 2007), 177.

30. Basil also notes the necessity of the Eucharist (*Mor.* 21.1).

31. See *Mor.* 80.22; *On Bap.* 1.3; and *Sh. Rul.* 172 and 309.

32. Augustine Holmes, *A Life Pleasing to God: The Spirituality of the Rules of St. Basil* (London: Darton, Longman & Todd, 2000), 118.

33. Ibid., 121.

34. Ibid., 82. On the Liturgy of St. Basil and its authenticity, see the interesting study of John R. K. Fenwick, *The Anaphoras of St. Basil and St. James: An Investigation of Their Common Origin*, Orientalia Christiana Analecta 240 (Rome: Pontificium Institutum Orientale, 1992), especially 19–30.

35. Trans. J. N. W. B. Robertson, *The Divine Liturgies*, altered by and cited in Holmes, *Life Pleasing to God*, 83.

36. Trans. Holmes, *Life Pleasing to God*, 79–80.

37. See ibid., 84.

38. Ibid.

39. Monica Wagner has a more concrete translation of this passage, and I take the sense of it from hers (*Saint Basil: Ascetical Works*, Fathers of the Church 9 [Washington, DC: Catholic University of America Press, 1962], 436).

Chapter 7: The Monastic Life

1. Augustine Holmes, *A Life Pleasing to God: The Spirituality of the Rules of St. Basil* (London: Darton, Longman & Todd, 2000), 196.

2. Robert Taft, *The Liturgy of the Hours in East and West: The Origins of the Divine Office and Its Meaning for Today* (Collegeville, MN: Liturgical Press, 1986), 84.

3. Philip Rousseau has provided the opposite approach, one that carefully and thoughtfully explores the long process whereby Basil arrived at his mature view (see *Basil of Caesarea* [Berkeley: University of California Press, 1994], 190–207).

4. This reason for the superiority of the common life seems, on the surface, identical with the second reason for its superiority—namely, that only in the life in common can one love as the Lord commands. I would not press this too far, but the two reasons may differ in that in the case of the command to love, Basil seems to have in mind the monastic community integral and unto itself—there is an internal consideration—while in the case of fulfilling all the commands, Basil mentions a number of groups of people who would not necessarily be members of the monastic community (the sick, travelers, the poor, mourners)—there is a consideration for those outside. It is clear that, for Basil, the common life is the only context wherein one can fulfill dominical obligations to fellow Christians and community members as well as to non-Christians and nonmembers.

5. The command to work can only be kept corporately because one is not allowed to work for one's own benefit but must work for the benefit of others (*Sh. Rul.* 207).

6. Basil refers to Romans 12:5 again in his answer to the question of whether there should be more than one monastic community in the same place. He answers that for a body to be properly fitted together and to function properly, it must have all the necessary parts (he mentions the tongue, eyes, and other necessary members). "Eyes," however, souls capable of leading a community, are hard to come by. In any case, even if a particular place has two or three such persons, a circumstance that Basil has never encountered, they should share the duty and burden of leading one community rather than lead separate ones (*Lg. Rul.* 35.1).

7. Silvas refers us to *Sh. Rul.* 155.Q on the hospice: "We who serve the infirm in the hospice are taught to serve them with the same disposition we would have towards brothers of the Lord. But if one being served is not so, how should we regard him?" (356).

8. Elm notes that Basil's mother, Emmelia, divested herself of her wealth by giving it to her children. Macrina, in turn, gave her share, either permanently or for her lifetime (after which it would revert to the family), to the local priest. Basil, Elm notes, "had to make five attempts

to divest himself of his fortune . . . [and] had publicly repudiated his social rank and lowered himself to a much inferior position" (Susanna Elm, *Virgins of God: The Making of Asceticism in Late Antiquity* [Oxford: Clarendon, 1996], 90).

9. Silvas notes the difficulty of translating the word. Rufinus takes it into Latin as *continentia* (*Reg. Bas.* 8, qu.), Garnier, as *temerantia*. Clarke takes it as "continence," and Way, as "continency." Silvas opts for "self-control," the rendering that, she says, is traditional in translations of the New Testament. She also lists self-restraint, self-discipline, and self-mastery as possibilities. See Silvas, 205n256.

10. In another place he defines it as the complete secession from one's own will (*Sh. Rul.* 128).

11. Basil mentions John (Matt. 3:4), Elijah (2 Kings 1:8), Peter (Acts 12:8), Paul (Acts 21:11), and Job (Job 38:3; 240:7).

12. Still another example of the priority of the gospel over the obligations of this world is the paying of taxes: the obligation of a citizen to pay taxes is vitiated by his joining the monastery (*Sh. Rul.* 94).

13. Stramara agrees with Garnier on the grounds that Basil's interpretation of 1 Corinthians 7:4 preserves a relationship of mutuality between husband and wife, while Clarke's view, Stramara says, implies that the husband could leave his wife for the monastery without her consent, but she could not leave him in the same way. Thus Clarke's interpretation destroys the mutuality and equality that Basil posits between man and woman (Daniel F. Stramara Jr., "Double Monasteries in the Greek East, Fourth through Eighth Centuries," *Journal of Early Christian Studies* 6 [1998]: 285). Of course the mutuality and equality would be preserved if Basil allowed the woman too to obey God rather than man.

14. The RSV has "utterance" instead of "word."

15. John H. Newman, "University Sermon XV: The Theory of Developments in Religious Doctrine," in *Fifteen Sermons Preached before the University of Oxford between AD 1826 and 1843* (New York: Longmans, Green, 1909), §27–28; 335. Newman preached this sermon in 1843, while still an Anglican, though he would soon thereafter retire to write *Essay on the Development of Doctrine*, after the writing of which he entered the Roman Church.

16. John H. Newman, *An Essay on the Development of Christian Doctrine*, 6th ed. (1878; repr., Notre Dame, IN: University of Notre Dame Press, 1989), 60.

17. Holmes notes with Gribomont that an appreciation for the office of the presider is a feature of Basil's more mature ascetic thought. *Shorter Rules* 114 is seen as evidence of an earlier form of obedience, mutual obedience (see Holmes, *Life Pleasing to God*, 169, 172).

18. Stramara, "Double Monasteries in the Greek East," 297.

19. Basil indicates that confession of sins is to be made not to just anyone, but only to those who have the ability to cure them (*Sh. Rul.* 229).

20. Basil writes: "The authority to forgive sins has not been given unconditionally but depends on the obedience of the penitent and his accord with the one entrusted with the care of the soul" (*Sh. Rul.* 15; 282).

21. Margaret Murphy holds that Basil did have sacramental confession (see *St. Basil and Monasticism* [Washington, DC: Catholic University of America Press, 1930], 96).

22. Silvas's extended comment on presbyters and presbyter-priests is very helpful.

> There is no doubt that when in his letters Basil refers to a "fellow-presbyter," he means a priest and that the *presbyters* of *Morals* 70.1 are certainly priests. Basil himself was already a priest during his second period as teacher of ascetics in Pontos, 363–65. As bishop, he ordained Peter a priest for Annisa in 371/72. Peter evidently continued as presbyter of the male section and priest-presbyter over both sections, while Makrina maintained a charismatic ascendency over the whole as the guiding genius and Peter's spiritual mother. *Lausiac History* 49.2 tells of Sissinius, a priest-presbyter presiding over a community of both men and women. On his return home to Cappadocia as an experienced ascetic, "he was considered worthy of the priesthood and he gathered together a community (*adelphotēs*) of men and women." (Silvas, 432n764)

23. The key texts are *Reg. Bas.* 21 and *Sh. Rul.* 288. The former, earlier, text has, "It *appears* necessary that sins be confessed to those entrusted with 'the stewardship of the mysteries of God' (1 Cor. 4:1; *Reg. Bas.* 21; 431; my emphasis). The latter, later, text has, "Therefore it *is* necessary . . ." (*Sh. Rul.* 288; 431; my emphasis).

24. Holmes, *Life Pleasing to God*, 190.

25. Holmes notes that in the practice of "excommunication from and within the communities, we thus see a typical conflation of concerns on the part of Basil the ascetic and bishop," for excommunication pertains especially to the office of bishop, as is clear in Basil's canonical letters (Holmes, *Life Pleasing to God*, 186).

26. It is not clear, at least to me, how often the monks would confess, but it seems obvious that far more time would be spent in work and prayer.

27. Murphy, *St. Basil and Monasticism*, 69.

28. Another example of this sort of thing is the meeting of a sister with an elder. The presider of the community of women is to be present at the meeting (*Sh. Rul.* 110).

29. It is not clear whether they prayed seven or eight times, for Basil may have described Lauds twice (*Lg. Rul.* 37.3–5). Taft takes the passage to yield seven rather than eight hours of prayer (*Liturgy of the Hours in East and West*, 86).

30. The first question, in particular, is whether one should receive "when something customary and according to nature happens" to him (*Sh. Rul.* 309.Q; 445). Silvas notes that the question here concerns sexual and reproductive matters and their implications for ritual cleanliness (Lev. 15). She concludes that "Basil's general principle seems to be that physical phenomena [including the menstruation of women] do not disbar one from Holy Communion unless they are due to wantonness or willful indulgence" (Silvas, 445n797).

31. Basil also mentions the custom of ascetics and laymen reserving the Eucharist in their homes and partaking of it when they see fit. Holmes treats the matter (see *Life Pleasing to God*, 234).

32. Basil here writes of the presider, but the text, I think, applies *mutandis mutatis* to all the monks.

Chapter 8: Tradition and Creativity

1. Mark DelCogliano, "Tradition and Polemic in Basil of Caesarea's Homily on the Theophany," *Vigiliae Christianae* 66 (2012): 31.

2. *La Tradition et la vie d'Église* (Paris: Arthème Fayard, 1963); trans. A. N. Woodrow, *The Meaning of Tradition* (San Francisco: Ignatius, 2004), 9–10.

3. See ep. 8.10 (NPNF 2, 8: 120): "Therefore the Holy Ghost is not a creature. If he is not a creature, He is of one essence and substance with the Father"; and ep. 8.11 (NPNF 2, 8: 121): "Now every temple is a temple of God, and if we are a temple of the Holy Ghost, then the Holy Ghost is God."

4. Thomas Weinandy argues that the (authentic) letters of Ignatius should be read in just this way. See "The Apostolic Christology of Ignatius of Antioch: The Road to Chalcedon," in *Trajectories through the New Testament and the Apostolic Fathers*, ed. A. F. Gregory and C. M. Tuckett, 72–84 (New York: Oxford University Press, 2005).

5. Newman, "University Sermon XV: The Theory of Developments in Religious Doctrine," in *Fifteen Sermons Preached before the University of Oxford between AD 1826 and 1843* (New York: Longmans, Green, 1909), §35; 342.

6. Ibid., §35; 342–43.

7. Ibid., 343.

8. Ibid. I think this text of Newman, I must confess, is a stroke of brilliance. It is, I believe, Newman's way of rescuing tradition (or at least some traditions) from the harsher consequences of the historical method. We could put it this way: the historical method tears apart what the tradition, even (or especially) in its historically tenuous instances, had put together. This tearing apart yields for us fantastic insights into the great figures of the Christian past and their thought, but the cost, very often, is a sense of continuity or overarching integrity. We get the historical (or theological) singular—what this or that theologian really said and thought and how this differs from what others said and thought—at the expense of how the theologian fits into the larger Christian tradition. Newman, in a way, tries to preserve the fruit of both the critical historical readings of the past and that of tradition-informed readings.

9. *Hom. gen. Chr.* 2: "Realize that God is in flesh for this reason: because the flesh that was cursed needed to be sanctified, the flesh that was weakened needed to be strengthened, the flesh that was alienated from God needed to be brought into affinity with him, the flesh that had fallen in paradise needed to be led back into heaven." This translation is Mark DelCogliano's; I am very grateful to him for the use of it before its publication.

10. The seven ways are wholesale adoption, adoption with tweaking, expansion, supplementation, abridgement, redeployment, and refutation (see DelCogliano, "Tradition and Polemic," 55).

11. Origen, *Homilies on Luke*, hom. 6.3; trans. Lienhard, 24.

12. Ibid.

13. See *Hom. gen. Chr.* 3; trans. DelCogliano: "So that Joseph could witness Mary's purity with his own eyes and she would not be subjected to ridicule as if she had defiled her virginity, she was given a betrothed who would defend her character."

14. See Ignatius, *Letter to the Ephesians* 6:4; and Origen, *Homilies on Luke*, hom. 6.4.

15. See *Hom. gen. Chr.* 3 and DelCogliano, "Tradition and Polemic," 33–34.

16. Origen, *Commentary on Matthew* 12:34; trans. John Patrick, in *The Gospel of Peter, The Diatesseron of Tatian, The Apocalypse of Peter, The Vision of Paul, The Apocalypses of the Virgin and Sedrach, The Testament of Abraham, The Acts of Xanthippe and Polyxena, The Narrative of Zosimus, The Apology of Aristides, The Epistles of Clement* (complete text), *Origen's Commentary on John, Books 1–10, and Commentary on Matthew, Books 1, 2, and 10–14*, ANF 9 (1896; repr., Peabody, MA: Hendrickson, 1994), 468.

17. DelCogliano notes something peculiar about Basil's borrowing: the point that Origen had made about "until" in Matthew 16:28 he also himself made about "until" in Matthew 1:25, but Basil uses the former text and not the latter. What is more, we have every reason to believe that the latter text was available to Basil (see DelCogliano, "Tradition and Polemic," 44–45).

18. Origen, *Homilies on Luke*, hom. 14.7; trans. Lienhard, 60.

19. *Hom. gen. Chr.* 5; trans. DelCogliano. DelCogliano notes that Basil's dependency here is ambiguous: Basil "could merely be offering a counter-definition of 'firstborn' based on Old Testament descriptions. But his extensive usage of Origen elsewhere suggests that perhaps in this case too he is drawing on him" ("Tradition and Polemic," 46).

20. See DelCogliano, "Tradition and Polemic," 46–47.

21. *Hom. gen. Chr.* 5; trans. DelCogliano.

22. Ibid.

23. DelCogliano, in his translation of this sermon, points out that, even though this tradition about Zechariah goes back to the apocryphal *Protoevangelium of James*, Basil seems to have gotten it through Origen. See also "Tradition and Polemic," 46–47.

24. See Origen, *Contra Celsum* 1.59; and DelCogliano, "Tradition and Polemic," 52–54.

25. See *Hom. gen. Chr.* 5–6.

26. DelCogliano, "Tradition and Polemic," 53.

27. *Hom. gen. Chr.* 6; trans. DelCogliano.

28. Here, again, I am indebted to Mark DelCogliano, who has demonstrated Basil's dependence here on Eusebius rather than Athanasius, in whose thought Proverbs 8:22 received much attention. See "Basil of Caesarea on Proverbs 8:22 and the Sources of Pro-Nicene Theology," *Journal of Theological Studies*, n.s., 59 (2008): 183–90.

29. See Eusebius, *Ecclesiastical Theology* 1.10.2; 3.1.1–3.2.8; 3.2.15; DelCogliano, "Basil of Caesarea on Proverbs 8:22," 185–89.

30. DelCogliano, "Basil of Caesarea on Proverbs 8:22," 190.

31. This point is made by DelCogliano (see "The Influence of Athansius and the Homoiousians on Basil of Caesarea's Decentralization of 'Unbegotten,'" *Journal of Early Christian Studies* 19 [2011]: 221–22).

32. "Homoiousian theology," DelCogliano writes, is "an anti-heteroousian restatement of Eusebian theology along Athanasian lines" (ibid., 202).

33. The fact that Basil of Ancrya, George of Laodicea, and Basil are all moving in the same theological direction (and in his own way we might include Athanasius in this list) is, I think, what Andrew Radde-Gallwitz is getting at when he says that the lines between theological parties were disappearing in Basil's time (*Basil of Caesarea: A Guide to His Life and Doctrine* [Eugene, OR: Cascade Books, 2012], 12).

34. See DelCogliano, "Influence of Athansius and the Homoiousians" 209–12. He argues for Basil's dependence on either Athanasius or Basil of Ancyra, but leans toward the position that St. Basil was immediately dependent on Basil of Ancyra and mediately dependent on Athanasius, for Basil of Ancyra used Athanasius.

35. George himself may have used Athanasius; though, if he did, he much altered what he borrowed (see ibid., 212–19).

36. See Epiphanius, *Panarion* 73.12–22; and DelCogliano, "Influence of Athansius and the Homoiousians," 219–20.

37. Johannes Zachhuber makes this point as does DelCogliano, as we saw, but in different ways (see Zachhuber, "Basil and the Three-Hypostases Tradition: Reconsidering the Origins of Cappadocian Theology, *Zeitschrift für Antikes Christentum* 5 [2001]: 65–85). Basil himself claims never to have changed the understanding of God that he received in childhood (ep. 223.3).

38. The best treatment of this issue in Athanasius is Khaled Anatolios, *Athanasius: The Coherence of His Thought* (New York: Routledge, 1998).

39. On the theme of a strict distinction between God and the world, see also *Ag. Eun.* 3.2.

40. The exposition on the Psalms attributed to Athanasius is thought to be spurious.

41. See Athanasius, *Contra gentes* 2. I pull this and the following examples from Anatolios, *Athanasius*, 32.

42. See, e.g., *Contra gentes* 3 and 7; and *De incarnatione* 4.

43. See, e.g., *Contra gentes* 41.

44. See, e.g., *De incarnatione* 6.

45. See Basil, *In Mamantem martyrem* 4.

46. See, e.g., *Contra gentes* 40; *De incarnatione* 42; *Ep. ad episcopos Aegypti et Libyae* (PG 25:564); *Orationes c. Ar.* (PG 26:28, 189, 205, 212, 224, 233). Lewis Ayres has argued that the real point, for Athanasius, of the technical language (*ek tēs ousias tou Patros* and *homoousios tō Patri*) in the creed of Nicaea is to secure the scriptural teaching that the Son is the true Son and Word, proper to and from the Father. See Lewis Ayres, "Athansius's Initial Defense of the Term *Homoousios*: Rereading the *De Decretis*," *Journal of Early Christian Studies* 12 (2004): 337–59.

47. Robertson thinks that ep. 8.3 shows the influence of *De synodis* 53, and he seems right (see his introduction to *De synodis*, NPNF 2, 4: 449). Ep. 8.3 reads:

> We in accordance with the true doctrine speak of the Son as neither like, nor unlike the Father. Each of these terms is equally impossible, for like and unlike are predicted in relation to quality and the divine is free from quality. We, on the contrary, confess identity of nature and accepting the consubstantiality, and rejecting the composition of the Father, God in substance, who begat the Son, God in substance. From this the consubstantiality is proved. For God in essence or substance is co-essential or consubstantial with God in essence or substance.

De synodis 53 has:

> For you know yourselves, and no one can dispute it, that Like is not predicated of essence, but of habits and qualities; for in the case of essences, we speak, not of likeness, but of identity. Man, for instance, is said to be like man, not in essence, but according to habit and character; for in essence men are of one nature. And again, man is not said to be unlike dog, but to be of a different nature. Accordingly while the former are of one nature and co-essential, the latter are different in both.

On the authenticity of ep. 8, see Wilhelm Bousset, *Apophthegmata. Studien zur Geschichte des ältesten Mönchtums* (Tübingen: J. C. B. Mohr, 1923), 335–41; and Robert Melcher, *Der achte Brief des hl. Basilius. Ein Werk des Evagrius Pontikus*, Münsterische Beiträge zur Theologie 1 (Münster i. W.: Aschendorff, 1923).

48. See *De synodis* 43.

49. See *De sententia Dionysii*.

50. On the relationship between *To Serap.* and *Con. Eun.* 3, see Marina Troiano, "Il *Contra Eunomium III* di Basilio di Cesarea e le *Epistolae ad Serapionem I–IV* di Atanasio di Alessandria: Nota Comparativa," *Augustinianum* 41 (2001): 59–91.

51. See *Con. Eun.* 3.1; and *To Serap.* 1.11–12.

52. See *Con. Eun.* 3.6; and *To Serap.* 1.15–21.

53. See *Con. Eun.* 3.5; and *To Serap.* 1.23; 1.28–31.

54. The RSV has "he who forms the mountains, and creates the wind."

55. So Troiano concludes that the common themes and use of Scripture do not justify a knowledge of or dependence on Athanasius by Basil ("Nota Comparativa," 91).

56. See Mark DelCogliano, "Basil of Caesarea, Didymus the Blind, and the Anti-Pneumatomachian Exegesis of Amos 4:13 and John 1:3," *Journal of Theological Studies*, n.s., 61 (2010): 644–58.

57. See Didymus, *On the Holy Spirit* 61–64, on John 1:3; and 65–73, on Amos 4:13.

58. *Tomus ad Antiochenos* 5 (NPNF 2, 4: 484).

59. W. K. L. Clarke, *St. Basil the Great: A Study in Monasticism* (Cambridge: Cambridge University Press, 1913), 122.

60. Ibid., 124. On Pachomius, see Philip Rousseau, *Pachomius: The Making of a Community in Fourth-Century Egypt* (Berkeley: University of California Press, 1985).

61. Jean Gribomont traces this view to H. Leclercq's article in the *Dictionnaire d'Archéologie* (see "Obéssance et Évangile selon s. Basile le Grand," *Supplément de la Vie spirituelle* 21 [1952]: 193).

62. Andrea Sterk, *Renouncing the World Yet Leading the Church: The Monk-Bishop in Late Antiquity* (Cambridge, MA: Harvard University Press, 2004), 42.

63. Ibid., 43. On the question of Basil and Pachomius, see also Paul J. Fedwick, *The Church and the Charisma of Leadership in Basil of Caesarea*, Studies and Texts 45 (Toronto: Pontifical Institute of Mediaeval Studies, 1979), 156–58.

64. E. Amand de Mendieta, "Le système cénobitique basilien compare au système cénobitique pachômien," *Revue de L'histoire des Religions* 152 (1957): 33.

65. This list is drawn from ibid., 69–71. Clarke draws up a similar list (see *Study in Monasticism*, 123–24).

66. On Basil and Eustathius, see also Charles A. Frazee, "Anatolian Asceticism in the Fourth Century: Eustathios of Sebastea and Basil of Caesarea," *Catholic Historical Review* 66 (1980): 16–33.

67. Sterk has written extensively on the monastic ideal of episcopal authority that Basil took over from Eustathius, that Basil himself embodied and promoted (see *Renouncing the World Yet Leading the Church*, 3–92).

68. De Mendieta, "Le système cénobitique basilien compare au système cénobitique pachômien," 73.

69. Stramara dates this change to 368: "By 368 the community as Annesi was no longer a familial ascetic retreat, but a fully functioning double monastery capable of absorbing new female and male members as well as of tending boys and girls" (Daniel F. Stramara Jr., "Double Monasteries in the Greek East, Fourth through Eighth Centuries," *Journal of Early Christian Studies* 6 [1998]: 283). His benchmark here is the great famine of 368–69 in Cappadocia and the response that the community at Annisa was able to mount.

70. Elm sees three points of difference between Basilian and Eustathian asceticism: a move to the countryside and away from the city; a distance, therefore, from doctrinal and ecclesial disputes; and a rejection of ascetic cohabitation (Susanna Elm, *Virgins of God: The Making of Asceticism in Late Antiquity* [Oxford: Clarendon, 1996], 210–11).

71. Stramara, "Double Monasteries in the Greek East," 276.

72. Holmes, *Life Pleasing to God*, 211. Holmes cites Basil of Ancyra's *On Virginity* from Susanna Elm's *Virgins of God* that is well worth repeating here:

> This is the greatest and most magnificent aspect of virginity, that it constitutes a manifestation already here on earth of the pure seed of the resurrection and the incorruptible life. If at the resurrection no one marries and is married but all are like the angels and become children of God (Matt. 22:30), then all those who lead the virginal life are already angels during their human life, while still ensconced in their corruptible flesh . . . surrounded by constant temptations. . . . Here, the virgins must be most highly admired. They have a female body, but they repress the appearance of their body through *askēsis*, and become, through their virtue, like men, to whom they are already created equal in their soul. And while men through *askēsis* become angels instead of men, so do women, through exercise (*dia tēs askēseōs*) of the same virtues, gain the same value as men. So, while in this present life they are equal to men in their soul only, but are hampered in achieving equality because of their female body, they will gain, through virtue, full equality with these men, who have already been made into the angels of the future life. Because if they become angel-like (*isangelous*), then those who practice asceticism in this life have already succeeded in being just like angels: they have castrated the female and male desires to cohabit through virtue and live among men on earth with naked souls. (Elm, *Virgins of God*, 120)

Silvas disagrees with Elm's assessment of Homoiousian asceticism, especially the latter's contention that the Homoiousians practiced the cohabitation of male and female ascetics (*syneisaktism*) (85–86). Silvas persuasively makes the point that Eustathius, one of these Homoiousians, has significantly moved away from his earlier extreme positions by the mid-360s. In his early extremism, however, it is well possible that he endorsed the practice of *syneisaktism*. This particular mistake is not mentioned at the Synod of Gangra, though women adopting male dress and hairstyle is (Gangra pref. 7, can. 13 and 17).

73. Holmes, *Life Pleasing to God*, 213.

74. For male and female cooperation in governance, see Stramara, "Double Monasteries in the Greek East," 297–301; for their prayer life together, see ibid., 302–6; and for their interactions through work, see ibid., 306–8.

75. Ibid., 311.

76. Ibid., 312.

77. Holmes, *Life Pleasing to God*, 110.

78. Holmes cites this text (ibid., 379–80).

79. *Skopos*, Holmes points out, appears only once in the New Testament but more than sixty times in the Asceticon (ibid., 113–14).

80. Ibid., 114.

81. J. E. Bamberger, "*MNĒMĒ-DIATHESIS*: The Psychic Dynamisms in the Ascetical Theology of St. Basil," *Orientalia Christiana Periodica* 34 (1968): 233–51.

82. Ibid., 235.

83. See ibid., 236; and *Lg. Rul.* 6.1–2.

84. Holmes expressed reservations about the originality of Basil's understanding of memory: we should "beware of attributing to him too unique a role in its [memory's] genesis" (*Life Pleasing to God*, 122–23).

85. Bamberger, "*MNĒMĒ-DIATHESIS*," 238, 248.

86. See ibid., 249–50.

87. Basil speaks of bad habits as having the force of nature, but the whole point of the Christian life is to arrive at God by replacing the bad habits with good ones, to replace habitual forgetfulness with habitual memory of God, habitual sin with habitual obedience to the commands of Christ (*Lg. Rul.* 6.1).

88. See Bamberger, "*MNĒMĒ-DIATHESIS*," 237–38, 241; and *Sh. Rul.* 281.

89. Bamberger, "*MNĒMĒ-DIATHESIS*," 243.

90. Bamberger cites this text (ibid., 242–43).

91. *Hom. in Mart. Jul.* 4; cited in Anne Gordon Keidel, "*Hesychia*, Prayer and Transformation in Basil of Caesarea," in *Studia Patristica 37, Papers Presented at the Thirteenth International Conference on Patristic Studies Held in Oxford, 1999: Cappadocian Writers, Other Greek Writers*, ed. M. F. Wiles and E. J. Yarnold (Louvain: Peeters, 2001), 116.

92. Elm, *Virgins of God*, 222.

Conclusion

1. Rousseau laments the distinction between ascetic works and homilies, just as I here am lamenting the distinction between ascetic and dogmatic works; he rightly points out that the homilies too are ascetic works (*Basil of Caesarea*, 91).

2. Peter W. Martens, "Interpreting Attentively: The Ascetic Character of Biblical Exegesis according to Origen and Basil of Caesarea," in *Origeniana Octava: Origen and the Alexandrian Tradition, Papers of the 8th International Origen Congress, Pisa, 27–31 August 2001*, vol. 2, ed. L. Perrone et al. (Louvain: Peeters, 2003), 1117.

3. I draw here on Andrea Sterk, *Renouncing the World Yet Leading the Church: The Monk-Bishop in Late Antiquity* (Cambridge, MA: Harvard University Press, 2004), 84–86.

Works Cited

Sources

Athanasius of Alexandria. *De synodis*. Translated by John Henry Newman. Revised by Archibald Robertson. In *Select Writings and Letters of Athanasius, Bishop of Alexandria*. NPNF, 2, 4. 1892. Reprint, Peabody, MA: Hendrickson, 1994.

———. *Letters to Serapion*. Translated by Mark DelCogliano, Andrew Radde-Gallwitz, and Lewis Ayres. In *Works on the Spirit: Athanasius and Didymus*. Popular Patristics, 43. Yonkers, NY: St. Vladimir's Seminary Press, 2011.

———. *Tomus ad Antiochenos*. Translated by John Henry Newman. Revised by Archibald Robertson. NPNF, 2, 4. 1892. Reprint, Peabody, MA: Hendrickson, 1994.

Augustine of Hippo. *Confessions*. Translated by Henry Chadwick. New York: Oxford University Press, 1991.

———. *Marriage and Virginity: The Excellence of Marriage, Holy Virginity, The Excellence of Widowhood, Adulterous Marriages, Continence*. Translated by Ray Kearney. The Works of St. Augustine: A Translation for the 21st Century, vol. 9, pt. 1. New York: New City Press, 1999.

———. *On Faith and Works*. Translated by Ray Kearney. In *On Christian Belief*. The Works of St. Augustine, vol. 8, pt. 1. Hyde Park, NY: New City Press, 2005.

Basil of Caesarea. *Against Eunomius*. Translated by Mark DelCogliano and Andrew Radde-Gallwitz. Fathers of the Church 122. Washington, DC: Catholic University of America Press, 2011.

———. Epistles. Translated by Roy J. Deferrari. In *Saint Basil, The Letters*, 4 vols. Loeb Classical Library. Cambridge, MA: Harvard University Press, 1926–34. Also translated by Blomfield Jackson. In *The Treatise De Spiritu Sancto, the Nine Homilies of the Hexaemeron and the Letters of Saint Basil the Great Archbishop of Caesarea*. NPNF 2, 8. 1895. Reprint, Peabody, MA: Hendrickson, 1994.

———. *Hexaëmeron 1–9*. Translated by Clare Agnes Way. In *St. Basil: Exegetic Homilies*. Fathers of the Church 46. Washington, DC: Catholic University of America Press, 1963.

———. *Hexaëmeron* 10–11. Translated by Nonna Verna Harrison. In *St. Basil the Great: On the Human Condition*. Popular Patristics 30. Crestwood, NY: St. Vladimir's Seminary Press, 2005.

———. *Homilia in Martyrem Iulitta.*

———. *Homilia in sanctam Christi generationem.*

———. *Homilies on the Psalms*. Translated by Way. In *Exegetic Homilies.*

———. *Homily against Anger*. Translated by Harrison. In *On the Human Condition.*

———. *Homily against Those Who Lend at Interest*. Translated by Schroeder. In *On Social Justice.*

———. *Homily, Attend to Yourself*. Translated by Harrison. In *On the Human Condition.*

———. *Homily Explaining that God Is Not the Cause of Evil*. Translated by Harrison. In *On the Human Condition.*

———. *Homily, I Will Tear Down These Barns*. Translated by C. Paul Schroeder. In *St. Basil the Great: On Social Justice*. Popular Patristics 38. Crestwood, NY: St. Vladimir's Seminary Press, 2009.

———. *Homily in a Time of Famine and Drought*. Translated by Schroeder. In *On Social Justice.*

———. *Homily on "In the Beginning Was the Word."* Translated by Mark DelCogliano. In *St. Basil the Great: On Christian Doctrine and Practice*. Popular Patristics 47. Yonkers, NY: St. Vladimir's Seminary Press, 2012.

———. *Homily, To the Rich*. Translated by Schroeder. In *On Social Justice.*

———. *Longer Rules*. Translated by Anna Silvas. *The Asketikon of St. Basil the Great*. Oxford Early Christian Studies. New York: Oxford University Press, 2005.

———. *Morals*. Translated by W. K. L. Clarke. In *The Ascetic Works of St. Basil*. London: SPCK, 1925.

———. *On Baptism*. Translated by M. Monica Wagner. In *Saint Basil, Ascetical Works*. Fathers of the Church 9. Washington, DC: Catholic University of America Press, 1962.

———. *On Faith*. Translated by Clarke. In *Ascetic Works of St. Basil.*

———. *On Judgment*. Translated by Clarke. In *Ascetic Works of St. Basil.*

———. *On the Holy Spirit*. Translated by Stephen M. Hildebrand. Popular Patristics 42. Yonkers, NY: St. Vladimir's Seminary Press, 2011.

———. *On the Renunciation of the World* (spurious). Translated by Clarke. In *Ascetic Works of St. Basil.*

———. *Protreptic on Baptism*. Translated by Thomas Halton. In *Baptism: Ancient Liturgies and Patristic Texts*, edited by André Hamman and Thomas Halton, 76–87. Staten Island, NY: Alba House, 1967.

———. *Regula Basilii* (Small Asceticon). Translated by Silvas. In *Asketikon of St. Basil.*

———. *Shorter Rules*. Translated by Silvas. In *Asketikon of St. Basil the Great.*

Decrees of the Ecumenical Councils, edited by Norman Tanner, Giuseppe Alberigo et al. Vol. 1, *Nicaea I to Lateran V*. Washington, DC: Georgetown University Press, 1990.

Epistle to Diognetus. Translated by Cyril Richardson. *Early Christian Fathers.* New York: Touchstone, 1996.

Eunomius of Cyzicus. *Apology.* Translated by Richard Paul Vaggione. In *Eunomius: The Extant Works.* Oxford Early Christian Texts. New York: Oxford University Press, 1987.

———. *Exposition of Faith.* Translated by Vaggione. In *Eunomius.*

Eusebius of Caesarea. *Letter to His Church concerning the Synod of Nicaea.* Translated by William Rusch. In *The Trinitarian Controversy.* Sources of Early Christian Thought. Philadelphia: Fortress, 1980.

Gangra, Synod of. Translated by Silvas. In *Asketikon of St. Basil the Great.*

Gregory of Nazianzus. Epistles. Translated by Charles Gordon Browne and James Edward Swallow. In *S. Cyril of Jerusalem, S. Gregory Nazianzen.* NPNF 2, 7. 1893. Reprint, Peabody, MA: Hendrickson, 1994.

———. *Orations.* Translated by Charles Gordon Browne and James Edward Swallow. NPNF 2, 7. 1893. Reprint, Peabody, MA: Hendrickson, 1994. Also in Gregory of Nazianzus, *On God and Christ: The Five Theological Orations and Two Letters to Cledonius.* Translated by Frederick Williams and Lionel Wickham. Popular Patristics 23. Crestwood, NY: St. Vladimir's Seminary Press, 2002.

Gregory of Nyssa. *Against Eunomius.* Translated by H. A. Wilson. In *Select Writings and Letters of Gregory, Bishop of Nyssa.* NPNF 2, 5. 1893. Reprint, Peabody, MA: Hendrickson, 1995.

———. *The Life of St. Macrina.* Translated by Kevin Corrigan. Toronto: Peregrina, 1998.

Origen. *Against Celsus.* Translated by Henry Chadwick. In *Origen: Contra Celsum.* Rev. ed. New York: Cambridge University Press, 1980.

———. *Commentary on Matthew.* Translated by John Patrick. In *The Gospel of Peter, The Diatesseron of Tatian, The Apocalypse of Peter, The Vision of Paul, The Apocalypses of the Virgin and Sedrach, The Testament of Abraham, The Acts of Xanthippe and Polyxena, The Narrative of Zosimus, The Apology of Aristides, The Epistles of Clement* (complete text), *Origen's Commentary on John, Books 1–10, and Commentary on Matthew, Books 1, 2, and 10–14.* ANF 9. 1896. Reprint, Peabody, MA: Hendrickson, 1994.

———. *Homilies on Luke.* Translated by Joseph T. Lienhard. Fathers of the Church 94. Washington, DC: Catholic University of America Press, 1996.

———. *On First Principles.* Translated by G. W. Butterworth. Gloucester, MA: Peter Smith, 1973.

Plato, *Timaeus.* Translated by Desmond Lee. In *Timaeus and Critias.* New York: Penguin, 1977.

Plotinus. *The Enneads: A New, Definitive Edition with Comparisons to Other Translations on Hundreds of Key Passages.* Translated by Stephen MacKenna. Burdett, NY: Larson, 1992.

Socrates. *Ecclesiastical History.* Anonymously translated in *Ecclesiastical History: A History of the Church in Seven Books, from the Accession of Constantine, AD 306, to the 36th year of Theodosius, Un., AD 445, including a period of 140 years*. London: Bagster, 1844. Revised by A. C. Zenos. *The Ecclesiastical History of Socrates Scholasticus*. In *Socrates, Sozomenus: Church Histories*. NPNF 2, 2. 1890. Reprint, Peabody, MA: Hendrickson, 1995.

Sozomen. *Ecclesiastical History*. Translated by Edward Walford. *Ecclesiastical History: A History of the Church in Nine Books, from AD 324 to AD 440*. London: Samuel Bagster & Sons, 1846. Revised by Chester D. Hartranft, *The Ecclesiastical History of Sozomen, comprising a History of the Church, from AD 323 to AD 425*. In *Socrates, Sozomenus: Church Histories*, NPNF 2, 2. 1890. Reprint, Peabody, MA: Hendrickson, 1995.

Tertullian. *On the Resurrection of the Flesh*. Translated by P. Holmes. In *Latin Christianity: Its Founder, Tertullian. Three Parts: I. Apologetic; II. Anti-Marcion; III. Ethical*, 545–96. ANF 3. Buffalo: Christian Literature Publishing, 1885. Reprint, Peabody, MA: Hendrickson, 1994.

Literature

Allison, Dale, Jr. *Resurrecting Jesus: The Earliest Christian Tradition and Its Interpreters*. New York: T&T Clark, 2005.

Amand de Mendieta, Emmanuel. "The Pair *KĒRYGMA* and *DOGMA* in the Theological Thought of St. Basil of Caesarea." *Journal of Theological Studies*, n.s., 16 (1965): 129–42.

———. "Le système cénobitique basilien compare au système cénobitique pachômien." *Revue de L'histoire des Religions* 152 (1957): 31–80.

———. *The "Unwritten" and "Secret" Apostolic Traditions in the Theological Thought of St. Basil of Caesarea*. Scottish Journal of Theology Occasional Papers 13. London: Oliver & Boyd, 1965.

Anatolios, Khaled. *Athanasius: The Coherence of His Thought*. New York: Routledge, 1998.

Auerbach, Erich. *Mimesis: The Representation of Reality in Western Literature*. Translated by Willard R. Trask. Princeton: Princeton University Press, 1953.

———. *Scenes from the Drama of European Literature*. Minneapolis: University of Minnesota Press, 1984.

Ayres, Lewis. "Athanasius' Initial Defense of the Term *Homoousios*: Rereading the *De Decretis*." *Journal of Early Christian Studies* 12 (2004): 337–59.

Bamberger, John Eudes. "*MNĒMĒ-DIATHESIS*: The Psychic Dynamisms in the Ascetical Theology of St. Basil." *Orientalia Christiana Periodica* 34 (1968): 233–51.

Barjeau, J. Philip de, *L'école exégétique d'Antioche*. Toulouse: Imprimerie A. Chauvin et Fils, 1898.

Behr, John. *The Nicene Faith*. The Formation of Christian Theology 2. Crestview, NY: St. Vladimir's Seminary Press, 2004.

Berger, M. *Die Schöpfungslehre des hl. Basilius des Grossen*. 2 vols. Rosenheim: Druck von M. Niedermayr, 1897–98.

Bernardi, Jean. *La Prédication des pères cappadociens: Le Prédicateur et son auditoire.* Publications de la Faculté des letters et sciences humaines de l'Université de Montpellier 30. Marseille: Presses universitaires de France, 1968.

Bousset, Wilhelm. *Apophthegmata. Studien zur Geschichte des ältesten Mönchtums.* Tübingen: J. C. B. Mohr, 1923.

Brown, Peter. *Augustine of Hippo: A Biography.* Rev. ed. Berkeley: University of California Press, 2000.

The Cambridge Companion to Plotinus. Edited by Lloyd P. Gerson. New York: Cambridge University Press, 1996.

Chadwick, Henry. "Florilegium." In *Reallexikon für Antike und Christentum*, edited by T. Klauser, 7:1131–60. Stuttgart: Hiersemann, 1969.

Clark, Elizabeth A. *The Origenist Controversy: The Cultural Construction of an Early Christian Debate.* Princeton: Princeton University Press, 1992.

Clark, Stephen. "Plotinus: Body and Soul." In *Cambridge Companion to Plotinus*, 275–91.

Claudel, Paul. *Œuvres en prose.* Edited by Jacques Petit and Charles Galpérine. Paris: Gallimard, Bibliothèque de la Pléiade, 1965.

Congar, Yves. *La Tradition et la vie d'Église.* Paris: Arthème Fayard, 1963. Translated by A. N. Woodrow. *The Meaning of Tradition.* San Francisco: Ignatius, 2004.

Corrigan, K. *Plotinus' Theory of Matter-Evil and the Question of Substance: Plato, Aristotle, and Alexander of Aphrodisias.* Recherches de Théologie Ancienne et Médiévale. Louvain: Peeters, 1996.

Courtonne, Yves. *Saint Basile et l'Hellénisme: Étude sur la recontre de la pensée chrétienne avec la sagesse antique dans l'Hexaméron de Basile le Grand.* Paris: Firmin Didot, 1934.

Daley, Brian. *The Hope of the Early Church: A Handbook of Patristic Eschatology.* New York: Cambridge University Press, 1991.

DelCogliano, Mark. "Basil of Caesarea, Didymus the Blind, and the Anti-Pneumatomachian Exegesis of Amos 4:13 and John 1:3." *Journal of Theological Studies*, n.s., 61 (2010): 644–58.

———. "Basil of Caesarea on Proverbs 8:22 and the Sources of Pro-Nicene Theology." *Journal of Theological Studies*, n.s., 59 (2008): 183–90.

———. *Basil of Caesarea's Anti-Eunomian Theory of Names: Christian Theology and Late-Antique Philosophy in the Fourth Century Trinitarian Controversy.* Supplements to Vigiliae Christianae 103. Boston: Brill, 2010.

———. "The Influence of Athanasius and the Homoiousians on Basil of Caesarea's Decentralization of 'Unbegotten.'" *Journal of Early Christian Studies* 19 (2011): 197–223.

———. "Tradition and Polemic in Basil of Caesarea's Homily on the Theophany." *Vigiliae Christianae* 66 (2012): 30–55.

Fedwick, Paul. "A Chronology of the Life and Works of Basil of Caesarea." In *Basil of Caesarea, Christian, Humanist, Ascetic: A Sixteen-Hundredth Anniversary*

Symposium. 2 vols. Edited by Paul Fedwick. Toronto: Pontifical Institute of Mediaeval Studies, 1981.

———. *The Church and the Charisma of Leadership in Basil of Caesarea.* Studies and Texts 45. Toronto: Pontifical Institute of Mediaeval Studies, 1979.

Fenwick, John R. K. *The Anaphoras of St. Basil and St. James: An Investigation of Their Common Origin.* Orientalia Christiana Analecta 240. Rome: Pontificium Institutum Orientale, 1992.

Fialon, E. *Étude historique et littéraire sur sainte Basile suivie de l'Hexaméron traduit en français.* Paris: Ernest Thorin, 1869.

Florovsky, Georges. "The Function of Tradition in the Ancient Church." *Greek Orthodox Theological Review* 9 (1963): 181–200.

Frank, Karl Suso. "Monastiche Reform im Altertum: Eustathius von Sebaste und Basilius von Caesarea." In *Reformatio Ecclesiae: Beiträge zu Kirchlichen Reformbemühungen von der Alten Kirche bis zur Neuzeit. Festgabe für Erwin Iserloh,* ed. Remigius Bäumer. Munich: Ferdinand Schöningh, 1980.

Frazee, Charles A. "Anatolian Asceticism in the Fourth Century: Eustathios of Sebastea and Basil of Caesarea." *Catholic Historical Review* 66 (1980): 16–33.

Gribomont, Jean. "Esotérisme et Tradition dans le Traité du Saint-Esprit de Saint Basile." In *Oecumenica, an Annual Symposium of Ecumenical Research,* 22–58. Minneapolis: Augsburg, 1967.

———. "Obéssance et Évangile selon s. Basile le Grand." *Supplément de la Vie spirituelle* 21 (1952): 192–215.

———. "Le Renoncement au monde dans l'idéal ascétique de s. Basile." *Irénikon* 31 (1958): 282–307; 460–75.

Hanson, R. P. C. "Basil's Doctrine of Tradition in Relation to the Holy Spirit." *Vigiliae Christianae* 22 (1968): 249–52.

———. *The Search for the Christian Doctrine of God: The Arian Controversy 318–381.* Edinburgh: T&T Clark, 1988. Reprint, Grand Rapids: Baker Academic, 2006.

Harrison, Verna. "Male and Female in Cappadocian Theology." *Journal of Theological Studies,* n.s., 41 (1990): 441–71.

Hennephof, H. *Textus byzantinos ad Iconomachiam pertinentes.* Leiden: Brill, 1969.

Henry, Nathalie. "A New Insight into the Growth of Ascetic Society in the Fourth Century AD: The Public Consecration of Virgins as a Means of Integration and Promotion of the Female Ascetic Movement." In Studia Patristica 35, *Papers Presented at the Thirteenth International Conference on Patristic Studies Held in Oxford, 1999.* Pt. 4, *Ascetica, Gnostica, Liturgica, Orientalia,* edited by M. F. Wiles and E. J. Yarnold, 102–9. Louvain: Peeters, 2001.

Hildebrand, Stephen M. "Scripture, Worship, and Liturgy in the Thought of St. Basil the Great." *Letter and Spirit* 7 (2011): 85–97.

———. *The Trinitarian Theology of Basil of Caesarea: A Synthesis of Greek Thought and Biblical Truth.* Washington, DC: Catholic University of America Press, 2007.

Holmes, Augustine. *A Life Pleasing to God: The Spirituality of the Rules of St. Basil.* London: Darton, Longman & Todd, 2000.

Kalligas, Paul. "Basil of Caesarea on the Semantics of Proper Names." In *Byzantine Philosophy and Its Ancient Sources*, edited by Katerina Ierodiakonou, 31–48. Oxford: Clarendon, 2002.

Kane, Michael A. "St. Basil's *On the Holy Spirit*: A Secret Tradition or the Rule of Faith?" *Diakonia* 35 (2002): 23–37.

Keidel, Anne Gordon. "*Hesychia*, Prayer and Transformation in Basil of Caesarea." In Studia Patristica 37, *Papers Presented at the Thirteenth International Conference on Patristic Studies Held in Oxford, 1999, Cappadocian Writers, Other Greek Writers*, edited by M. F. Wiles and E. J. Yarnold, 110–20. Louvain: Peeters, 2001.

Lèbe, Léon. "S. Basile et ses *Règles Morales*." *Revue bénédictine* 75 (1965): 193–200.

Levie, Jean. *Les sources de la septième et le huitième homélies de saint Basile sur l'Hexaméron*. Extrait du Musée belge, 1920. Louvain: F. Ceuterick, 1920.

Lewis, Stephen. "*Quid animo satis?* A Question that Generates an Education." Lecture, Franciscan University of Steubenville, Steubenville, OH, November 18, 2011.

Lienhard, Joseph T. "The 'Arian' Controversy: Some Categories Reconsidered." *Theological Studies* 48 (1987): 415–37.

———. *Contra Marcellum: Marcellus of Ancyra and Fourth-Century Theology*. Washington, DC: Catholic University of America Press, 1999.

Lim, Richard. "The Politics of Interpretation in Basil of Caesarea's *Hexaemeron*." *Vigiliae Christianae* 44 (1990): 351–70.

Loofs, F. *Eustathius von Sebaste und die Chronologie der Basilius-Briefe*. Halle: Niemeyer, 1898.

Ludlow, Morwenna. "Demons, Evil, and Liminity in Cappadocian Theology." *Journal of Early Christian Studies* 20 (2012): 179–211.

Martens, Peter W. "Interpreting Attentively: The Ascetic Character of Biblical Exegesis according to Origen and Basil of Caesarea." In *Origeniana Octava: Origen and the Alexandrian Tradition, Papers of the 8th International Origen Congress, Pisa, 27–31 August 2001*, edited by L. Perrone et al. 2 vols. Louvain: Peeters, 2003.

Melcher, Robert. *Der achte Brief des hl. Basilius. Ein Werk des Evagrius Ponticus*. Münsterische Beiträge zur Theologie 1. Münster i. W.: Aschendorff, 1923.

Meredith, Anthony. "Asceticism—Christian and Greek." *Journal of Theological Studies*, n.s., 27 (1976): 312–32.

———. "Gregory of Nazianzus and Gregory of Nyssa on Basil." In *Studia Patristica 32, Papers Presented at the Twelfth International Conference on Patristic Studies Held in Oxford 1995. Athanasius and His Opponents, Cappadocian Fathers, Other Greek Writers after Nicaea*, edited by Elizabeth A. Livingstone, 163–69. Louvain: Peeters, 1997.

Murphy, Margaret. *St. Basil and Monasticism*. Washington, DC: Catholic University of America Press, 1930.

Newman, John Henry. *An Essay on the Development of Doctrine*. 6th ed. 1878. Reprint, Notre Dame, IN: University of Notre Dame Press, 1989.

———. "University Sermon XV, 'The Theory of Developments in Religious Doctrine.'" In *Fifteen Sermons Preached before the University of Oxford between AD 1826 and 1843*. New York: Longmans, Green, 1909.

O'Brien, Denis. "Plotinus on Matter and Evil." In *Cambridge Companion to Plotinus*.

———. *Plotinus on the Origin of Matter: An Exercise in the Interpretation of the Enneads*. Elenchos: Collana di testi e studi sul pensiero antico 22. Naples: Centro di studio del pensiero antico, 1991.

O'Keefe, John J. "'A Letter that Killeth': Toward a Reassessment of Antiochene Exegesis, or Diodore, Theodore, and Theodoret on the Psalms." *Journal of Early Christian Studies* 8 (2000): 83–104.

O'Meara, Dominic J. *Plotinus: An Introduction to the Enneads*. Oxford: Clarendon, 1995.

Pistorius, P. V. *Plotinus and Neoplatonism: An Introductory Study*. Cambridge: Bowes & Bowes, 1952.

Radde-Gallwitz, Andrew. *Basil of Caesarea: A Guide to His Life and Doctrine*. Eugene, OR: Cascade Books, 2012.

———. *Basil of Caesarea, Gregory of Nyssa, and the Transformation of Divine Simplicity*. Oxford Early Christian Studies. New York: Oxford University Press, 2009.

———. "Creed as Apology: The Pneumatological Letters of Basil of Caesarea and Gregory of Nyssa." Paper presented at the Boston Colloquy for Historical Theology, Boston College, July 30, 2011.

Rist, John M. "Plato Says that We Have Tripartite Souls. If He Is Right, What Can We Do About It?" In *SOPHIÊS MAIÊTORES. "Chercheurs de Sagesse." Hommage à Jean Pépin*, edited by M.-O. Goulet-Cazé, G. Madec, and D. O'Brien, 103–24. Paris: Institut d'Études Augustiniennes, 1992.

———. *Plotinus: The Road to Reality*. New York: Cambridge University Press, 1967.

Robbins, Frank. "Hexaemeral Literature." PhD diss., University of Chicago, 1912.

Robertson, David G. "Relatives in Basil of Caesarea." In *Studia Patristica 37, Paper Presented at the Thirteenth International Conference on Patristic Studies Held in Oxford, 1999, Cappadocian Writers, Other Greek Writers*, edited by Maurice F. Wiles and Edward J. Yarnold, 277–87. Louvain: Peeters, 2001.

Robertson, Jon M. *Christ as Mediator: A Study of the Theologies of Eusebius of Caesarea, Marcellus of Ancyra and Athanasius of Alexandria*. Oxford Theological Monographs. New York: Oxford University Press, 2007.

Rousseau, Philip. *Basil of Caesarea*. Berkeley: University of California Press, 1994.

———. "Human Nature and Its Material Setting in Basil of Caesarea's Sermons on the Creation." *Heythrop Journal* 49 (2008): 222–39.

———. *Pachomius: The Making of a Community in Fourth-Century Egypt*. Berkeley: University of California Press, 1985.

Ruaro, Enrica. "'Lovers of the Body': The Platonic Primacy of Soul vs. the Christian Affirmation of the Body." In *Conversations Platonic and Neoplatonic: Intellect, Soul, and Nature. Papers from 6th Annual Conference of the International Society for Neoplatonic Studies*, edited by John F. Finamore and Robert M. Berchman, 155–69. Sankt Augustin: Academia Verlag, 2010.

———. "'Resurrection: The Hope of Worms.' The Dispute between Celsus and Origen on the Resurrection of the Body." In *Perspectives sur le néoplatonisme: International Society of Neoplatonic Studies. Acts du colloque de 2006*, edited by Martin Achard, Wayne Hankey, and Jean-Marc Narbonne, 111–22. Québec: Les Presses de l'Université Laval, 2009.

Schäublin, Christoph. *Untersuchungen zu Methode und Herkunft der Antiochenischen Exegese.* Cologne-Bonn: Peter Hanstein, 1974.

Schönborn, Christoph. *God's Human Face: The Christ-Icon.* Translated by Lothar Krauth. San Francisco: Ignatius, 1994.

Schwyzer, H.-R. "Zu Plotins Deutung der sogenannten platonischen Materie." In *Zetesis: Festschrift E. de Strijcker*, edited by Th. Lefevre, 266–80. Antwerp: De Nederlandsche Boeklandel, 1973.

Shear, Theodore Leslie. *The Influence of Plato on St. Basil.* Baltimore: J. H. Furst, 1906.

Sterk, Andrea. *Renouncing the World Yet Leading the Church: The Monk-Bishop in Late Antiquity.* Cambridge, MA: Harvard University Press, 2004.

Stramara, Daniel F., Jr. "Double Monasteries in the Greek East, Fourth through Eighth Centuries." *Journal of Early Christian Studies* 6 (1998): 269–312.

Taft, Robert. *The Liturgy of the Hours in East and West: The Origins of the Divine Office and Its Meaning for Today.* Collegeville, MN: Liturgical Press, 1986.

Tieck, A. "Basil of Caesarea and the Bible." PhD diss., Columbia University, 1953.

Troiano, Marina. "Il *Contra Eunomium III* di Basilio di Cesarea e le *Epistolae ad Serapionem I–IV* di Atanasio di Alessandria: Nota Comparativa." *Augustinianum* 41 (2001): 59–91.

Vaggione, Richard Paul. *Eunomius of Cyzicus and the Nicene Revolution.* Oxford Early Christian Studies. New York: Oxford University Press, 2002.

Weinandy, Thomas. "The Apostolic Christology of Ignatius of Antioch: The Road to Chalcedon." In *Trajectories through the New Testament and the Apostolic Fathers*, ed. A. F. Gregory and C. M. Tuckett, 72–84. New York: Oxford University Press, 2005.

Wiles, Maurice. "Eunomius: Hair-splitting Dialectician or Defender of the Accessibility of Salvation?" In *The Making of Orthodoxy: Essays in Honour of Henry Chadwick*, ed. Rowan Williams, 157–72. New York: Cambridge University Press, 1989.

Young, Frances M. *The Art of Performance: Towards a Theology of Holy Scripture.* London: Darton, Longman & Todd, 1990. Reprinted as *Virtuoso Theology: The Bible and Interpretation.* Cleveland, OH: Pilgrim Press, 1993.

———. *Biblical Exegesis and the Formation of Christian Culture.* New York: Cambridge University Press, 1997.

———. "Exegetical Method and Scriptural Proof: The Bible in Doctrinal Debate." In *Studia Patristica 29, Papers Presented to the Tenth International Conference on Patristic Studies Held in Oxford 1987*, edited by Elizabeth A. Livingstone, 291–304. Louvain: Peeters, 1989.

————. *From Nicaea to Chalcedon: A Guide to the Literature and Its Background.* London: SCM, 1983. Revised with Andrew Teal. Grand Rapids: Baker Academic, 2010.

————. "The Rhetorical Schools and Their Influence on Patristic Exegesis." In *The Making of Orthodoxy: Essays in Honour of Henry Chadwick*, edited by Rowan Williams, 182–99. New York: Cambridge University Press, 1989.

Zachhuber, Johannes. "Basil and the Three-Hypostases Tradition: Reconsidering the Origins of Cappadocian Theology." *Zeitschrift für antikes Christentum* 5 (2001): 65–85.

Index